# THE AMERICAN ADOLESCENT

# THE DORSEY SERIES IN ANTHROPOLOGY AND SOCIOLOGY

EDITOR

ROBIN M. WILLIAMS, JR.
*Cornell University*

ARGYRIS  *Understanding Organizational Behavior*

ADAMS & PREISS (eds.)  *Human Organization Research* (Published for the Society for Applied Anthropology)

HSU (ed.)  *Psychological Anthropology: Approaches to Culture and Personality*

BELL (ed.)  *The Sociology of Education: A Sourcebook*

HAGEN  *On the Theory of Social Change: How Economic Growth Begins*

BELL  *Marriage and Family Interaction*

BARNOUW  *Culture and Personality*

GOTTLIEB & RAMSEY  *The American Adolescent*

JACOBS  *Pattern in Cultural Anthropology*

JOHNSON  *Crime, Correction, and Society*

SALISBURY  *Religion in American Culture: A Sociological Interpretation*

BREER & LOCKE  *Task Experience as a Source of Attitudes*

WILSON  *Sociology: Rules, Roles, and Relationships*

SHOSTAK  *Sociology in Action: Case Studies in Social Problems and Directed Social Change*

# THE
# AMERICAN
# ADOLESCENT

By

## DAVID GOTTLIEB, Ph.D.

Associate Professor
of Sociology and Education
Michigan State University

*and*

## CHARLES E. RAMSEY, Ph.D.

Professor of Sociology
Colorado State University

## 1964

## THE DORSEY PRESS, INC.

Homewood, Illinois

First Printing, May, 1964
Second Printing May, 1965
Third Printing July, 1966

Library of Congress Catalog Card No. 64–17255

PRINTED IN THE UNITED STATES OF AMERICA

# PREFACE

Youth is a universal phenomenon and through the ages a major task faced by every society is the socialization of its young.

For the most part the formal training of youth is left to adults. When the young meet the standards and demands of adults there is little conflict between the generations. When, however, youth do not fulfill the expectations of adults there is both intergenerational conflict and concern for the future of the society.

Recently we have seen evidence in our country, as well as in other industrialized societies, that the socialization process is not running too smoothly.

The purpose of this book is to examine the various phases of adolescent development within a sociological context. To this end, chapters dealing with age and sex roles, occupational choice, courtship and marriage, and the educational process are included. In addition, we will be dealing with the concept of "youth cultures" as it operates for different kinds of adolescents in varying types of social settings.

While the work is presented as a "sociological text," it has been written in a manner that should be comprehensible and meaningful to both the behavioral scientist and the layman.

Our goal was to move beyond a theoretical formulation of youth behavior and to note areas where the gap between the generations might be lessened.

The three case studies presented in Chapter III are intended to pinpoint differences and similarities among American youth in our contemporary society. It is hoped that their stories will provide the basis for extensive discussion among students who are concerned with the study of youth.

Chapter XII deals with minority groups and adolescent culture. This chapter was prepared by Dr. Francis A. J. Ianni of the U.S. Office of Education. Dr. Ianni's comments will provide valuable insights into how the adolescent culture operates among youth from different racial and ethnic backgrounds.

The final two chapters of this book are directed at identifying social areas in which young people have participated in some significant manner. The examples provided in these two chapters are not meant to be all-inclusive but rather they are indicative of what can be done in order to involve adolescents in the mainstream of American life.

As tradition demands, it is necessary for the authors to identify individuals who have contributed to the preparation of this work. To mention by name the many people who have played some role in the task of assembling the material presented here would be difficult indeed. For this reason a more general acknowledgment must follow: To our colleagues who have read portions of the manuscript and have offered their comments, we are indeed indebted. To the many students who have read sections of this work within various sociology classes, and who have voiced their critical opinions, we say "thank you for your assistance."

To both groups we offer the hope that the final product will be of benefit to those who are concerned with the study and education of American youth.

March 15, 1964

DAVID GOTTLIEB
Michigan State University

CHARLES RAMSEY
Colorado State University

# TABLE OF CONTENTS

## PART I.  ADOLESCENT SOCIETY

vii

# PART III.   AREAS OF CONFLICT AND RESOLUTION

# PART IV.   BRIDGING THE GAP BETWEEN ADOLESCENTS AND THE WORLD IN WHICH THEY LIVE

# Chapter I

# ADOLESCENTS AND THE
# ADULT WORLD

Despite the fact there has been a growing public concern with the plight and condition of our young, it seems safe to say that throughout the ages a similar protest has been raised by members of the adult society. The apparently increased sound may be attributed to the popular media and the professional exaggeration of the situation by numerous individuals, agencies, and, in all probability, an overly aroused adult community which is attempting—in part at least—to compensate for some of its own shortcomings.

There has always been a concern for the young and for the age of youth. This concern is based partially on the almost universal notion that youth is—or at least should be—a time of innocence and a time of experiment. This is the period when the body is strong and the spirit viable and dynamic. On the symbolic side, we see youth identified with the springtime of the year—the time of emergence and growth, the period when all is fresh, clean, and pure. Winter, on the other hand, comes to represent age--the eventual conclusion of the life cycle—the winter is cold and the winter is hard. In song we see this symbolism emphasized again and again: "It's a long, long time from May to September," and when September comes, it is frequently too late.

A second reason for concern with youth stems from the fact that every society, regardless of industrial complexity, cultural heritage, or social structure, must, if it is to survive, train the young for the taking on of responsible adult roles. It is apparent to all that without the constant integration of the young into the social system there can be little hope for the continuation of the tribe, community, or society.

Concern for the plight of the young is not unique to the present era nor to American society alone. The fact of the matter is that every nation, and this is most true of those undergoing industrial emergence, has some youth-adult conflict. England has its "teddy boys,"

1

France its *"blousons noirs;"* in Sweden the delinquent youth are called *"raggare,"* in Germany the *"halbstarken;"* and Japan has its "thunder boys." The Russians are not spared and many a Soviet newspaper makes reference to the *"stilyagi,"* a group of youth who do not seem too enthusiastic in embracing Marxist-Lenin doctrine.

Prior to a more detailed examination of the factors which might help explain this continuous struggle in the socialization of our young, let us review, in some detail, how youth have been viewed over time and the kinds of concerns which have been expressed by members of the adult society. We begin with the Bible, the Old Testament. Here in the section titled Proverbs, we find the words of Solomon, the son of David.

Hear my son, the instruction of thy father
And forsake not the teaching of thy mother:
For they shall be a chaplet of grace unto
thy head, And chains about thy neck.

My son, if sinners intice thee, Consent
thou not.
If they say: "Come with us,
Let us lie in wait of blood,
Let us lurk for the innocent without cause;
Let us swallow them up alive as the grave,
And whole, as those that go down into the pit;
We shall find all precious substance,
We shall fill our houses with spoil;
Cast in thy lot among us; Let us all have one purse."
My son walk not thou in the way with them
Estrain thy foot from their path;
For their feet run to evil,
And they make haste to shed blood.

We note in this passage two interesting factors. First, we find words dealing with the importance of heeding one's parents and second, some excellent insights as to the pressures which might come about when one heeds the words of peers. This, as we shall see later, may be the basic conflict in youth cultures. To what extent does one or is one able to identify with the values of the adult society when pressures of the age-grade peer society become overbearing? Further comments about heeding one's parents and remaining on the path of goodness are found in Shakespeare's *Hamlet*. The act is the first, scene three; Polonius speaks to his son Laertes who is leaving for France:

Look thou character. Give thy thoughts no tongue,
Not any unproportioned thought his act.
Be thou familiar but by no means vulgar;

Those friends thou hast, and their adoption tried,
Grapple them to thy soul with hoops of steel;
But do not dull thy palm with entertainment
Of each new hatch'd, unfledg'd comrade. Beware
Of entrance to a quarrel, but being in, bear't,
That the opposed may be aware of thee. Give
Every man thine ear, but few thy voice;
Take each man's censure, but reserve thy judgement.
Costly thy habit as thy purse can buy,
But not expressed in fancy; rich, not gaudy;
For the apparel oft proclaims the man, . . .
Neither a borrower nor lender be;
For loan oft loses both itself and friend, and
Borrow dulls the ego of husbandry. This above all:
To thine own self be true, and it must follow as
The night the day, thou canst not then be false to any
man.
Farewell; my blessing season this in thee.

And if we care to go back some 2,500 years we will find Socrates, in this instance not so very sympathetic to youth, expressing sentiments not unlike some heard today.

Children now love luxury. They have bad manners, contempt for authority. They show disrespect for elders, and love chatter in place of exercise. Children are now tyrants, not the servants of their households.

Moving to our own country, we can see sufficient evidence that even before the introduction of the factory system, the mass media, suburbs and slums, there were problems with youth. In her discussion of *Child Life in Colonial Days*, Alice Morse Earle presents some interesting observations as to how some youth behaved and how they were corrected by adults.[1]

The "correction" approach was primarily punitive based on the following kind of logic:

I would rather have the rod to be the general terror to all, to make them learn, than to tell a child, if you do this, or that, you will be more esteemed than your brothers and sisters. The rod produces an effect which terminates in itself. A child is afraid of being whipped, and gets his task, and there's an end on't. Whereas, by exciting emulation and comparisons of superiority, you lay the foundation of lasting mischief; you make brothers and sisters hate each other.[2]

Birch rods were the order of the day and could be purchased from street venders. In some cases the child to be punished was forced to pay the price of the rod. One Boston master struck his scholars on the head with a ruler until this was forbidden by the school directors; he then whipped the soles of the students' feet, and "roared out in

[1] Alice Morse Earle, *Child Life in Colonial Days* (New York: The Macmillan Co., 1899).
[2] *Ibid.*, p. 194.

the ecstasy of cruelty, 'Oh! the Caitiffs! (a mean and dispicable person) it is good for them'."[3]

Other innovations in methods of punishment were soon to follow. Some schoolmasters would send the ill-behaving student outdoors to find a small branch of a tree. A split was made at the severed end of the branch, and the offending student's nose was placed in the cleft end. Another approach was to yoke two offenders together in a yoke made with two bows similar to an ox yoke. On some occasions a boy and girl were "yoked together." "Whispering sticks" were used in some schoolrooms to preserve quiet. These were wooden gags to be tied in the mouth with strings, somewhat as a bit is placed in a horse's mouth. Yet another approach was used by one schoolteacher who even at that time was somewhat aware of group dynamics in relation to the classroom setting. A Reverend John Barnard, student of schoolmaster Ezekiel Cheever, related the following incident:

> I was a very naughty boy, much given to play, in so much that Master Cheever openly declared, "You, Barnard, I know you can do well enough if you will, but you are so full of play, you hinder your classmates from getting their lessons, therefore if any of them cannot perform their duty, I shall correct you for it." One day one of my classmates did not look at his book, and could not say his lesson, though I called upon him once and again to mind his book. Whereupon our master beat me. . . . The boy was pleased with my being corrected and persisted in his neglect for which I still was beaten and that for several days. I thought in justice I ought to correct the boy and compel him to a better temper; therefore after school was done I went to him and told him I had been beaten several times for his neglect and since master would not correct him, I would, and then drubbed him heartily.[4]

With few exceptions the most serious offenses committed by these youngsters were chatting in class, failure to memorize biblical quotations, failure to greet adults with the proper salutation, and failure to agree with the schoolmaster.

While the offenses of colonial youth were less dramatic and less violent than those committed by some youth today, it was not too long before "rumbles" were to occur in some American communities. Excerpts from the *New York Times* reflect the tone of these incidents: "New York City has gangs with such names as the 'Dead Rabbits' and the 'Bowery Boys.' In this year [1857] there was a pitched battle between rival gangs in the streets which caused the state militia to be called out."[5]

The problem of violent youth was not unique to New York City. A *New York Times* article of the same year indicates that New Orleans

[3] *Ibid.*, p. 197.
[4] *Ibid.*, p. 200.
[5] *The New York Times*, June 4, 1854.

was faced with its own brand of youth terrorism. "The most infamous outrages have been perpetuated for months past in New Orleans with perfect impunity . . . gangs of youthful scoundrels have filled the streets day and night, assailing, robbing, and stabbing peaceful citizens."[6]

One writer suggested there was a general decline of moral values among the population and this was reflected in the behavior of youth as well as adults. "Obedience to the law is very little practiced today; neither the statute nor the moral law is regarded; everyone wants to do as he pleases. Hence the contentions against authority, the disobedience of employees against employers, the disregard of school and family, and the dreadful want of reverence toward old age. You pass by the pupils just dismissed from school and listen to the conversation of half-grown boys, and observe how even girls push older people from the sidewalk; how some talk to well-meaning older people who criticize their behavior and upbraid them for their vicious conduct, and you will admit the outlook is very sad."[7]

By the early 1900's and with the rapid influx of migrants to this country we are able to note a change in the flavor of written materials dealing with youth. This was a period of rapid social change in America. Not only were thousands coming to this country from various sections of the world but there was in addition an internal migration which marked the emergence of our complex urban society.

For the most part the emphasis in these documents is on the special problems faced by youth who suddenly find themselves in a new and foreign setting. Several authors refer to the crowded city conditions and the fact that there is little physical room for recreation or opportunity for organized leisure-time activities. Other writers note how youth from different ethnic minority groups are forced to choose between the values of the "old country" as expressed by parents and the demands of the absorbing society.

One way of bridging the gap between the demands of the new world and the traditions of the old is found in the letter a young immigrant boy writes to his parents:

Dearest Parents:
    Please do not be angry with me for what I shall write. I write you that it is hard to live alone, so please find some girl for me, but an orderly and honest one, for in America there is not even one single, orderly girl. . . .

Some time later he learns from his parents that they have found him a suitable mate and he responds:

---
[6] *The New York Times,* July, 1858.
[7] *Education Magazine,* 1883.

I thank you kindly for your letter, for it was happy. As to the girl, although I don't know her, my companion who knows her, says that she is stately and pretty, and I believe him, as well as you my parents. . . . Please inform we which one [of the sisters] is to come, the older or the younger one, whether Alesandra or Stanislawa.[8]

For many of the young the problem was not so easily resolved. Several early sociological writers deal with the conflict which developed between parents and children. Nels Anderson, in his study of the hobo, relates the experience of one young man who broke home ties because he was unable to cope with the expectations of his parents.

W. left home when he was sixteen. He was the oldest of a family of five boys and three girls. His father owned a farm in Michigan and was usually hard pressed for means. He needed help at home and so W. was kept out of school a great deal. When he did go to school it was hard for him to learn. When the father saw the younger boys were passing W. in school he decided that it was time wasted to send W. to school. W. was big for his age and the father imposed more work on him than on the other boys who were smaller. W. felt that he was not getting a square deal so he ran away.[9]

Burgess and Locke note how, for one family at least, the transition between the Old and New Worlds manifests itself in dramatic social disorganization. In this instance they are dealing with the case history of an Italian family.

. . . . The third son is in Leavenworth; he is an original "42" [a notorious criminal gang which was located on the West Side of Chicago]. He finished two years of high school. At this point his family moved only about three blocks but into the midst of the "42" gang. Here the boy picked up delinquent cronies, cultivated new pleasures and habits, became delinquent and ended up as a big time robber, the accomplice in professional stick ups, the pal of notorious, big gangsters. There was nothing the family could do to save this boy. The family affections were always too strong to throw him out or disown him. Repeatedly, the family made big sacrifices for bonds and lawyers and "fixers" only to find themselves in the same situation soon again. Finally nothing could save him from a prison sentence.[10]

An analysis of written materials from the early 1900's would indicate that many adults saw industrialization and the growth of the city as the most salient factors in the breakdown in wholesome youth behavior. It was within the boundaries of the city that the youngster would be tempted by the "bright lights" and "evil influences;" it was the factory system and an opportunity to earn money outside of the home which was to give youth a sense of independence and a means

---

[8] Robert Ezra Park, *Human Communities* (Glencoe, Ill.: The Free Press, 1952).

[9] Nels Anderson, *The Hobo: The Sociology of the Homeless Man* (Chicago: The University of Chicago Press, 1923) pp. 83–84.

[10] Ernest W. Burgess and Harvey J. Locke, *The Family: From Institution to Companionship* (New York: The American Book Company, 1945) p. 124.

to break away from the family or origin. To support this point, examples were cited of farm youth who remained not only "physically straight but morally firm." One critic of urban youth made the following observations:

> One has only to compare the broken, bent and depraved youth of the city with the honest and firm farm child to see what evil the city offers. On the farm the young person learns to respect work and to disregard sinful influences. The air about him is fresh and he does not breathe the stench of the factory or narcotics. He can take pride in the accomplishments of his work and the pleasures of his family. In the city, youth are always subject to the wicked and have little opportunity for wholesome outdoor play.[11]

One of the most severe critics of the city and its impact on youth was Jane Addams, founder of Hull House in Chicago. In her book, *The Spirit of Youth and the City Streets*, Miss Addams attacked both the politician and the layman for their indifference to the tragic plight of youth in the city. Not unlike others of this period, Miss Addams dealt with the unique problem confronting immigrant and economically deprived youth.[12]

For Miss Addams the central problem stemmed from the fact that unlike other periods of time when communities provided organized play and activity for youth, the contemporary city no longer fulfilled this responsibility. Added to this was the phenomenon of industrialization, a stimulus for bringing together young people from all sections of the earth—young people who were to be the labor supply for the countless factories and workshops located in these new urban areas.

> Never before in civilization have such numbers of young girls been suddenly released from the protection of the home and permitted to walk unattended upon city streets and to work under alien roofs; for the first time they are being prized more for their labor power than for their innocence, their tender beauty, their ephemeral gaiety. . . .
> Never before have such numbers of young boys earned money independently of the family life, and felt themselves free to spend it as they choose in the midst of vice deliberately disguised as pleasure.[13]

Miss Addams perceived the city as a network of organizations directed at the exploitation of youth. On the one hand were the factories where young people worked long hours for meager rewards, and on the other were the countless "places" established for leisure-time activities.

---

[11] *Agricultural Record, 1912*, Annual Report of the Ohio State Board of Agriculture, p. 476.
[12] Jane Addams, *The Spirit of Youth and the City Streets* (New York: The Macmillan Co., 1910).
[13] *Ibid.*, pp. 5–6.

In every city arise so-called "places"—"gin places," they are called in fiction; in Chicago we euphemistically say merely "places," in which alcohol is dispensed, not to allay thirst, but, ostensibly to stimulate gaiety, it is sold really in order to empty pockets. Huge dance halls are opened to which hundreds of young people are attracted, many of whom stand wistfully outside a roped circle, for it requires five cents to procure within it for five minutes the sense of allurement and intoxication which is sold in lieu of innocent pleasure.[14]

Aside from the "places" noted above, Miss Addams was also critical of the theater, which she described as "the house of dreams." Within the theatre, she averred, young people could "satisfy that craving for a conception of life higher than that which the actual world offers them."[15]

Being limited in contact, with few sources of pleasure and relaxation, the youngster could build, in fantasy at least, a life based on the actions of the observed theater characters. Here the lonely young girl could identify with the romantic heroine while the boy sought to take on the characteristics of the dominant male. For Miss Addams, however, the real danger was not so much the fantasy but what she saw as a transference of screen behavior to the actual behavior of the young person. She recalled the following incident:

Three boys aged nine, eleven, and thirteen years, who had recently seen depicted the adventures of frontier life including the holding up of a stage coach and the lassoing of the driver, spent weeks planning to lasso, murder, and rob a neighborhood milkman, who started on his route at four o'clock in the morning. They made their headquarters in a barn and saved enough money to buy a revolver, adopting as their watchword the phrase "dead men tell no tales." One spring morning the conspirators, with their faces covered with black cloth, lay, "in ambush" for the milkman. Fortunately for him, as the lariat was thrown the horse shied, and, although the shot was appropriately fired, the milkman's life was saved.[16]

Clearly the "house of dreams" was to Miss Addams a source of "direct influence" upon the behavior of these boys.

As is the case in contemporary research dealing with adolescents, most early investigators concentrated on the behavior of male youth. One exception was W. I. Thomas, a psychological sociologist from the University of Chicago.[17] Thomas held that "every individual has a vast variety of wishes which can be satisfied only by his incorporation in society." He saw the four paramount wishes as the desire for new experience; the desire for security; the desire for response; and the desire for recognition.

Thomas never really made clear the relationship between these

---

[14] *Ibid.,* pp. 6–7.
[15] *Ibid.,* p. 76.
[16] *Ibid.,* p. 93.
[17] William I. Thomas, *The Unadjusted Girl* (Boston: Little, Brown, & Co., 1937), p. 4.

wishes and personal attitudes. He seemed to view the wishes as a motor element—a starting point for social activity. He saw society (family and community) as having two primary functions in regard to these wishes. First, the group must suppress those wishes and activities in conflict with the prevailing normative order; second, it must encourage those wishes and actions seen as desirable. Thomas noted that in the more primitive or folk societies, conflict between individual wishes and societal expectations is kept at a minimum since there is little change in the "moral code" from one generation to the next. The problem arises—and here Thomas is in harmony with many others who have dealt with the impact of industrialization on personality disorganization—when technical innovations, mass communications, and bureaucratic organizations lead to a breakdown in value continuity. Once this disruption occurs the individual is no longer able to depend on traditional modes of behavior but must, according to Thomas, redefine the situation and adopt new forms of behavior. For the immigrant the conflict between old and new cultures becomes most traumatic, resulting, in many instances, in an abandonment of traditional values. In his study of *The Unadjusted Girl,* Thomas presents vivid case histories of adolescents caught in the web of acculturation.

When I left Europe my little sister's last words were, "Here in Hell, I will dream through the nights that far, far, across the ocean, my loving brother lives happily." And my last words were, "I shall forget my right hand if I ever forget you."

I suffered not a little in the golden land. . . . Five years passed. I loyally served the God of Gold, saved some money and sent for my sister. For three years I believed myself the happiest of men. . . . My sister bloomed like a rose in May and she was kind and motherly to me. We were tied by a bond of the highest love and on my part that love had until now remained the same. But listen what a terrible thing occurred.

About a year ago I noticed a marked change in my sister—both physically and spiritually. She grew pale, her eyes lost their fire and her attitude toward me changed also. She began to neglect her work (I taught her a good trade), until half a year ago she entirely gave up the work. This angered me very much and I began to shadow her in order to discover the mystery of her life, for she had recently avoided talking to me, particularly of her life. I concluded that she kept company with a boy and that caused her trouble.

But I soon noticed that she was wearing such expensive things that a boy could not afford to buy them. She had a couple of diamond rings and plenty of other jewelry. I investigated until I discovered, oh, horrible! that my sister was a prostitute.

You can understand that I want to drag her out of the mire, but . . . she tells me that I do not understand life. She cannot conceive why it should be considered indecent to sell one's body in this manner. When I point out to her the end that awaits her she says in the first place it is not more harmful than working by steam for twelve to fourteen hours; in the second place, even if it were so, she enjoys life more. One must take as much as possible out of life. When I call her attention to the horrible degradation she replies that in the shop, too, we are humiliated by the foreman, and so on.

I know that if I could convince her that I am right, she would be willing to emerge from the swamp, but I am unfortunately too inadequate in words, she being a good speaker, and I am usually defeated.[18]

By 1915 there was a marked decline in the number of immigrants arriving in this country. With this decline came a period of relative stability among the migrants who had settled in American cities. Within the boundaries of ethnic ghettos the various minority groups established, in miniature, the culture of the Old World. In their own quarters they could speak their own language, eat their own kinds of foods, read their own newspapers, and establish their own organizations. Here is a brief description of the ethnic groups found in the city of Cleveland during this period of time:

> In the anonymous masses that make up the living city, Cleveland is almost a Midwest anomaly. The white stock of native parentage comprises only a quarter of the population; eight percent are Negroes and the remaining 67 percent are either foreign born or the offspring of foreign or mixed parentage. Once almost entirely Nordic or Celtic in makeup, Cleveland was transformed by the expanding steel industry into one of the most racially diversified communities in the United States. Forty-eight nationalities have representatives here; more than forty languages are spoken in the city. First in number are the Czechoslovaks followed by the Poles, Italians, Germans, Yugoslavs, Irish and Hungarians. Where they concentrate in nationality groups, their native tongues are spoken almost as commonly as English.[19]

The concentration of various ethnic groups within different sections of the city seems to have brought about a change in how youth were perceived by adults. For one thing there was a shift from an emphasis on individual behavior to a concern with group or gang behavior. Secondly, there was growing recognition of the fact that despite industrialization and the dilemmas of acculturation, youth from different ethnic and socioeconomic groups behaved differently. It was this latter factor which seems to have acted as a stimulus for a number of sociological studies dealing with the socialization process among youth from different backgrounds.

The literature pertaining to youth for this period of American life is indeed rich. Not only are there the numerous case studies conducted by social scientists but in addition there exists a variety of novels dealing with youth.

Among the case studies are several which have become classics for students of adolescent behavior. Included are Clifford R. Shaw's

---

[18] *Ibid.*, pp. 88–89.

[19] *The Ohio Guide,* American Guide Series (New York: Oxford University Press, 1923), p. 217.

*The Jackroller,* the autobiography of a young delinquent, and *The Natural History of a Delinquent Career,* a study of the effect of family life, gang association, and neighborhood conditions on the evolution of a criminal career.[20]

A third study which deals with youth gangs is the monumental work undertaken by Frederic M. Thrasher which appeared in 1927. Thrasher's discussion of the origin and dynamics of the gang was based on a survey of some 1,300 Chicago youth gangs and clubs.[21]

In discussing the "roots of the gang" Thrasher stated that "the gang represents the spontaneous effort of boys to create a society for themselves where none adequate to their needs exists."[22] Indirectly he took the position that the various agencies responsible for the socialization of the child, i.e., the family, the church, and the school, have failed in fulfilling the needs of the young, hence their involvement in gang associations.

> The gang functions with reference to these conditions in two ways: It offers a substitute for what society fails to give; and it provides a relief from suppression and distasteful behavior. It fills a gap and affords an escape.[23]

While the gang appears to hold some appeal for all economically deprived youth, Thrasher suggested that members of some ethnic groups are less likely than others to organize gangs.

> The Jewish gangs, which belong to this region are less numerous than those of other slum areas, due, it is said to the more individualistic spirit of the Jews, but more likely to better organized recreation and family life than is found among the poorer classes of other immigrant groups.[24]

Although Thrasher made only brief mention of a separate youth society, his work, as we shall later see, appears to anticipate contemporary adolescent research which places great emphasis on the existence of distinct adolescent subcultures.

Social scientists were not alone, however, in identifying the breakdown of social institutions as the major force for moving youth into intimate peer associations. The American novelist James T. Farrell, who created the character Studs Lonigan, took a position very much like that expressed by Thrasher. In discussing his conception of Studs —an American boy of Irish-Catholic extraction—he notes the following:

---

[20] Clifford R. Shaw, *The Jackroller* (Chicago: The University of Chicago Press, 1929). *The Natural History of a Delinquent Career* (Chicago: The University of Chicago Press, 1931).

[21] Frederic M. Thrasher, *The Gang* (Chicago: The University of Chicago Press, 1927).

[22] *Ibid.,* p. 37.

[23] *Ibid.,* p. 39.

[24] *Ibid.,* p. 12.

The important institutions in the education of Studs Lonigan were the home and the family, the church, the school, and the playground. These institutions broke down and did not serve their desired function. The streets became a potent educative factor in the boy's life.[25]

Farrell portrayed Studs as an adolescent typical of his time and class. Much of his daily life is centered about the activities of his gang. Within his peer group he is able to maintain a level of prestige that cannot be found in the classroom or the occupational market. In large part the gang's unity is based on a rejection of and hostility toward all others in the society. Parents are labeled "gaffers"—people unable to understand the needs and desires of the young. Teachers, clergymen, policemen, and politicians are not spared the scorn of the gang. The only acceptable people seem to be other Irish-Catholic youth who hold the types of values endorsed by Studs and his group. There is, in other words, little sympathy for other youth who, in all probability, face the same dilemmas Studs encountered. Farrell indicated how this hostility operates in exchange between Studs and Kenny:

> What beach'll we go to? asked Studs.
> Fifty-first Street, said Kenny.
> Ain't there a lot of Jews there? asked Studs.
> Where ain't there kikes? They're all over. You watch. First it's the hebes, and then it's the niggers that's gonna overrun the southside, Kenny said.
> And then where 'ull a white man go to, asked Studs.
> He'll have to go to Africa or . . . Jew-rusalem, said Kenny. . . .
> Afterward Studs said:
> If we go to Jackson Park, it might be better.
> There's Polacks there, said Killarney.[26]

From the passage noted above we can see in addition to the expressed hostility toward others some further evidence that youth are not necessarily cut of a common cloth and that differences in race, religion, class, and ethnic background may help account for some of the variation in adolescent behavior.

The extent to which differences existed among the various ethnic groups can be seen in the work of the urban sociologist Louis Wirth and the writings of such novelists as Meyer Levin and Michael Gold.[27]

Gold's book deals with the Jews of New York's east side. These were the people of the ghetto who came to America to escape the oppressions of their homelands. America was visualized as the true land of "milk and honey," "where the streets were paved with gold." This

---

[25] James T. Farrell, *Studs Lonigan* (New York: The Modern Library, 1932), p. xiii. By permission of Vanguard Press, Inc.

[26] *Ibid.*, pp. 141–42.

[27] Louis Wirth, *The Ghetto* (Chicago: University of Chicago Press, 1928); Meyer Levin, *The Old Bunch* (New York: Macfadden, 1937); Michael Gold, *Jews Without Money* (New York: Horace Liveright, 1930).

was to be the land of opportunity where one could succeed if he was diligent and hard driving. For many Jewish parents the ultimate goal was to have a son attend college and enter a profession. In fear of having their children influenced by "outsiders" who might hold contrary values, Jewish parents reinforced the idea of a cultural ghetto. Again and again they reminded their children that the Jews were different from the gentiles and it was best to remain detached. Gold noted how this opposition to others as expressed by adults was internalized by one Jewish adolescent:

My mother was opposed to the Italians, Irish, Germans and every other variety of Christian with whom we were surrounded. "May eight and eighty black years fall on these goys!" she said, her black eyes flashing. "They live like pigs; they have ruined the world. And they hate and kill Jews. They may seem friendly, but behind our backs they laugh at us. I know them well. I have seen them in Hungary."

The East Side never forgot Europe. We children heard endless tales of the pogroms. Joey Cohen, who was born in Russia, could himself remember one.

The Christians had hammered a nail into his uncle's head, and killed him. When we passed a Christian church we were careful to spit three times; otherwise bad luck was sure to befall us. We were obsessed by wild stories of how the Christians loved to kidnap Jewish children, to burn a cross on each cheek with a redhot poker. They also cut off children's ears and made a kind of soup.

"In the old days," my mother said, "the Christians hunted the Jews like rabbits. They would gather thousands in a big marketplace, and stuff pork down their throats with swords, and ask the Jews to be baptized. The Jews refused of course. So they were burnt in great fires, and the Christians laughed, danced and made merry when they saw the poor Jews burning up like candles. Such are the Christians. May they burn some day too."

These impressions sank into my heart, and in my bad dreams during the hot summer nights, dark Christian ogres the size of tenements moved all around me. They sat on my chest, and clutched my throat with slimy remorseless fingers, shrieking, "Jew, Jew, Jew!"

And I would spend long daylight hours wondering why the Christians hated us so, and form noble plans of how I would lead valiant Jewish armies when I grew up, in defense of the Jews.[28]

While our emphasis here has been on literature dealing with immigrant youth, it should be noted that the more affluent American-born adolescent was not spared the critical and frequently negative evaluation of adults. This was the "flapper" group, bell-bottom trousers, raccoon coats, "twenty-one skidoo" and "oh, you kid." Generally these young people were seen as wasters who were overindulged and who made little worthy contribution to themselves, their families, or their society. The activities of this group are described in the works of F. Scott Fitzgerald, Ernest Hemingway, and Sinclair Lewis. From the more empirical side we have again the work of

---

[28] Gold, *op. cit.*, pp. 164–65.

Thrasher who related some of the leisure time pursuits of one such youthful group.

> The Fusileers were college fellows with few congenial friends and some women attached, who stuck closely together for two or three years. They were bound together by ties of sincere friendship and by common standards of conduct. Several of them were fraternity men, but they dared not let their "brothers" know of this relationship. They were hard drinkers and rounders, and they wanted complete freedom from traditional morality.
>
> The chief activities and interests of the group were of the festivity type. The first year they held frequent parties on the south shore at the home of one of the members whose parents were away for the summer. One autumn, two or three nights a week, they collected at the Smiths before starting out in their cars to make the rounds of the cabarets.
>
> There was an unwritten law among the men not to interfere with each other's women, and this was carefully observed, for what was one girl more or less? The girls for the most part, were well to do and moved in the best society.[29]

Gradually each of the ethnic groups was to become partially absorbed and integrated into the dominant American culture. While there are still traces of these early ethnic ghettoes in our communities, they are not so easily identified as in years passed. The processes of acculturation have washed away many institutions and customs of these ethnic groups.

Foreign-language papers which were once popular in American cities have slowly gone out of business or have replaced the old language and format with English and a content more acceptable to an American audience. The fraternal and benevolent ethnic organizations which were once very much part of the immigrants' life have all but disappeared. Foreign foods have been replaced with American menus and certain dishes are no longer served by the children of foreign parents.

With the children of immigrant parents entering and passing through American educational systems, the process of acculturation is expedited. Few adults of ethnic extraction speak the language of their parents nor are they eager for their children to retain the traditions. By the early 1940's, an expressed concern with ethnic groups had become relatively insignificant. From that period of time to the early 1950's when we witnessed a new kind of migrant—the Negro, the Puerto Rican, the Mexican, and the Southern white—the research emphasis and popular-novel orientation of youth literature has been on studies dealing with the impact of social class on youth values, attitudes, and behavior.

Although there were a variety of studies dealing with the phenomenon of social status in American communities, we will be concerned here with two which dealt specifically with American adolescents.

---

[29] Thrasher, *op. cit.* (from a manuscript prepared by a member of the group), p. 51.

The first is *Middletown: A Study in American Culture*, by Helen M. and Robert S. Lynd.[30]

During the years 1924 and 1925, the Lynds, using the techniques of the cultural anthropologist, carried on a detailed investigation of Middletown, a Midwestern industrial city of about 38,000 population. The Middletown study focuses on social class analysis, among other areas, and on "training the young." The Lynds point out that the people of Middletown are very much concerned that the young have an education. They note that in 1925 "no less than 45% of all money expended by the city was devoted to its schools."[31]

Of importance to our discussion is the chapter dealing with school life where the Lynds comment that "the school is taking over more and more of the child's waking life. Both high school and grades have departed from the attitude of fifty years ago, when the Board directed teachers to encourage children to leave for home once formal studies and class work was completed for the day."[32] The many activities of the school act, according to the Lynds, as an agent for socializing young from the various social strata into one common cultural group. Obviously there are differences in which students will become involved in these extracurricular activities, since youth from the working class are more likely to hold part-time jobs that prevent entrance into the many school activities. Next, as we might anticipate, working class youth are hesitant due to a lack of social skills, sophistication, and financial support to engage in the many programs of the school.

Despite the social class variations, the Lynds make it explicit that most members of the adult community see education as the "guarantee" factor in insuring social mobility. The fact that the high school has moved from a rigid, formal educational institution to one that embraces numerous social events does not seem to disturb parents. On the contrary, a number of parents suggest that too much intellectual stimulation is dangerous and that the adolescent period should be a time of fun and excitement.

And yet when one looks more closely at this dominant belief in the magic of formal schooling, it appears that it is not what actually goes on in the schoolroom that these many voices laud. Literacy, yes, they want their children to be able to "read the newspapers, write a letter and perform the ordinary operations of arithmetic," but, beyond that, many of them are little interested in what the schools teach. This thing, education—appears to be desired frequently not for the specific content but as a symbol—by the working class as an open sesame

---

[30] Helen Merrill Lynd and Robert S. Lynd, *Middletown: A Study in American Culture* (New York: Harcourt, Brace & Co., 1929).

[31] *Ibid.*, p. 182.

[32] *Ibid.*, p. 211.

that will mysteriously admit their children to a world closed to them, and by the business class as a heavily sanctioned aid in getting on further economically or socially in the world.[33]

While the Lynds emphasized the school as the institution for bringing about a minimization of social class differences, August Hollingshead, in his study, *Elmtown's Youth*, takes the position that the high school acts as a source for furthering the gap between youth from the various class groups.[34]

Hollingshead focused on the relationship of adolescents to the social structure in a Midwestern community which is also analyzed in *Democracy in Jonesville.*

The analysis involved 390 high school students, 345 adolescents who had withdrawn from the school, and the 535 families of these adolescents.

The relationship between class level and patterns of school attendence, attrition, dating, school activity involvement, employment, career expectations, and peer association is the focus of attention. These data, supplemented by case histories, provide the foundation for the conclusion that opportunities for the successful attainment of desirable rewards and values (those held by members of the middle class) vary positively with the individual's position on the social-class ladder.

Hollingshead proposes two explanations for the failure of the lower-class adolescent to rise above his present status position. First is the lower-class socialization process, which Hollingshead believes does not properly fit the working-class adolescent for satisfactory educational and occupational adjustment. Second, middle-class adults in the school enforce their class values by "putting down" the lower-class adolescents.

Finally, Hollingshead presents evidence to support his initial working hypothesis that youngsters manifest within the social structure of the school the attitudes, values, and behavior patterns pursued by their parents in the larger society.

Much of the criticism of these two studies stems from the authors' assumption that the relatively small communities analyzed are an adequate sampling from which generalizations can be made to all of American society. Furthermore, the data do not fully support the hypothesis that variations in school dropout, curriculum selection, friendship choices, extracurricular activity participation, and other variables relevant to education are determined by social class posi-

---

[33] *Ibid.*, pp. 210–20.
[34] August Hollingshead, *Elmtown's Youth* (New York: John Wiley & Sons, 1949).

tion or unjust school policies. From the first-order (two variables) tables presented, in most instances it is difficult to pinpoint just what causal relationships exist. Generally the authors fail to consider other factors once a relationship is found between social class and some dependent variable.

Hollingshead's discussion of social class and pattern of friendship among Elmtown's high school youth illustrates the limitations of this analysis. He shows that most students maintain clique associations within their own social class, but he also finds clique homogeneity in respect to school class. In other words, freshmen are more likely to maintain friendship ties with other freshmen; sophomores with sophomores; juniors with juniors; and seniors with seniors. Thus, both social class and school class are related to clique associations. Since attrition increases with years in school and is highest for the lower classes, we should not be surprised to find social class tied in with friendship patterns. We cannot, however, be certain whether the observed differences result from social-class discrimination or from the fact that over time fewer and fewer lower-class students are around to choose as friends. A tighter analysis would have examined the correlation between social class and clique relationships with year in school (freshman, sophomore, etc.) controlled. We would speculate that over time social class differences would become less important in determining friendship choices than would post-high school plans, school activity involvement, and academic interests, or other reference group variables.

These studies also fail to make clear just what in the students' socioeconomic status leads to variations in attitudes, norms, and behavior. Is it, for example, a question of finances alone? Will capable lower-class students who are given financial assistance express as strong an interest in college as students from the more affluent families? Or is it rather a question of the values stressed by parents from the different class groups? To what extent do members of lower classes hold educational values and attitudes similar to the middle class, which is the relevant reference group for educational matters? Could difference in educational level be due simply to differences in educational sophistication among individuals from the various social strata? Middle-class parents, because of their own college experiences and community positions, may have a better understanding of how schools operate, where you get information, whom you speak to in the academic bureaucracy, how you fill out applications, and so on.

Probably each of these factors is at play in the total operation of social class and education. The problem, however, is to determine the saliency of each and measure its impact as the student moves through the various stages of the educational program.

Finally (and here the authors of the works cited above cannot be held accountable), there have been many changes in our schools and communities during the past three decades.

Granting the limitations of these investigations, their value should not be minimized. They are among the first of a series of systematic, empirical research studies dealing with social stratification in the United States. Both studies, in addition, provide valuable insights as to how socioeconomic differences influence human behavior. Finally, and most important to this discussion, these studies are rich in data describing the dynamics of the adolescent society as observed in American high schools. In later sections of this book we will, of course, deal with the question of the relation of social class, religion, race, and region of origin to adolescent behavior.

While sociologists continued to pursue the group or peer phenomenon in youth behavior, psychologists, as well as psychoanalysts, have concentrated on the individual adolescent. Perhaps under the influence of the Freudian theory of the relative completeness of the personality structure at the conclusion of puberty, many psychological studies of adolescent development have emphasized the theme of stress and personality turmoil.[35] Generally one gets the impression from the psychological and psychoanalytical literature that the second decade of life is filled with a variety of conflicts. Emotional instability and deviant behavior are said to be the results of rapid physiological change. The observed disordered behavior of adolescents is said to be a social expression of the period of sex maturation. The position seems to be that since this is a time when the body is strong and growing there is a need for stimulation beyond that offered by the institutions involved in the young person's socialization. Not finding sufficient satisfaction within the accepted activities provided by the social system, the adolescent must seek out other stimuli in order to ease his frustration. Involvement in sexual promiscuity, drinking, crime, and other forms of unconventional or deviant behavior is, according to some of these writers, the inevitable result of the search for greater need fulfillment.

The validity of these propositions is questionable since they imply a universal mode of behavior for all adolescents. In other words, if

---

[35] See Sigmund Freud, "Three Contributions to the Theory of Sex," *The Basic Writings of Sigmund Freud*, translated and edited, with an introduction by A. A. Brill (New York: Random House, 1938), especially pp. 620 ff.; for negative evidence see William H. Sewell, "Infant Training and the Personality of the Child," *American Journal of Sociology*, LVIII (1952), pp. 150–59.

it is merely a question of biological development then why do not all adolescents in every society behave in a similar manner? In his discussion of adolescent behavior E. B. Reuter raises a number of issues with regard to both the idea of adolescence as a time of stress and the biological-social proposition.[36] He first challenges the prevailing adult notion that adolescence is indeed a period of "storm and stress." Reuter points out that the information adults usually get about young people comes from the mass media where the emphasis is placed on failure. Stories of Heroin peddlers, gang fights, school dropouts, and early marriages are better sellers than those dealing with responsible behavior. In addition, Reuter points out that much psychological and psychoanalytical writing is done by those who have only limited contact with young people. He feels that this writing may be further biased by the fact that these contacts are frequently with maladjusted youth.

As for the idea of social behavior being primarily a product of biological maturation, Reuter states the following:

> If such a dependent relation obtains, three things will be found: (1) the mental disorder will appear in all children; (2) the physical adolescence and the social maladjustment will coincide or follow a uniform time sequence, and (3) the same characteristics will mark the age period in all civilizations. Such seems not to be the case.[37]

The periods of the late 1940's, 1950's, and early 1960's, reveal some slight modifications in how youth are observed by adults. The great difference between these periods and the earlier times discussed, however, is not found so much in the conclusions drawn but rather in the research techniques employed by behavioral scientists.

In great part, the current methodology employed in youth research reflects the many refinements in the technology of behavioral science. We note a stronger emphasis on quantitative, systematic, and empirical studies. While progress has been made in the techniques of youth research, little new seems to be available in accounting for the variations and similarities in how youth go about the business of taking their place in the social order.

In this, the concluding section of our discussion of youth in an adult world, we will deal with some of the more recent and unique propositions offered by students of adolescent behavior.

Kingsley Davis, in his paper, "Sociology of Parent Youth Conflict," contends that in societies where merit is the criterion for status there

---

[36] E. B. Reuter, "The Sociology of Adolescence," *American Journal of Sociology*, Vol. 43, 1937, pp. 414–27.

[37] *Ibid.*, p. 416.

will be some conflict between the generations regarding the rightful incumbency to positions of status and prestige.[38] In other words, a social system which offers rewards on the basis of achievement rather than ascribed criteria will, in all probability, encounter disputes between age groups. In the primitive society, where age is the primary criterion for prestige and power, the conflict is minimized. In a society such as ours, however, where formal education and training are the primary sources for social mobility status, tensions are likely to occur.

For example, we frequently find younger people in positions of power in formal organizations and work situations, in many cases as supervisers of older people who deeply resent this type of power-control relationship. Such terms as "he's still wet behind the ears," "his mother's milk is still on his lips," and "young whipper-snapper" reflect this age-group conflict.

At times the status anomalies may take a reverse form. In this case the young person with higher formal education and socioeconomic background may be subordinate to an older person who possesses lower education. An example is found in the work of Gottlieb and Rossi [39] where the authors point out that military organizations using large complements of technically trained individuals can often be characterized by status anomalies in which persons of inferior social status are placed above persons with superior status. They found that while the relationship appeared harmonious between the formal authority structure and the broad social statuses of individual soldiers at a paratrooper training base, the social structure observed at an urban-centered command headquarters was quite different. At the paratrooper base the younger men held the lowest military ranks, came generally from low socioeconomic backgrounds, and rarely had gone beyond high school. The officers at this base were older, usually came from middle-class families, and had higher formal education. In contrast, at the command headquarters the younger privates tended to have more formal education than did the older noncommissioned officers who were their direct supervisors; and their socioeconomic background was markedly different. The distinct difference in education and social class helped to create a situation whereby men with

---

[38] Kingsley Davis, "Sociology of Parent Youth Conflict," *American Sociological Review*, Vol. 5 (August, 1940). See also his paper, "Adolescence and the Social Structure," *The Annals of the American Academy of Political and Social Science*, Vol. 236 (November, 1944).

[39] David Gottlieb and Peter H. Rossi, *Study of the Bases of Changing Food Attitudes*, Quartermaster Food and Container Institute for the Armed Forces (Chicago: 1959), Contract No. DA 19-129-qm-1117.

lower formal status were engaged in high-prestige activities since they had the skills needed for these jobs while the men with the higher formal status were involved in the more routine and lowest-prestige activities. This situation created problems and conflicts for both groups. On the one hand the younger men resented the idea of taking orders from those whom they perceived as having less ability and responsibility than they themselves; the older men felt both intimidated by the knowledge and skill of the enlisted man and angered at the lack of respect the younger soldiers paid to their formal rank.

Kingsley Davis holds that since adults see themselves as having a greater stake in the ongoing social order they tend more to realism than do the young. Youth standing, in a sense, outside of the system appear—at least in the eyes of adults—to take the position they are not responsible for the dysfunction and problems of the society. In addition, adults feel that youth are not satisfied with the role of silent partners but would rather stand on the sidelines heaping scorn on the actions of the adult world.

Erikson, Block, and Niederhoffer, as well as others, emphasize the problem of self-identity on the part of youth as an important source of youth tension. This position maintains our society does not make precise the exact status or role of the adolescent. There is uncertainty whether the adolescent is still a child or to be accepted as a full-fledged member of the adult community. In this situation of ambiguity, adolescents find it difficult to establish their own self concept and are confused as to the role they are expected to play.[40]

Pitirim Sorokin and others stress the adult normative standard regarding adolescent sexual behavior as a source of youth frustration. Youth, according to these authors, exist in a sex-obsessed culture which stimulates their sexual promiscuity while at the same time parents attempt to repress this sexual interest.[41]

In the area of contemporary gang behavior we see further evidence that little new is being offered in explaining why these youth act the way they do. The reasons for gang formation proposed today are really no different than those suggested by Thrasher, Shaw, or Jane Addams some thirty-five years ago. The only changes seem to be in the names taken by the gangs, the innovations in armament (which reflect technological advances in destructive weapons), and the ethnic background of gang members. In Thrasher's study of Chicago

[40] Erik Erikson, "New Perspectives for Research in Juvenile Delinquency," eds. Helen Witmer and Ruth Kotinsky (Publication No. 356) (Washington, D.C.: Children's Bureau, 1956); Herbert Block and Arthur Niederhoffer, *The Gang* (New York: Philosophical Library, 1958).

[41] Pitirim Sorokin, *The American Sex Revolution* (Boston: Sargent, 1956).

gangs he notes that with few exceptions gangs either had no formal name or they took the name of the street where they "hang out." [42] Contemporary urban gangs, on the other hand, seem to take great pride in naming their group. Some highly publicized gangs in New York have carried the names Egyptian Kings, Jesters, Playboys, Balkans, Black Knights, Villains, Scorpions, Mighty Hoods, and Politicians.

As for weapons, the change appears great. In the days of Thrasher's *Gang* and William Whyte's *Street Corner Society*, the ultimate weapons were sticks, rocks, and—on some occasions—bottles. Some gang members felt the use of anything but fists for fighting indicated cowardice. Gang members today, however, rely on the more violent and fatal instruments of fighting: a variety of knives, guns, chains, steel pipes, broken bottles, and so forth.

The ethnic and racial background of today's gang members is primarily Negro, Mexican, Puerto Rican, and in some cases southern whites.

As to why they behave the way they do, we have the comments of a sociologist who worked with gangs in New York City.

> Today's violent delinquent is a displaced person—suspicious, fearful, and not willing or able to establish a concrete human relationship. The formation of the violent gang, with its impermanence, its possibilities for hollow glory, its limited expectations of any responsibility on the part of its members, is all inviting to youths who have difficulty fitting into a more integrated and clearly defined world. [43]

As noted earlier, this explanation is very much like that offered by those who watched the integration of ethnic youth in the earlier decades of this century.

Finally, we have the work of James S. Coleman, whose study of high school students does much to pinpoint the dimensions of the adolescent society. [44]

In his book, *The Adolescent Society*, Coleman makes the following statement: "With his fellows, he [the adolescent] comes to constitute a small society, one that has most of its important interactions within itself, and maintains only a few threads of connection with the outside adult society." [45]

Although some sociologists would question the sweeping nature of Coleman's statement, few would disagree with the idea that adoles-

---

[42] Thrasher, *op. cit.*, p. 10.

[43] Lewis Yablonsky, *The Violent Gang* (New York: The Macmillan Company, 1962), p. 4.

[44] James S. Coleman, *The Adolescent Society* (New York: The Free Press of Glencoe, 1961).

[45] *Ibid.*, p. 3.

cents do find much of their day-to-day activities centered within the structure of peer relationships.

In the following chapter and through the course of this book we will deal in greater detail with the question of youth culture—its emergence and impact. In addition, we will examine the propositions that more than one youth culture exists and that these cultures have different kinds of effects on youth from different backgrounds, communities, and societies.

## SUMMARY AND CONCLUSIONS

Through the course of this chapter we have attempted to show how youth have been perceived and evaluated by adults through the course of American history. Generally, we would have to accept the idea that many adults see the adolescent period as a time of stress and strain, with young people struggling to attain a comfortable position within the total societal setting. We also indicated that while the characters have changed the plot, the adolescent drama has been much the same throughout the years. The industrial revolution and urbanization have been clearly seen as primary factors in accounting for many of the dilemmas involved in the transition from child to adult. Finally, we have indicated that there does appear to be a general consensus among those who have studied youth that much of what the adolescent feels and does is in part a product not only of family involvements but of interaction with his fellows.

To these reasons for adult–youth conflict we would propose three additional factors.

Adults, whether they verbalize it or not, see themselves as responsible for the actions and activities of their offspring. The old, time-worn adage, "The apple does not fall far from the tree," has some significance here. In this case it means that if the child fails, look to the parent. This notion prevails despite the fact that numerous professionals in different areas of child behavior and development have stated in numerous instances that family background and conditioning will not always be the determining factor in how young people behave, what they think, and what they do.

Some sort of guilt blanket settles over parents; hence they are quick to comment on the poor status of today's youth. By constantly reminding each other how difficult it is to work with the young they hope to resolve or ease their own personal dissonance in time of youth–adult tensions. In a sense, adults attempt to have the best of two worlds. If the child does not measure up to adult expectations they say, "What can you expect with the way young people act today?" Or they will take the position that they did everything possible for their child but he was influenced by someone else's evil children. On the other hand, if the child excels the parents can take extra pleasure in the fact that in a world so filled with negative youth behavior they were able to come up with a well-behaved child.

Within this framework we can see the workings of the total social system in terms of enforcement of norms and values. No doubt some parents would just as soon disassociate themselves from the behavior of their children, if they were not constantly reminded by other adults that parents are indeed responsible for their children. It is interesting to note, for example, how difficult it is for any parent to accept the fact that his child has failed or has some personal adjustment shortcoming. Many teachers have faced irate parents—parents who insist that if the child fails, look to the teacher, or to the prevailing system of education. This situation has led to the development of a new language in parent-teacher public relations. The teacher must never say a child is bad but rather that he has not as yet found his element; never say he is a failure, rather he has untapped resources and great potential. The teacher may never say he does not get along with his peers; we declare instead that the child tends to be independent, original, or creative. One reason for the dilemma of the adult lies in the fact that despite his personal convictions, the society will not allow the parent to go unmarked once the child deviates from expected norms.

A second reason for the youth–adult breach stems from the fact that ours is a rapidly changing and complex industrial society, a society with an intricate and elaborate division of labor. Within this type of social system, the young, if they are eventually to take on the role of adult, must learn some occupational skill. As the society becomes technologically more complex there is less need for the young to rely on parents for occupational mobility. Increasingly fewer and fewer occupational skills can be handed down from father to son so the young must go beyond the home in order to attain the proficiencies which are crucial to mature adult role playing.

Part of this change is tied in with a total value alteration occurring in our society. We are less dependent on age as a basis for the allocation of roles and statuses and we are less dependent on the ascribed status that goes with one's family background. Ours is a relatively open class system where mobility is encouraged and facilitated—the child is not bound to the status of his parents but can move up and out on his own. It is a society where achievement becomes more and more important. In addition, ours is a society where youth and being youthful are held to be highly important. We emulate youth; we imitate youth. We try by all means—be it Metrecal, fashions, the Frug, or what have you—to stay with the young, to "be sociable." In traditional American society, and today in many more-primitive cultures, age and being older are correlated with wisdom. The elders of the community are emulated and heeded. In our society, and in the emergent industrial nations of the world, youth takes the upper hand since they are the most recent recipients of the kind of knowledge important to the functioning of the society. Part of the adult dilemma lies in the fact that adults see the discrepancy between allocated statuses and total societal needs. Elders may have the higher formal status but the young are the ones who stand on the new frontiers. This discrepancy becomes all the more intensified when there is an apparent need for young people, as in the case of war. In the times of national survival youth must take on responsibility for the protection and welfare of the total society.

A final factor which might help explain the continuous strain between youth and adults lies in the adults' recognition that much of youth culture represents a reflection of adult behavior and values. In many instances young people imitate—in their own style—the actions and ideas of adults. We can readily see an example of this phenomenon in the comments of a male adolescent apprehended by the police for his part in the desecration of a Chicago synagogue.

My father was always talking about the kikes and how the Jews were running everything. Whenever we walked by this Jewish church he would say something about how the Jews were talking this funny language so that Gentiles wouldn't understand what the Jews were up to. Once he said that all of the Gentiles in the neighborhood should get together and throw the Jews the hell out of Chicago before they drive the Gentiles out. Me and my buddy just decided one night that we would bust in and tear the place apart.[46]

Too often, and perhaps too late, parents see in the behavior of their children the acting out of ideas, values, and attitudes which have been part of the young person's socialization. For some parents, admission of the role they might have played in the actions of their children is a burden too difficult to accept. Rejection of this responsibility frequently takes the form of more intensive attacks on the total youth society and other socialization agencies outside the home.

---

[46] From an Anti-Defamation League interview transcript, 1960.

# Chapter II

# THE CONTEMPORARY ADOLESCENT SOCIETY

We have noted in our earlier discussion that a number of authors dealing with the problem of the socialization of the young refer to a distinct youth society. The emphasis on degree of detachment from other age groups appears to be the question these writers most frequently debate. Some take the position there really is very little difference in the expressed values and norms of a particular adolescent group and its parents. August Hollingshead, in his study of Elmtown, proposes that with few exceptions most adolescents in their behavior reflect the "class culture" of their parents. He identifies five social class groups in the Elmtown community and then goes on to show that the social class position of the adolescent's parents directly and extensively influence his behavior in relation to the school, the church, the job, recreation, peers, and family.[1]

Bernard Rosen, on the other hand, dealing with a sample of Jewish youth in regard to their observance or nonobservance of certain religious traditions, comes to the opposite conclusion. His findings suggest that the peer group exerts a greater influence on the choice of the adolescent in this matter than do parents.[2]

Burton Clark refers in his work to three subcultures operating within the American high school: the "fun subculture," the "academic subculture," and the "delinquent subculture."[3] The determinants of the fun subculture seem to be a concern with the many extracurricular activities of the school as opposed to a concern with the more intellectual matters. The fun subculture is built around athletic events, school dances, the selection of a "queen," informal clubs, sororities, fraternities, and a general concern with "building school spirit." The

---

[1] August Hollingshead, *Elmtown's Youth* (New York: John Wiley & Sons, 1949).
[2] Bernard C. Rosen, "Conflicting Group Membership: A Study of Parent-Peer Group Cross Pressures," *American Sociological Review*, XX (April, 1955), 155–61.
[3] Burton R. Clark, *Educating the Expert Society* (San Francisco: Chandler Publishing Co., 1962).

academic subculture, as might be anticipated, is centered around the more formal or traditional aspects of the learning process. Students who fall into this category are seen as primarily concerned with attaining knowledge and with intellectual pursuits. In many American high schools these students are identified by teachers as "the more serious type," while their peers may refer to them as "grinds," "creeps," "drags," or "finks." The delinquent subculture, as perceived by Clark, includes an active rejection of social as well as educational activities and an open rebellion against the formal educational establishment. These are the students who not only reject the rules of the school system but also flaunt them. The overt behavioral form is one of challenge and scorn.

Other authors, whether they are writing of Negro adolescents, members of different ethnic groups, or different religious groups, propose that for each of the youth segments studied, more than one subculture or life style appears to be in operation. Clearly then, American youth cannot be cast as a single type and there is danger in making broad, sweeping generalizations applicable to all youth. Sex, socioeconomic status, ethnicity, residence, education . . . . each of these will no doubt play some part in the norms and behavior of young people. Throughout the course of this book an attempt will be made to point out both the differences and similarities found among various youth throughout our society. Our goal at this point, however, is to deal with certain variables associated with the emergence of a youth culture in our society; to show how various scholars in the field of youth research respond to the proposition of a youth culture; and to cite several behavioral areas where we can see manifestations of this youth culture.

## THE EMERGENCE OF A YOUTH CULTURE

Perhaps the most vital task faced by any society, once it has established an efficient system of social control, is training the young for responsible adulthood. If the demand for human resources exceeds the supply in a given society, that society will be unable to maintain itself over time.

While the necessity of child training is incumbent on all societies, the means by which this training is accomplished vary greatly. A nation incorporating the caste system and limiting social mobility is likely to limit formal education to an elite group. The primitive agricultural society's educational processes will be limited and nontechnical in content.

In our society, a number of unique factors contribute to the problem of training the young. First, ours is a highly industrialized society with a complete division of labor. Second, we pride ourselves on the fact that ours is an open class society with great potential for individual occupational and social mobility. Third, our society has public school systems which not only make education available to all but actually demand attendance up to a given age, regardless of child and parental preferences. Finally, our society does not allocate certain jobs to certain people but allows free selection of occupation, regardless of the needs of the labor force.

Prior to the industrial revolution, training for adulthood was primarily the responsibility of the family. A father could teach his son a trade and this training could take place within the boundaries of the family. Not only would the family supply occupational training, it would also determine the kinds of values, norms, and attitudes transmitted to the child. Family and community identification ran high and the homogeneity of population reduced the areas of potential youth-adult conflict to a minimum.

After the industrial revolution, the developing complexity and the demand for occupational specialists brought about a dramatic shift in the nature, location, and agents of child training. The expanding technological sector required more individuals with special skills— skills which were unknown in the "good old days;" skills which could not be passed from father to son. Thus parents could no longer give their children the occupational, and in many cases the social, skills required in an increasingly technical, urban society.

The result of the increased specialization and innovations in most occupational fields led to centralization of training facilities in institutions which could afford the expenditures necessary for personnel and equipment. In short, the school took on the role of training the young for positions in the adult world.

As the years progress, and occupational roles in our society require an even higher level of training, there will be more and more to learn and less and less need for semi- and unskilled persons. Thus, the institution that took over the role of training the youth will require their students' presence for longer periods of time.

Setting apart the young in schools for extended periods of time has had a dramatic effect on the child of high school age. Outside of the training aspect of the school new functions have been added: it keeps youth out of the labor market; it provides a degree of entertainment for the community; it teaches "social skills" and "builds the whole man;" and lately it has become an ideal market place for manufacturers and merchants. Within the context of the school the adolescent is forced into extended contact with his peers and is, in a sense, isolated from the total societal complex. Over time and through continued interaction this "closed corporation" of interacting individuals takes on the characteristics of a small, private society. It develops its own ways of doing things and new things to do. It becomes a society with a subculture which is not lacking in ritual, symbols, fashions, languages, and values.

## A "POLL" OF SCHOLARS REGARDING YOUTH CULTURE

In general, the notion of adolescent subcultures has been well received among students of adolescent behavior, but dissenting voices are still heard. Several years ago Frederick Elkin and William Westley, in their article, "The Myth of Adolescent Culture."[4] rejected the notion of an adolescent culture which cuts across all class lines along with the notion of the adolescent period as a time of "storm and stress," on the basis of data collected in a suburban Canadian community which indicated little or no parent-adolescent conflict and a distinct continuity of socialization.

What appears to be a direct contradiction to the Elkin and Westley thesis is found in James S. Coleman's large-scale study of adolescent society.[5]

While differences in interpretation are not new to the behavioral sciences, it is of interest to note that both authors rely on the criterion of significant differences between the actions and values of youth and the expectations of adults. Elkin and Westley, finding few differences, reject the subcultural notion while Coleman, finding distinct differences, accepts the youth culture idea.

Feeling that clarification of the notion of adolescent culture was critical in understanding the social structural framework within which adolescents operate, David Gottlieb and Jon Reeves decided to "poll" a number of social scientists well known for their interest in adolescent behavior.[6] A nonrandom selection of some twenty social scientists was asked—noting the Coleman and Elkin-Westley points of view—for their comments on the existence of an adolescent culture and the criteria they would utilize to establish the validity of the notion.

The responses indicated that, in general, the notion of the ex-

[4] Frederick Elkin and William Westley, "The Myth of Adolescent Culture," *American Sociological Review*, Vol. 20 (1955). See also by the same authors, "The Protection Environment and Adolescent Socialization," *Social Forces*, Vol. 35 (1957).

[5] James S. Coleman, *The Adolescent Society* (Glencoe. Ill.: The Free Press of Glencoe, 1961), p. 3.

[6] David Gottlieb and Jon Reeves, *Adolescent Behavior in Urban Areas* (New York: The Free Press of Glencoe, 1963).

istence of an adolescent subculture is accepted by many professionals. A number of the social scientists stressed that probably more than one subculture exists, if one looks for variations in socioeconomic, ethnic, and religious background as well as for differences in age, residence, and perhaps school attended.

There also seemed to be general agreement that the operational criteria used to identify and establish the existence of the subculture should involve observed differences in values and behavior between adolescents and adults.

Mitigating the general agreement are comments which revealed hesitation due to questions of terminology and semantics— that is, "Exactly what do we mean by culture or subculture?" Robert Hess of the University of Chicago remarked that he would not accept the notion if ". . . you use the term *adolescent culture* to mean a set of values that are independent of the values of adult society, and to imply that these values are transmitted from one generation to another (i.e., are socialized)." But if we take the term to indicate patterns of behavior which are different from adult values, as well as a distinct psychosocial phase of life, there is, for Hess, a strong argument for the existence of adolescent culture or subculture.

H. H. Remmers, Director of the Purdue Opinion Panel, also feels that the existence of the culture is basically a matter of semantics and operational definition.

A second factor which stimulated some comment is whether great or significant differences really exist between the attitudes and values endorsed by adolescents and those held by adults. While there are differences, just how great are they? Bernice Neugarten of Chicago takes the view that ". . . the notion of an adolescent subculture that operates separately from, or in defiance of, the adult's subculture is a much exaggerated phenomemon." She holds that the peer group teaches the adult culture and that the adolescent has basically the same values found in the adult world. H. H. Remmers feels that the behavioral differences can be understood in terms of "differential social behavioral norms." For him, there are greater similarities than differences between adults and adolescents. "My impression is that teenagers are trying very hard to 'learn the rules of the game' of the adult world."

Another respondent looks at the question of differences and, citing nineteenth- and early twentieth-century literature, contends there is probably less of a gap between generations today than there was at the turn of the century. While he feels there is greater psychological understanding between the generations today he also thinks that the penetration of the high school has given great impetus to the social system of adolescents.

Muzafer Sherif of the University of Oklahoma notes that the supposition of the existence of an adolescent culture is an empirical question and that its answer depends upon the definition of "culture." Any culture, for Sherif, presupposes at least (1) some system of status and role relations and (2) some distinctive values or norms. These normative systems can then be measured by (1) uniformities of behavior within a defined range of acceptance, (2) reactions to deviations outside of that range, and (3) the sanctions for acceptable and deviant behavior. Sherif goes on to comment that, depending on the adolescent's location in the social scheme, adolescent culture will inevitably reflect various aspects of the dominant adult status and norm systems. He concludes with this statement on his research position: "In any specific situation, I would favor intensive study of the distinctiveness of the status and norm systems and also the extent of its linkage to pre-existing adult values or norms."

In discussing the methodological problems in the measurement of differences, Ruth S. Cavan notes that the term "subculture" is too loose and has too many meanings; it seems to imply basic conformity to the main culture with deviations in some areas and, in addition, varying degrees of conflict with the main culture. In speaking of the measurement of differences she says:

> What is the standard against which one should measure adolescent deviating cultural forms? The parents' culture? The culture of the specific ethnic group to which the parents belong? Or the general American culture? If the last, what is this culture? Sociologists sometimes speak of a middle class Protestant ethos as the standard. But a rather large proportion of the population is neither middle class nor Protestant and in fact may be opposed to this particular ethos.

Miss Cavan accepts a variety of subcultures, each related to a specific social situation of stability or change. Her subcultures reflect varying degrees of congruence, conflict, and destructiveness.

Albert K. Cohen, author of *Delinquent Boys: The Culture of the Gang*, adds yet another dimension when he looks at "what we mean by a subculture." [7]

> The key question is: What do we mean by a subculture? It cannot mean that there are distinct adolescent patterns of behaving, no matter how different they are from those of adults, if those differences are merely ways of conforming to age-specific role expectations. I like to put it in terms of game model. If people are playing different positions their behavior may differ greatly but the differences derive from the same set of rules or cultural understandings. Even if people are playing different games, their cultures are not necessarily different.

---

[7] Albert K. Cohen, *Delinquent Boys: The Culture of the Gang* (Glencoe, Ill.: The Free Press of Glencoe, 1955).

Each culture provides rules for different sorts of games, including rules about who may play them and under what conditions, and also rules defining the relative prestige of different games. So, if I play basketball today and hockey tomorrow, my culture has not changed. I am merely engaged in different activities, which run off, to be sure, according to different "rules of the game," but the rules that define both games are part of the repertoire of the same culture.

The fact that there are "adolescent social systems" does not, *of itself,* mean that there is a distinct adolescent culture. Adults may avoid involvement in such systems or eschew the activities because they are "childish," "kid stuff," etc., and yet both they and the kids may see the involvement of *kids* in systems of this sort as quite appropriate. I am quite sure that a great deal of what is interpreted as a distinct "youth culture" is implicit in the *common* culture in this way, and is not "subcultural." It seems to me equally clear, however, that there are distinct adolescent subcultures. The distinctions may be distinctions of *emphasis,* of *relative* valuation, etc., but that does not make them less distinct. I would say, then, that the culture of young people is largely the common culture they share with their parents, but marked, here and there, with differences in subcultural emphasis. These differences may be trifling or they may be of very great consequence.

A sufficient test for *me* that the cultures of young people are significantly different from *my* culture is that I don't understand much of what goes on amongst them, and much of what I see I am upset by. I don't understand because I simply don't know what rules they play by, where this or that "fits in," although *they* obviously know. And equally obviously I and most other adults place very different value upon certain games, or certain ways of playing them, than do the kids.

It is, however, very difficult, it seems to me, to set up workable *operational* criteria for subcultural distinctiveness, whether we are concerned with possible cultural differences between adults and children, or possible differences among youth cultures. The reason, as indicated, is that differences in the sorts of activities in which people engage, the goals to which they are oriented, the criteria by which they evaluate themselves, etc., need not indicate that they are responding to different cultures.

In the response to this "poll" we noted a general acceptance of specific age-grade behavior patterns which can be accepted as an indication of a distinct subculture. Most respondents felt that, while there was much overlapping, adolescent behavior and values do set youth apart from other age groups.

In most cases the critical point in accepting or rejecting the notion of adolescent subcultures lies in the observance of distinct differences between adolescents and some other age group, typically adults. However, a number of difficulties arise from this approach. First, how are we to define "differences?" Second, differences in what? Third, how do we isolate values or behaviors which are solely the product of adolescent peer contact from those learned from adults? Fourth, what is accomplished if we finally do note areas of difference between adolescents and adults? Will this prove the adolescent peer group has more influence on educational aspirations than parental influence has? Will this allow us to predict an adolescent's behavior when faced with the pressures of his peers and the desires of his parents? Actually, a description of differences will do little more than reveal where adolescents agree or disagree with adults.

In our approach, the question of the existence of an adolescent culture should not depend on degrees or types of differences found between adolescents and adults. For us, differences may be sufficient but they are not necessary in investigating adolescent behavior. In the case of the adolescent the question is not deviation from some universal norm but rather how involvement in and commitment to the peer group influence the behavior and beliefs of the participant. Once we can pinpoint areas of influence and how they operate we will be better able to evaluate the meaning of adolescent cultures.

## SOME EXAMPLES OF YOUTH CULTURE IN ACTION

Even though variations do exist in the behavior of youth it is possible to identify a number of areas where the actions of adolescents are distinct in style from those of other age groups. In these situations the norm of acceptance or preference is set for the most part by members of the adolescent group and deviation from these standards is likely to bring about peer-imposed sanctions.

Before presenting these youth-centered activities, though, it is important to remind the reader that regardless of the areas discussed we will always find youth who do not "go along" with the group.

We begin this portion of youth culture behavior with a discussion of the adolescent as a consumer.

### The Adolescent as a Consumer

Many agencies and institutions in our society are established specifically to provide commodities for youth. Schools provide both educational and social goods for young people. Religious institutions attempt to provide young people with a set of ethical and moral beliefs. Manufacturers come up with a variety of products which they hope to sell to youth. Through the mass media we see a variety of magazines, radio and television programs, and books directed at the youth market. In each case the end goal is to "sell" a particular product, idea, sentiment, or attitude to the young consumer. Interestingly enough, while the motivations of the adult seller will vary there is much similarity in the methods used in selling the product.

The teacher, the clergy, the clothing manufacturer, the disc jockey, and the magazine publisher adopt similar merchandizing programs. In most instances the appeal is made not to the individual but to the group; the youngster is reminded again and again that a particular product will enable him to stand in good stead with his peers. He can prevent isolation and minimize "that left-out feeling" by buying or accepting the commodity being offered. Young people are encouraged to stay in school so they will not be left behind when their friends finish high school and go on to college. Religion is sometimes offered as the answer for young people who are unable to find their place in the social setting of the school or neighborhood; by joining the church youth group the individual will be able to meet and interact with other young people. Disc jockeys are quick to emphasize the peer group in their attempt to create a following. Personal requests and dedications, school activity announcements, and the latest happenings in the "rock-and-roll world" are used to hold their listener. By keeping in touch the youngster stays aware of the latest in music and social events. The clothing manufacturer endorses the same approach in stressing, "This fall loafer shoes are out and those in the know will be wearing white bucks." The many "teen magazines" often stress the peer-group orientation. By reading this article or that column the adolescent can learn what "the teen-age world" thinks about a singer, the latest dance fad, hair styles, kissing on the first date, and so on. In each case we can see that manufacturers and sellers of youth-directed products recognize that adolescents are very much influenced by their peers and by the social system in which they function. In addition, there is a real awareness that youth are a potent economic source in our society.

The adolescent does at times seem to be a slave to fashion and fad and quite vulnerable to the slighest variation in clothing and grooming trends. We can observe how new clothing fashions are introduced and the processes by which the youth society adopts them. In many instances, and this seems most true of girls, the primary motivating factor for accepting the latest fashion is a desire for group approval. By keeping in style with the current trends the adolescent makes it clear to his peers that he is not "square" but rather aware of what is passé and what is acceptable. In many high schools and colleges students are judged by their visible presentation of self. Entrance into the more exclusive or prestige cliques is determined not so much by academic or intellectual qualities as by how the young person looks and what he wears. While little empirical evidence is available as to just who sets the current fashions and fads among young people, it is generally felt they originate from the upper socioeconomic groups. From a structural point of view the flow of clothing fashions is seen to move down from the more affluent adolescents to members of the lower social class groups.

An added factor to the diffusion of clothing fashions and fads is geographic region. Several years ago, for example, while the "Ivy League" look was rapidly accepted by adolescents in the East and West it was not readily endorsed by youth in the Midwest and South. Regardless of the pattern of adaption, however, it is fairly apparent that concern with peer approval is very much related to what young people wear and how they wear it.

In her study of certain psychological factors related to clothing and appearance among adolescent girls, Sylvia S. Silverman [8] found that all age groups (girls ranging in age from seven to twelve in a suburban high school) conformed closely in the style of dress for daily wear, with sweaters and skirts, socks, and flat-heeled shoes the predominant style. The use of make-up increased with age, but lipstick and powder were used even at twelve. With slight variations in age groups, the motives in clothing and grooming revolved around the desire for approval and a desire for sexual attractiveness. Economic differences were reflected only in luxury items. Finally, Miss Silverman found that those adolescent girls with high ratings in clothing and grooming awareness were more likely to be members of prestige groups and perceived as leaders by their peers.

Coleman reports similar findings in his study of adolescents from a number of Midwest high schools. He notes that "appearance," including both clothing and grooming, was seen by many of his respondents as important to membership in "the leading crowd." Coleman adds that although dress styles may at times differ from one school to the next the importance of clothing was always stressed by adolescents.[9] Again, we are able to see that even though one group of adolescents favors style A while another prefers style B, there is conformity to the prevailing fashion, and this conformity is very much based on peer-group evaluations.

The adolescent's preference for media seems to center on a desire for the light or fantastic as opposed to the more serious or educational content. Paul I. Lyness indicates that while girls prefer stories dealing with love, glamor, and private life exposés, boys have a stronger preference for violence and adventure.[10]

Although differences exist in desired theme content preferred by males and females there are similarities in how the youth society

[8] Sylvia S. Silverman, *Clothing and Appearance: Their Psychological Implications for Teen-Age Girls* (New York: Bureau of Publications, Teachers College, Columbia University, 1945).

[9] Coleman, *op. cit.*

[10] Paul I. Lyness, "Patterns in the Mass Communication Tastes of the Young Audience," *Journal of Educational Psychology*, XLII (December, 1951), pp. 449–67.

functions to hold both groups to certain kinds of magazines. We see the impact of the peer group among certain groups of boys in their endorsement of particular sport and hot-rod magazines. Knowledge of current athletic heroes and the latest innovations in hot-rod components is gained through the continued reading of these magazines. Generally, however, the magazine market seems to have the greater appeal among female adolescents. The fact that girls have less social mobility than boys and are more restricted in activity involvement is no doubt related to their greater involvement with certain media. The most popular magazines among young girls deal with movie stars, singing idols, dating behavior, and personal grooming. This interest reflects the adolescent girl's greater concern for approval from members of her own sex than from boys. The greater activity allowed boys leads to a situation where girls must be more dependent on other girls for social involvement. While boys have access to athletic activities, hot rods, and other extracurricular programs, girls are restricted in their range of social participation. In many instances the adolescent female is placed in a position where entrance into a social activity must await the actions of a male. Each of these factors contributes to the adolescent girl's greater dependency on outside sources for aid in the fulfillment of desired goals and activities. The many teen and movie magazines supply the kinds of information and cues the young girls seeks. In addition, these media and their romantic love themes provide the young girl another area for personal involvement, even though at the fantasy level.

The female orientation of the teen magazine is rather apparent and can be readily seen from a review of cover photos, ads, and content. The covers usually portray some young, popular male hero. The Beatles, Elvis Presley, Bobby Darin, Ricky Nelson, Edd Byrnes, Fabian, Frankie Avalon, Troy Donahue, Paul Anka, and Dion are among those publicized during the last few years. Rarely do females appear on the cover of these magazines. The articles, as mentioned earlier, provide advice on behavior and grooming. Typical subjects include "How to Make Him Care," "Crushes: Good or Bad?", "High School Marriages," "Ten Dates You Can Do Without," "How to be Smooth," "How Not to Kiss a Boy," and "Ten Rules for Playing the Field." [11] In addition, each of these magazines carries a special section for questions submitted by readers. For the most part the questions center about the readers' desire for help in three distinct areas: relationship with boys, grooming, and getting along with parents.

---

[11] See Charles H. Brown, "Self-Portrait: The Teen Type Magazine," *The Annals,* Vol. 338 (November, 1961) pp. 13–21.

The teen magazines stimulate a group-centered interest among readers in several ways. First, by publishing the letters of young subscribers others come to recognize the problems they face are not unique. The quoted letter which follows is typical of how this identification with others operates among some adolescent girls: [12]

Dear Editor,
. . . Less than a year ago, I was the shyest person in the world. . . . Then I started reading your magazine, TEEN WORLD, and I discovered that I wasn't the only one who had this problem of shyness. . . .

The second method by which peer cohesiveness is encouraged is in the formation of "fan clubs." Through these organizations, with members throughout the world, young people are able to channel both their energies and their emotions around some young popular male. The teen magazine serves the function of clearing house for these groups, noting where the different fan clubs are located and where photos of the worshipped hero can be obtained and presenting stories dealing with the private life of the idol.

A third method for stimulating group involvement through these magazines is in the development of "pen-pal" programs. Virtually all teen magazines contain several pages devoted to the names, ages, and hobbies of readers who are interested in coming in contact with other young people. Typically, vital statistics are included describing the color of eyes and hair as well as the height and weight of the individual. Two examples of "pen-pal" requests are noted below; the first from a fifteen-year-old girl and the second from an eighteen-year-old boy:

I really dig chocolate cake, which isn't too good for a gal who wants to be an actress-model. I'm 15, have green eyes and enjoy horseback riding with my friends.

My favorite hobby is diving and I'd like to make a splash with you! I'm 18, nuts about Annette (formerly with the Walt Disney Mouseketeers), traveling, and barbecued beef. Please send a picture.

As there are variations in the behavior of youth so are there differences in the audiences these magazines attempt to reach. From a content analysis of format, advertisements, and letters to the editor we are able to note that magazine appeals are purposely directed to youth of different ages and social class backgrounds. In this respect these magazines are similar to the magazines geared to older adult groups. *Teen*, for example, is presented as "Young America's Beauty-Fashion and Entertainment Magazine." It is directed at the suburban middle-class youngster and includes stories not unlike those found

---

[12] *Ibid.*, p. 16.

in *McCalls, Vogue, Redbook,* and *The Ladies Home Journal.* As is the case with these adult magazines, the characters presented in the stories are sophisticated, well-dressed, and aware of the most current trends in clothing and grooming. There is little emphasis on popular idols, no pen-pal section or fan-club activity. A typical issue will include ads for automobiles, expensive jewelry, hope chests, and cocktail dresses. There is no hard sell and a minimum of the flash and color of other teen magazines.

In contrast to *Teen* are *Dig, Teen Pin-Ups,* and *Teen Album.* These magazines, resembling in many respects such publications as *True Story, True Romance, Modern Screen,* and *Hollywood Romances,* are clearly directed at younger adolescents and those from either rural or working-class families. They are for the youngster who no doubt is limited both in access to material things and in the many social activities of the affluent adolescent. There are no full-page advertisements for automobiles, hope chests, expensive clothes or jewelry. In fact, these magazines contain very few advertisements with the exception of those for inexpensive trinkets, ointments for the prevention of acne, and cheap cosmetics. There are few short stories and most content is devoted to items about young movie stars and recording idols. These are flashy magazines with provocative headlines such as: "The Night Haley Shocked Hollywood," "Connie Stevens: A Girl Can Go Too Far—I Know," "Exclusive: Why Dick Chamberlain Fears His Past."

Popular music is still another place where the adolescent plays the role of an active consumer. Each year young people invest millions of dollars in the latest popular recordings. Through the constant playing of certain hit songs and the comments of the disc jockeys the adolescent comes to learn which songs are the most popular. In some cases the best-selling number is not the one recorded by the superior vocalist but rather by the current singing idol. As we shall see in a later chapter, the theme and content of these songs are not unrelated to their popularity among many adolescents. For the moment, however, we will be concerned with the part played by the peer group in maintaining solidarity in respect to some vocalist or song.

Coleman's work with adolescents indicates a high degree of consensus among young people as to what kinds of music they prefer. About two thirds of the young people interviewed chose either "rock and roll" or "other popular music" as their preference. Less than one tenth of all Coleman's sample selected "classical" music as their first choice.[13]

[13] Coleman, *op. cit.,* p. 23.

The impact of the peer group on which songs are endorsed or purchased is shown in the work of John Johnstone and Elihu Katz,[14] who reported that peer group affiliation acts as an influence on which disc jockey adolescents listen to and the kinds of recordings they purchase.

Coleman's study deals in some detail with the importance of popular music among adolescents. For one thing, he notes that while hit songs are vital to all adolescents they seem to have particular significance for girls. The explanation offered is related to the adolescent girls' greater desire for reinforcement of the romantic role. Coleman proposes that the adolescent males' involvement with cars is similar to the girls' involvement with popular music. Both use these as their involvements within the structure of the youth culture. An interest in and awareness of cars and popular music are ways in which the adolescent finds his place in the youth culture. Finally, popular music as well as the many school and community dances act to bring young people together and to further the cohesiveness of the youth society.

### The Adolescent as a Builder of School and Community Spirit

Because much of the adolescent culture finds its roots and activities within the high school it is not surprising that one salient area of the youth culture is centered about the school. In this case it is not so much the academic programs as the countless extracurricular and social functions that have become an integral part of many American high schools and communities. It should be recognized that the high school and college do more than just provide formal education for the youngster. On the contrary, the current trend in many educational institutions is on the development of the "well-rounded individual." The school provides a multitude of extras for the student. Athletic events, social clubs, dances, community plays, and exhibits are but a few. These activities serve several purposes: they help create a feeling of esprit among students; they do much, especially in smaller communities, to stimulate community solidarity; they act as areas for the further operation of the youth culture.

Athletic events are certainly a primary source for building school spirit among students. Through pep rallies, school cheers, and the declarations of adults within and outside the school, youngsters are constantly encouraged to support their team. In addition to this are the growing phenomena of playoffs and statewide championships which are heavily publicized by the press, radio, and television. While

---

[14] John Johnstone and Elihu Katz, "Youth and Popular Music: A Study in the Sociology of Taste," *American Journal of Sociology*, LXII (May, 1957), pp. 563–68.

this competition between schools may stimulate a greater verbal attachment to his school on the part of the individual student, it also creates a number of serious problems. For one, the competition has reached a point in some communities of open violence between students from different schools. The situation is most explosive where the competition is between different racial groups. In one community known to the authors white students shouted insults such as "jungle bunnies" and "Here are the apes from Congo High" at a team of Negro basketball players. The game ended in a series of fights between students from two schools. In other instances the pressure of competition has been such that student-players and nonplayers alike have been unable to concentrate on studies in anticipation of the next game. One high school principal tells us that through much of the football and basketball seasons formal education comes to a virtual halt in his school.

The athletic competition seems to have a similar effect on adult members of the community, although this seems most true of smaller communities. The culmination of state playoffs manifests itself in the mass migration of adults from all over the state to the place where the final games are to be played. Local newspapers give wide coverage to these events and sports bulletins noting the latest scores are repeated on the hour. What occurs in some communities can be seen from the following newspaper excerpt:

Not all ghost towns are out West. This Shiawassee County town might look like home to a passing Texan or an Arizona cowpoke about 8 o'clock tonight.

The townspeople have been struck with basketball fever ever since its high school Ramblers won the district championship. They haven't recuperated since.

Leaving only a corporal's guard behind, the whole town will be in Lansing tonight to see the Ramblers play Houghton at the Civic Center in a Class C semi-final game.

. . . From the town's undertaker to its president, the garage mechanic to the supermarket clerk, there is complete support and enthusiasm for the team.

. . . Up and down Main Street the enthusiasm and excitement continues. All conversation is directed to basketball. Some stores closed in mid-afternoon so that people could leave early enough to get a seat for the tournament game.

Athletic competition as well as other extracurricular activity serves the dual purpose of building school and community spirit. At the same time, however, it does much to keep the youth culture alive. Within the framework of these athletic and social activities youth are given an opportunity for further personal interaction. School dances become a source for learning more about the latest fashions and fads in dance, music, dating patterns, and clothing styles. The social activities add to the formation and maintenance of student cliques and private clubs. The athletic events and the support they receive from peers as well as adults aid in convincing students that prestige within the school goes not to the scholar or the serious citizen but rather to the boy who can run with a football or shoot baskets or to the girl who is selected as cheerleader. The rewards for athletic achievement are visibility, publicity, and the wearing of a school letter. These rewards are more than a match for those given the outstanding student or the serious student citizen who in many schools is shown little public recognition. The scholar may find his name on the principal's list or may receive a lapel pin or certificate, but rarely is he granted the attention, privileges, and prestige offered the athlete or popular boy and girl.

### The Adolescent as a Responsible Citizen

The areas of youth society emphasized to this point have portrayed the adolescent in large part as someone frivolous, subject to the whims of style and fad, and generally unconcerned with the world in which he lives. As was mentioned earlier, this popular image may be partially explained by the picture most frequently presented of American youth. It would be ethically wrong and empirically incorrect to allow this generalized impression of youth as irresponsible and unconcerned to prevail without presenting some contrasting information.

There are numerous examples of situations where young people have been involved in programs and activities concerned with improving the community and its institutions. Although many of these activities have community involvement as but one part of a total youth program, contributions are made by young people. National programs such as the Boy Scouts, 4-H, Hi-Y are supplemented by a variety of local school, church, and group work agencies. As part of their over-all function each of these organizations attempts, to some degree, to involve the adolescent in activities which enable him to work toward the betterment of his community—activities such as working with the aged, being a social service volunteer or hospital aide, collecting funds for the economically limited or physically handicapped. On a less publicized level are the activities of such organizations as the American Friends Service Committee in which youth from different communities work as teachers, roadbuilders, farmhands, and general aides in the total community development of depressed areas.

More recently we have witnessed the organization and operation of the Peace Corps. Thousands of young people have applied to the Peace Corps and many are now engaged in purposeful activities throughout the world. In many cases these are well-educated youth who are in a position to earn more than adequate salaries in their field of specialized training. Each, in fact, delays immediate material gratification for the opportunity to help others.

Similar domestic programs can be found in some American communities. Students from several Ivy League colleges have devoted their time and energy, without financial reward, to work with the socioeconomically deprived in major urban areas. These college students act as educational assistants by helping young people who are having difficulty both at home and in school. Another group of college students has spent summers in Prince Edward County, Virginia, attempting to give some formal education to Negro youngsters who were "locked out" of their schools by segregation policies. Lately we have seen the emergence of a Student Education Corps at one large state university. Organized and directed by students, this corps has the purpose of supplying teachers in economically deprived communities with the talents and skills of college students. Within this program college volunteers act as teacher aides in preparing science, dance, art, drama, music, and recreational programs.

To these contributions of young people as responsible citizens a number of others could be provided, not the least of which is the part played by youth in times of war and national crisis.

Aside from the efforts of youth organized in groups, many young people make some contribution as individuals to their community: adolescents who work as volunteers in youth centers, read to the blind, serve in hospitals, schools, and other community agencies.

In noting the more serious efforts of young people we have attempted to indicate that given the opportunity many young people will act as responsible citizens. The major problem does not seem to be a lack of zeal or motivation on the part of the young but rather a shortage of worthwhile and meaningful activities in which they can become a part. If we limit youth involvement to the purely social and athletic programs provided by schools and communities it follows that these will be the activities which will attract and hold young people. Sufficient evidence is certainly on hand to verify the proposition that given an opportunity to play the role of citizen of the community and nation, many young people will turn their creative efforts to significant pursuits.

### Summary and Conclusions

In this chapter we have examined the processes by which youth cultures have arisen and operated in our society. We took the position that although there were distinct qualities and patterns in the behavior of youth, it would be wrong to talk in terms of a single youth culture; rather, there will be variations influenced by the young person's background. We also dealt with the analytical problem involved in the definition and empirical validation of the notion of a youth culture. From our poll we note that there is general agreement as to the existence of a youth culture but some hedging as to how it functions, how it is best studied, and how different it really is from other age groupings. Finally, materials were presented dealing with certain behavioral areas where we are able to see how this youth culture operates in respect to the total societal setting.

From this discussion it should be clear that youth are most often seen as unconcerned and uninvolved in the more serious functions of the society because of two factors: first, the more hectic and deviant activities of young people are the most likely to come to the attention of the population, and second, few channels are open to young people which will allow them to take on responsible roles within the framework of their communities and schools.

# Chapter III

# THREE CASE STUDIES

In the previous chapter we discussed certain of the more universal characteristics of the American adolescent. It was noted that although there are many similarities in the life style of adolescents, distinct differences can be found. In part, these observed differences reflect the earlier experiences of the individual and the manner in which he goes about the business of goal fulfillment. Variations in family background, school, and leisure-time patterns of the youngster will certainly have an effect on the adolescent. It is important, then, that the reader recognize that while we can make certain broad generalizations about young people with respect to specific behavior patterns there will be variations as we move from one group of adolescents to the next.

In this chapter we will examine the developmental experiences of three young people. Each differs from the other in regard to family background, religion, socioeconomic status, and community of origin. Each has encountered different kinds of encouragements and impediments. Each has pursued certain ends and employed a variety of means in order to attain these goals. The three have in common the fact they were born in the United States and are now in the process of completing their college studies. Our purpose in presenting these histories is to give the reader some added insights as to how different types of youth view themselves, their peers, and the society in which they live. It is hoped that these three presentations will shed some light on the impact of the various forces that play a part in the socialization of the young.

The method employed to relate the experiences of our three young people is known as the case-history technique. In relating their experiences they deal with what they see as the salient factors in their lives. Little restriction was placed on what they were to write about. Each was told to discuss his background, his ideas, and his aspirations. The case histories are presented as written by these young people with editing limited to changing certain names and places.

In selecting these case studies we were motivated by a desire to give the reader an intimate look at the lives and experiences of young people who differed in many respects. The choice of a Caucasian of Greek ethnic origin, a girl who came from an affluent Protestant background, and a Negro who experienced high school integration in the Deep South was quite deliberate. It is our belief that by telling their stories those involved in the understanding of human behavior can better identify and evaluate the variables influencing the behavior of young people.

The first case history deals with a young man who describes his life in a medium-sized industrial community. He relates his earlier experiences as a member of a youth gang and discusses the factors he sees as playing an important role in his moving away from that gang. The second history is the work of a young woman who tells of her life in a fairly well-to-do American suburb. She discusses her involvement in school activities at both the high school and college level and finally identifies those factors which she feels were most salient in bringing about changes in her attitudes, values, and aspirations. The final personal history differs from the others in that we identify the author and the people he writes of since their names have been discussed in a variety of newspaper and magazine articles. The author, who is a Negro, deals with his experiences and impressions as a young adolescent going through the dramatic events of high school integration in a Southern community.

## CASE STUDY #1: GANG LEADER AND COLLEGE HERO

I was born in a medium-sized factory city in the Midwest. My parents had little formal education, both of them coming to this country from their native Greece. They arrived in America when they were quite young and like many others from Greece they settled in the city where I was born. My father is part of a long line of men who have worked both as shoe builders and shoe repairers. We lived in an old house near the center of town. It was not a slum section but it certainly was not the finest section of the town. I guess most people would call it a working-class neighborhood. There were three children; my older sister who is now married, a twin brother who died when he was three years old, and myself. I can recall little of my brother but I remember the night he died. Till this day no one is really sure as to what caused his death. The doctors felt that it was probably a disease of the blood. Aside from my immediate family there were lots of other relatives—aunts, uncles, cousins and some great uncles. Being of Greek descent they were pretty close and there was a lot of contact between the family. We would have family picnics and big parties celebrating weddings, births, and most any happy occasion. I know there was and still is to a lesser degree a lot of pressure for "keeping it in the family." When the older boys and girls began to go out on dates the older people were there to make sure that they went with other Greeks. It seemed like the greatest crime you could commit was to marry someone who was not Greek.

I had an older cousin who met a girl while he was in the Army. She was a nice girl but she was not Greek. He was pretty serious about her and after getting out of the service he went to see her in Boston. All of the relatives got together and worked out the strategy for keeping them apart. When he got back home they told him they had made special arrangements for him to get a job in California. One of my uncles had a cousin in California who owned a radio and television repair shop. They called him on the phone and told him that they had to do something about my cousin and this girl. The Californian relative said not to worry and to send him out and that he would take care of everything. When they told my cousin he got pretty angry and said he would not go and they had no business to tell him who he should marry. He said they were old-fashioned and they did not understand that things were different in this country. They really did not argue with him but they just continued to wear him down. They told him that he could marry this girl if he wanted to but that first he should have a job. My aunt kept pounding at him that if he was so sure he loved this girl he should not be afraid to go away from her for a while. She said that if the girl was true and he really loved her the separation wouldn't mean a thing. In a few weeks my cousin was on his way to Los Angeles. He took the job and it was not long before he married a Greek girl. The relative in California did a good job. I think the importance of marrying your own is still a big thing with my family but I don't think it is what it used to be. I have gone out with girls who were not Greek and my parents have never really tried to stop me. Maybe they are at a point where they know it would be useless to try.

The relationships between the relatives was a very close one but it was not limited to relatives alone. An important thing here was the Greek clan. My parents belonged to a fraternal organization and it was within this group and the family that they had all of their social life. They did not go to movies. They did go to church. As for myself, I went to church when I was very young but stopped when I was about eight.

When I was a kid (about five or six), I first started spending a lot of time away from the house. My father worked long hours and my mother helped him and was always busy. There was not much for kids to do around the house so most of us spent our time outside. We never did anything wrong, just general playing of games like hide and seek and kick the can. The pattern of being outside and away from the house was one that started early for all of the kids in my neighborhood. Most of us came from families where our folks never took us places. Sometimes there would be a picnic at the park or a clan party but that was about the extent of it. It was not that they did not care about us but that they were either working all the time or they could not afford it, or they did not know where to take us or what we would enjoy. My folks were concerned about me but they never really knew how to deal with me. They seldom gave me any specific kinds of instructions but would always tell me to be good and to stay out of trouble. This was the kind of thing that went on for years, their telling me to be good and to stay out of trouble.

In grade school I was an average student. I seldom got into trouble with the exception of little things like running in the hall or laughing or talking in class. Usually we were all pretty well behaved in class. I think we were afraid of the teachers. They were older women and they would not take any fooling around. I remember we used to talk about the teachers and say that none of them could smile and that if they did their faces would cave in. As I grew older I was closer with the same boys that I played with when I was in grade school. The big thing that held us together then was baseball and basketball. In baseball we were part of a Little League team. Later most of us still played ball when we were in high school. It was about the time we entered high school that we really became a gang. Before that time we never really did anything bad—some fights and a little stealing but that was it. None of us drank and only a few of the guys would smoke. By the time we were fourteen and fifteen most of the fellows were smoking and drinking. Things really changed. We caused a lot of trouble both in and out of school. The boys began to do more drinking and looking for girls. We were not interested in just necking with a girl; we wanted one who would go all the way. We also broke further away from our parents. We would come home for supper, eat in a hurry, and take off again. I did my homework but I don't think the others did much of their schoolwork. My folks, especially my mother, would try to keep some control over me but I always got out of the house. My father never said much—I don't think he knew what I was doing.

For the most part the guys I ran with did not like school and they made their feelings very clear. They skipped school, they argued with the teachers, and they had a lot of trouble with the principal. One buddy of mine gave a teacher such a bad time that she just stood in front of the class and cried. These guys never did any homework and looked forward to the time when they could quit school. I was an average student but not too interested in my studies. For me the most important thing about high school was the fact that I could play football and basketball. This was the main reason why I did my homework and tried to get passing grades. I played varsity and that was one of the reasons the other fellows in the group looked up to me. Not only that, I was passing my classes and that was something they could not do. Both of these reasons, my doing well in sports, which was something they respected, and my passing grades, something they could not understand, gave me prestige with the gang. They thought that I was pretty cool in that I could hit it off with the teachers and still do well in athletics. In addition kids who were not in the gang paid a lot of attention to me and that was still another reason that the boys thought I was something special.

This division between the kids in the high school was really important. We would call these kids the cake eaters or church goers. They were the middle-class kids who had the money and clothes. The biggest kick we got was when we could shake them up. These good kids would never have anything to do with us. I think it was more our rejecting them than their putting us down. One thing was certain —any girl who wanted to keep her reputation would not be seen in public with any guy from the gang. I say in public because some of these well-to-do girls did spend time with us. They would make us promise that we would not say anything about it. It was funny how many of them who were with us would have flipped if they knew that the night before we were with one of their girl friends. I think the main reason they wanted to be with us was that we were different. They thought we were pretty exciting and wild.

As far as girls went we did little dating. We stayed away from school dances or the places where high school kids would hang out. We usually picked up some girls or we drove downtown and found some older women. We never wasted time with formalities. Most girls knew pretty quickly exactly what the boys were interested in.

In about the junior year of high school we began to branch out in our activities. We did a higher level of stealing and there was more violence. I remember one night we went to a church where they were having a youth dance. While everyone else was dancing we cleaned out the kitchen of the church. We took the coffee maker, silverware, pots and pans, knives, candlestick holders, and finally the carpet from another room. From this kind of stealing we got into "rolling queers" [homosexuals]. The idea was to drive downtown and find the places where these guys hung out. We would get to know them, have a few drinks, and later jump them and take their money and any jewelry. The idea was to have a few drinks with them, get the guy high, and then take off on him after getting his stuff. There were times when I had about six watches. One night when we were working on a queer the police came up the alley. They made the boys stand with their hands against the wall and they began to search them. I managed to get away and watched the whole thing from a doorway. Later the boys told me that the police took them down to the station and questioned them. The police asked who else had been involved. No one gave them any information. This was one thing that you never did, tell on any other guy. Being caught by the police was a new experience and some of the fellows were less enthusiastic about trying the same thing again. Some of the guys though, did it again and again.

Right up to the time I finished high school the gang stayed together. The other fellows continued to do a lot of drinking and running around. This was most true of the ones who dropped out of high school. Some of them got jobs and with the money they made they really lived it up. I had thought about quitting school but did not for two reasons. First, my older sister was important in that she kept at me and insisted that I do my work and think about college. Next, I had done fairly well in athletics and a number of colleges were interested in me. I feel pretty sure that if it had not been for the athletic scholarship I would never have gone to college.

Of the eight boys in the gang two of us finished high school. The other fellow started college, lasted one year and quit, and then went into the army. I am the only one in the group who stayed in college. Two of the other fellows got married before they were twenty and both were separated from their wives within a year. At the present time the others are either in the army or working in factories or in city jobs.

The average age of the group is now about twenty-two. Two more have married during the last few years and they seem settled. Another is now engaged. The gang has slowly fallen apart. There are three members who continue to be very close. While they no longer are involved in stealing or rolling queers they still do a lot of drinking and looking for women. The three of them are very much alike in that they never think in terms of the future but rather they live for the day. There have been a number of times that we have talked and they say that if they had to do it again they would have finished high school and tried for college. They all seem realistic about their futures. They do not expect to get rich and they do not kid themselves about being happily married men. In a sense I seem to still be the leader of this group. Even though we are not as close as we once were, whenever I come home they come to the house. Most of them, even the ones that are married, drive up to the campus for the home football games. They think college life is a great thing, not because of the academic advantages but because of the good life. They see all the coeds and what seems to be a lot of fun. I do not think they are envious of me but rather they seem pleased that one of the boys made it. I get the feeling that they feel that they played an important part in my success.

I have tried to understand in my own mind why it was different for me. Why did I not end up in the same situation as those who were so close to me? There are probably a number of reasons. My sister and the athletic scholarship were certainly important. Another reason I think is that once I got to college I felt alone. I was not ready for college; not so much the feeling that I could not make it academically, but in terms of the social aspect. I had no relatives who had gone to college and as a result I knew little of the informal aspects of college life. In high school I did little dating and I was not very sophisticated about meeting nice girls or even talking with them. I felt out of it and thought seriously about taking off and going home. There were many hours during the day and during the evening that I kept to myself. At first I spent a lot of time going to movies or just walking around. Pretty soon I got tired of the movies and I began to read. My reading was not limited to my course work or required extra reading but instead I read everything that came to my attention. At one point I got started on religion and I began to read the Bible, the old and the new; I read portions of Buber, Tillich, Niebuhr and Pope. Another time it was existentialism or Buddhism. I would read just so I could argue with the author. I would take the position of the antagonist and look for the weaknesses of the author's argument. It became a way of filling the time and perhaps a way for making reading more acceptable to me. Between football, classes, and reading I kept busy.

A number of people, both teammates and others, talked to me about being a kind of hermit. I rarely went out on dates and I never went out with the boys after a game. I guess the only time I really felt relaxed was when I was at home or by myself. At home I would look forward to being with some of the guys I used to go with. But each visit seemed to be filled with more and more tension. I knew that I was moving away from the boys and there was little that we could talk about.

Through football I received a great deal of attention and publicity. The attention did little, I think, to change my way of thinking or acting. In fact I even became more detatched from campus events than I had been when I first arrived. I did some dating but I was never sure that the girl was reacting to me as a person or as a well-publicized athlete.

Now I have just about completed my college career and I have a fairly good idea as to the kind of work I would want to do. I feel that I would want to go into some area of education. More exactly I would like to work with young people who come from backgrounds similar to my own. The major problem I think will be in finding my social place. I want to be able to find people that I can feel comfortable with. At the present time I feel like someone who is standing with his feet spread wide apart—one leg in one world, the other leg in yet another world.

## CASE STUDY #2: FROM SUBURB TO SORORITY

I was raised in a suburb not far from a very large city in the Midwest. For the most part the homes in my neighborhood were quite large and the section was restricted. The restrictions were enforced in order to minimize the number of Jews who might move into the community. It was taken for granted that Negroes would never even attempt to move in. Most of the homes were single units, surrounded by spacious grounds, some with paved driveways circling the entire house. The residents of this community were white, most of them being from one of the Protestant faiths. Several people in the area had chauffeurs, most had maids.

In terms of socioeconomic background, the people in this community would fall into the range of upper middle class and higher. My father was an executive with a nationally known steel company. My closest friends had fathers who were either professionals or successful businessmen. Most of the mothers, including my own, were college graduates. My mother went to an elite private college in the East. Mother is one of these very busy women with membership in a number of civic and social organizations. Even as young children (I have an older brother and sister) we were aware of her many activities. Usually our maid would look after us during the day or when we came home from school. The schools that I attended were new and rich and they had all kinds of equipment and modern facilities.

As a very young child I spent most of my free time with other children in the neighborhood. We rode our tricycles, did some roller skating, or just played different games. On Saturdays we would go to the movies but only if the picture was one that my mother felt I should see. Sundays I attended Sunday school.

As I grew older my mother enrolled me in a ballet class and I also became a member of the Brownies. This was the beginning of a whole series of clubs, activities, and organizations which I was to join. The importance of these many activities was stressed by my mother who saw in them a means by which I could learn to get along with other people and with the right kind of people. I recall the many times my mother emphasized the importance of my being in contact with people who were of the right background. It was not so much her being a total snob but the fact that she felt that a person from a well-educated family had responsibilities to herself and others. My mother was proud of the fact that she was doing things in the community and that she was making some use of her college training. She felt strongly that no girl should just get married and have children but that they should also be busy with outside programs and activities.

The kids that were part of the ballet class and the Brownie troop were the same ones that I knew in school. We did many things together. Most of these same girls were my high school classmates. I think that our high school clique really had its start before we even got to high school. When I was about ten the kinds of things we did for enjoyment began to change. I started to think that the games we were playing were silly and immature. More important I began to think about boys and what they thought of me. This was true of most of my girl friends. At first we would comment about how silly the boys were and then we would talk about which ones were cute and which ones we liked. Up to this time we never really had anything to do with boys except that we saw them in school. The boys spent most of their time playing baseball or football and never really paid any attention to us that we knew of. In about the sixth grade we did start to have dances with the boys. These were always strange in that the boys did not want to ask the girls and the girls would act silly when a boy approached. Finally the teacher gave a number to each of the boys and to each of the girls; you then would have to dance with the person who had your number. I felt very awkward at first and uncomfortable about the whole thing. The teacher would always tell us that learning to dance was very important and that we should think of this as a very important part of our regular education and schoolwork. There was a lot of giggling during the dances and most of the boys would act as if dancing with a girl would bring about some disaster.

In terms of family life I would say we were a very closely knit group. My mother was really the one who took the responsibility for our doing homework, making our beds, and our keeping neat and clean. We ate dinner as a family unless my father was out of town for business. Weekends my father and mother played golf. We always took trips as a family; one summer we drove to California and for my thirteenth birthday we all went to Jamaica. For three summers I went to a girls' camp but that was during the times I was in elementary school. We had a number of relatives and on most holidays we would all get together. My mother would take us to plays and concerts for young people. In addition she was pretty insistent that we visit the library.

By the time we were thirteen years of age most of the girls that I went around with had become fairly sophisticated in respect to clothing, grooming, and sex. We were quite concerned with how we looked and made it a point of wearing the latest fashions. As for sex, this was something that my mother had discussed with me a number of times. She was never hesitant about it and pointed out that she knew that it was something I would be concerned with. She said many girls would go too far with boys and that this kind of behavior could destroy a girl's reputation. She said that she knew I would kiss boys and that she did not think there was anything really wrong with that. Her main point was that intimate sexual relations were something to be set aside until you find the one you love and the one you plan to marry. There was a great discrepancy between how our mothers viewed sex and the attitudes of the girls. We would not of course advertise what we did with boys but I think it would be fair to say that by the time we were fifteen or sixteen, most of us had done some heavy necking and petting. We would have many parties and dances and each of these would be followed with the kids pairing off and necking. I think that the limit at that time was necking and petting, but you could never be sure of what everyone else was doing. My mother was right about one thing—as soon as a girl was labeled as being "hot," her prestige with the other students went way down. I know of a number of girls who had spent miserable days in high school because someone started a story about them. I say a story because the boys would always overexaggerate anything they did with a girl.

All through high school there were many social activities and parties. There were school activities and others that took place outside of the school. We were no longer members of any formal organization with the exception of our high school sorority. There were several of these sororities in our high school even though they were outlawed by the school. As much as possible we would try to imitate the college sororities. We had teas, initiation, pins, and so forth. The girls in our sorority were considered the best dressed and best looking girls in the school. We were very particular about who we let into the group. At the tea we looked the girls over very carefully—how they dressed, their make-up, and the kinds of families they came from. Once the tea was over we would go through the names of the rushees and talk about each one. We never stressed schoolwork but we certainly would not take a girl who was doing poor work. I should point out that we were snobs in every respect. We would not take a girl who did not have what we called a "good personality." This meant that she had to be good looking, dress nicely, know how to talk with boys, and be a person who had a good reputation. We did not want wall-flowers and we did not want "drags." At this stage of our lives (sixteen), another thing that was important was having a car of your own or at least having the use of a family car. A number of the girls received their own cars on their sixteenth birthday.

As a sorority we did a number of things, mostly social, having parties of all kinds. One of the most popular events was having a weekend at the cottage. The girls would go up on Friday evening and spend the whole weekend at a cottage owned by one of the parents. On Saturday the boys we invited would come up. They would bring food and on a number of occasions, liquor. We would swim, go sailing, dance, and just have a full day of fun. The drinking was not serious and we were very careful not to get drunk. Our parents knew about the boys being there but they would never come up to chaperone or just drop in. I think our parents would have been too embarrassed to check up on us. My mother, for example, would tell me again and again that she trusted me and knew that I would do nothing that would bring embarrassment to myself or my family. Things like drinking were taken for granted as was the necking and petting. Of course the girls in the sorority made certain that no girl went too far.

In high school we were a fairly active group. We never really had much to do with student government or the more academic clubs like science or the square clubs like band or glee club. Our girls were cheerleaders or senior queens or the queen of the prom. We were pretty good students but few of the girls ever made the honor roll. I know that if we wanted to we could have done much better work in school but this was not our primary interest. Our main concern was being identified as the leaders in the social events of the school.

Only one of the girls in our group became engaged before we graduated from high school. Her engagement was short-lived however, and part of her breaking off with the boy was because of pressure from the group. We really put the pressure on, telling her that people would think that she got engaged because she had to. There were always rumors floating around the school about girls who dropped out of school because they were pregnant. We told her that this was the kind of thing that people would say about her. I do not think we were as much concerned about her personally as to what her action would do to the status of the sorority. She finally broke off with the boy; he was a college student. A number of us did go steady with different boys while we were in high school but all of these relationships were of a short duration. By the time we became juniors and seniors in high school we were doing little dating with high school boys. Most of us started to go out with college fellows either on the weekend at home or by going up to a campus for the weekend. This was another factor that gave our group prestige, especially with the other girls; we were dating college boys.

All of the girls in our sorority went to college. It was graduation from high school and the shift to different colleges that put an end to our particular group. The sorority itself is still in existence and from what I have seen and heard they are still the big thing in the high school.

For me, life in college was not too different from high school with the exception that I worked a little harder and was not living at home. The college I attend is not too tough academically but you do have to work. Before coming to college I knew I was going to pledge a sorority and I knew which sorority it would be. My mother had been a member of the same sorority while she was in college and it was taken for granted that I would pledge the same group.

As I mentioned earlier, college life was not too different from high school. My first year I lived in the dorm but most of the girls I spent time with were either in a sorority or were going to pledge. I dated the same kinds of boys that I had dated during my senior year of high school. They were mostly from fraternities. The dates and social activities were very similar to high school but perhaps on a more advanced level. There was more sexual play and more drinking and less talk. Once I was in the sorority I moved into the house and became a fullfledged active member. My sorority was considered one of the better ones in the school. We did not have the total reputation of being "party girls" but we were never considered "dogs." All in all we were a popular group. Not unlike the high school sorority there was a great deal of concern with the behavior of the girls. Again no one could really be sure how far a girl had gone but whenever there was some indication that one of the girls was getting a bad name the pressures were applied. Again it was not so much what this would do to the girl but instead what it would mean to the reputation of the house. The emphasis on grades was not too important with the exception that we wanted to avoid academic probation. The girls in the house were not involved in student government, campus UN, or any of the academic honor societies. Again, not unlike high school, the emphasis was placed on social skills and achievements. For example each year one of our girls competed in the selection for the homecoming queen.

It was probably the continuation of the same kinds of activities which I had been so much a part of in high school that led me to the point where I slowly became disenchanted with the sorority and shifted to a different kind of orientation. I had come to the point where it was all so routine—the same kind of life and activities each and every day. The boys were the same. It was always some party, or grasser, or dance, or something with the Greeks. The sings and homecoming events were of the same nature. In about my third year of college I began to move away from the girls. I missed some meetings, I failed to attend a tea, and I did not do my full share in the preparation of the homecoming float.

I continued to live at the house but it was obvious to my sorority sisters that a change was taking place. I became more critical of the kinds of things we were doing. Finally, I was at a point where I was conducting open warfare with the entire Greek system. My behavior at first was tolerated with many of the girls proposing that I was going through a stage. After a while it became clear to them that I was no longer with it. At first I was fined for missing certain meetings; after that I was asked to consider leaving the house. I finally did, prior to my senior year.

In place of the sorority and its functions I found something else. I guess it was the other end of the continuum. I began to hang around where the college beats were supposed to be. I had never really known people like this nor had I at any time talked with people like the beats. I was fascinated by their appearance, their lack of concern for convention, and what I thought was their acceptance of people not on the basis of how they looked and what they wore but in terms of the kind of person they were. Over time I managed to become an accepted part of this group. My former sorority sisters would see me and ask how I was doing. Old dates—once they found out about my new interests—avoided me like the plague. After a while my closest sorority sisters tended to avoid me. It is only fair to admit that the rejection was initiated by me and that they viewed me as someone who had given up the good life for one marginal to say the least. As for my parents, they were quick to notice the change. The change was a total one in terms of dress, grooming, and interests. When I came home for the weekend I would not be on the phone lining up dates; instead I kept to myself and did a great deal of reading. Not unlike my sorority sisters my parents were sure this was a stage and that I would grow out of it. After a few months they were less certain and began to take an active interest in what I was thinking and doing. I think my mother's major concern was that I would take off with some wild beat and live in sin. I assured her that while there was a change in certain intellectual and social ideas I was not about to submerge myself in a pit of evil and sin.

I must be honest in saying that parts of this beat approach were rather frightening to me. I disliked the use of obscene language even though it was proposed that this was a rejection of the phonyness of middle-class morality. Next, I did not care too much for the boys. Once the talk was through their interests were no different from that of the Greeks and they were less subtle in making their interests known. In addition some of the conversation seemed so futile and immature. There was a great deal of griping but rarely would anyone come up with any purposeful or constructive suggestions. After a while I moved away from this group and think I have reached some sort of balance. I now place a greater emphasis on the importance of intellectual matters than I did before but I do not want to be part of some isolated or fringe group. This year I will be finishing my BA degree. My grades are such that I have been accepted into graduate school. When my studies are completed I hope to do some free-lance writing, get married, and be a good wife and mother.

## CASE STUDY #3: A NEGRO IN AMERICA

My association with Little Rock, Arkansas, begins September 21, 1941. This was the date of my birth but my family ties go back much further than that—at least four generations of residence in Little Rock itself and over six generations of residence in Arkansas. I would assume that this would qualify me as one of the first families of the area —but this is not quite the case. As far as I can tell, the main reason that I have not been awarded first-family status is the color of my skin. I am a Negro living in America, which, at the time I was born, was a sure handicap.

The main purpose for writing this history is to acquaint the reader with my participation in the Little Rock crisis, 1957. This, as you remember, was the first attempted desegregation of public schools in Little Rock. I was one of nine students that entered Little Rock Central that year. But before I can give an adequate story of the crisis, I must give you some background information on myself and on Little Rock.

Reliving one's childhood is sometimes difficult because of the problem deciding just what is important to tell. The things that I thought important as a child somehow don't seem quite as important as I grow older. However, there are a few things that seem to stand out as easily discernible and important events in one way or another.

My family tends to be small as far as Southern families are in size. I have an older sister and a younger brother. My mother as a girl grew up in Little Rock and my father moved to Little Rock in his teens from the town of Helena, Arkansas. The long ties to Little Rock are all on my mother's side of the family. My grandfather was very active in civic affairs in Little Rock for quite a long while. He was also one of the first Negro letter carriers in Little Rock, and consequently, the desire to institute change was planted within the family long before direct action was evolved as a means of protest. In fact, I remember an incident related to me when I was very young concerning my grandfather. Once, when he attempted to vote in an election, he was threatened and hit over the head with a pistol . . . all because he wanted to exercise his rights as an American citizen.

When I consider the fact that my father was a veteran of World War I, it becomes difficult to understand how this country can be so slow in giving me what is rightfully mine, complete freedom. My father saw duty in France—although the troops were segregated at the time. He reached the eleventh grade and had to drop out of school to support his family. My mother attended elementary through high school in Little Rock and then went to Wilberforce, a Methodist church school, for two years. At that time the number of Negroes that went to college was very small and especially those who went away from home to college was even smaller. She finished first in her high school class along with her only sister. My aunt was a very influential person in my life—especially my school life. Both my mother and my aunt attended Wilberforce and after two years came back to Little Rock and began teaching school. Both my mother and aunt have taught school in the Little Rock system since they were about nineteen years of age. My aunt died in 1959.

My parents didn't decide to start a family right away—consequently, my brother and I were not born until my father was in his forties. My father was a custodian at the post office and sometimes waited table for private parties of the very wealthy in Little Rock. I remember that usually Christmas and New Years he was not at home during the day because he had to serve a party. However, the food he would bring back would compensate somewhat for his absence. It was not everyone that was exposed to lobsters at my age—especially with lobsters being the delicacy that they were. When I look back and think of the sacrifices my folks made to try and give us an outlook so that we wouldn't be swept under by racial prejudice, I can't help but be thankful for the courage against such tremendous odds.

During my preschool years my mother did not teach but stayed home with my brother and me. This was the only time in her life that she was not teaching. Consequently, she taught me how to read at an early age. So by the time I entered the first grade, I had read most of the first-grade primers. Because of this, my association with the first grade lasted only one day and I was immediately passed to the second grade.

Many present-day school administrators frown on skipping grades as being detrimental to the development of the child. In some cases, the age gradation made in this society did leave me with a bitter taste. But it always involved areas outside of school, such as Sunday School or the Boy Scouts. The differences that were made between twelve and thirteen-year-old children often left me with children one grade lower than those of my own class who I was familiar with. So a number of times, I told a "little white lie" about my age. I guess this is one of the reasons I had a desire to grow up early. But this is sort of moving the cart before the horse, so I would like to shift back to my preschool days.

An incident occurred when I was about four or five that focused in to me the differences between Negro and white people. I was downtown with my mother. While she was busy shopping, a white boy about the same age as I was began to play with me. As children are able to do under almost any circumstances, we had a "ball of a time." Then his mother came along and jerked him away telling him not to play with "those dirty people." The "dirty people" didn't make a real impression upon me at the time. But the fact that we were having fun together and she pulled him away did make a very lasting impression.

The Negro child in the South isn't very old when he learns "what the score is." By the time the Negro child attends school, the world of segregation is very real—the back of busses, separate water fountains—at first very confusing. These incidents upset me but there was enough cushion in my immediate surroundings to soothe the edge.

While I was in elementary school my mother went on to obtain her masters degree. Before I was born she had completed the other two years of college at Arkansas A.M. & N., the state Negro college. She earned her masters degree from the University of Arkansas. At the time she graduated from the university, the Negro students were not allowed to participate in the graduation ceremony (the degree was obtained during the summers, and the ceremonies were held at the main campus, Fayetville). When one thinks that there are Negro students attending the main campus now, this may seem like a moot point, but the rate of progress in the South has to be measured by a different yardstick than what applies to the rest of the country.

When I was eleven my father died; some of the role of the man of the house fell on my shoulders and I guess at this point I began to think of problems other youths my age were not as concerned about.

Another incident that sticks out in my mind concerning segregation is the refusal of the city park commissioner to allow my family and me the pleasure of listening to a band concert in the city park. One hot summer evening my mother remembered reading in the paper about a series of concerts being held in the bandshell. Since she was a music lover, she thought it would be a good idea for all of us to go. We were all seated when the park commissioner came over and told us Negroes couldn't attend the concert because the city required segregated seating. When I thought about the incident, it seemed very strange that the segregationist talks about the inherent inability of the Negro to appreciate "good music." And yet, here was a situation of a Negro family attempting to enjoy some of the things the segregationists claim that we as a race lack appreciation of.

As I mentioned, the edge of the sword was somewhat smoothed—not that we had things handed to us on the proverbial "silver platter." In fact, my brother and I have had summer jobs ever since we were ten or eleven. Two years before that we sold papers. It was a Negro weekly paper, *The Chicago Defender*. My mother saw to it that we all were given a firm religious training and were very active in the church. We were members of Bethel African Methodist Episcopal Church—the Methodist church is another segregated institution. My membership in the church helped a great deal in my growth and development.

By the time I entered high school, my sister had finished college at the age of nineteen. She graduated with honors from Hampton Institute, Hampton, Virginia. She is now teaching elementary school in Baltimore, Maryland. So the influence of teachers was all around me. The desire to achieve in school was well entrenched within my framework long before I entered high school. My brother was three years behind me in school. He later finished high school and went into the air force.

The two years I spent at Horace Mann were very exciting. I played in the band for five years, including the three in junior high. Also, I was active in student government. I never thought of myself as being a really bright student, but somehow I managed to make the honor society. Until I was fifteen, I remained very active with the Boy Scouts. In fact, I was able to achieve the rank of Eagle Scout. This gave me valuable experience in working with people and meeting the adult leaders of the community. My biggest enjoyment in school was the formation of a jazz club by a group of boys and girls in my class. Even today it has maintained a close togetherness.

All of the above was meant to give the reader a brief insight into some of my family background. Now I would like to give the reader a brief glimpse of Little Rock before the crisis.

To get a picture of Little Rock, Arkansas, you must imagine a city of about 100,000 people—not too hurried by a steady pace of life—a Southern city, a transitional city, desiring to enjoy the economic improvement of industrialization but not willing to make the accompanying sacrifices. Integration was not a complete stranger to Little Rock before 1957. It had quietly invaded the public transportation system in 1956 and the public library in 1955. The University of Arkansas was integrated on the graduate level as early as 1949 (medical and law schools). Yet, there are other facts that dim the picture of Arkansas as a more forward Southern state.

The Negro population of Little Rock is 25,000 . . . about one-fourth of the total population. Many people have observed that Southern towns are not characterized by the racial ghettoes so prevalent in Northern cities. This observation also applies to Little Rock. My own neighborhood is bordered by homes of white families. Many times I played basketball with the children of these families in the nearby "white" junior high basketball court. There is some variance in the contact between whites and Negroes in Little Rock. A Negro boy is very apt to play with a white child whose parents employ Negro domestics. Therefore, in some cases, the white adult community in Little Rock carries a stereotyped impression of the Negro as a servant.

These distinct kinds of contact result in conflicting images in the minds of most white citizens. In this setting, the Little Rock school board decided to integrate the public schools on the high school level in compliance with the 1954 Supreme Court decision . . . in September, 1957.

My first introduction to desegregation of the high school came in the fall of 1956, my junior year at Horace Mann High School. At this time, the school board requested the names of all students living within the boundaries of Central High School who wished to attend the all-white school. Many of my classmates were very apprehensive about signing and consequently spending their senior year pioneering the Negro cause. But a few of the curious ones, perhaps more curious than brave, gave their names to make up a list from which a few would be chosen to attend Central. The students were to be chosen on the basis of academic records, social adjustment and maturity, and the extent of their high school activities—supposedly the "cream of the crop." From September, 1956, to the spring of 1957, no one knew who would be selected and how many would attend. Then in August, 1957, I met the group of students who were to become my constant companions for the coming year and crisis. Seated in the superintendent's office of the Little Rock public schools, I first became acquainted with the others—Elizabeth Eckford, Minnie Jean Brown, Jefferson Thomas, Melba Patillo, Terrance Roberts, Thelma Mothershead, Gloria Ray, Carlotta Walls, and me, Ernest Green. Together, we made up the "Little Rock Nine." Here, we were all told that we were selected from the large list of students as the ones best prepared to make the breakthrough in integrating the previously all-white high school. Being told all of this by the superintendent of the schools, we wondered why the teachers hadn't recognized our hidden talents and given us better grades. At the time, there were five more students that had been accepted by the school board, but these five dropped out before school started. Two of them were seniors. All of the five dropped out because they believed that the pressure would be too great.

With the number finally reduced to nine, the beginning of the Little Rock crisis takes form. At this point I would like to discuss the crisis and the participants.

Elizabeth, Minnie Jean, Melba, and Thelma were all eleventh graders when we entered Central. Elizabeth is the young lady that was pictured all across the world as facing the angry mob the first day. This became a symbol of Little Rock many years after 1957. Minnie Jean was the most outspoken of all the students. A vivid example of her explosive honesty occurred in December at Central High. Minnie was constantly pestered by one white student in particular. The boy was very small in stature but possessed a large vocabulary of ready insults. Minnie was getting fed up with his constant harassment. One day, while eating lunch, she retaliated by pouring soup over his head. For this she was suspended by the school board and eventually dismissed for the rest of the school year. She finished the rest of her high school days at New Lincoln, a private school in New York. Her expenses were covered by a scholarship. The Negro students viewed her act as one of unquestionable heroism. To-day all of the girls are in colleges throughout the country; Elizabeth in Ohio, Minnie and Thelma in Illinois, and Melba in California.

The two other girls, Gloria and Carlotta, were in the tenth grade. Both young ladies turned out to be excellent students, one making the honor roll and the other doing very well in a science project. Both are pursuing careers in biological sciences. Carlotta is attending school in Denver and Gloria is attending in Chicago.

That leaves the two boys, Terrence and Jefferson. Terrence was an eleventh grader and Jefferson was in the tenth. Terrence was probably the brightest of the boys. I remember him especially for the drive and vigor with which he tackled his Spanish lessons. Throughout the entire crisis he maintained good grades. To describe Terrence, one must picture a six-foot frame, rather thin—with a very comical, cynical outlook about things around him. He continually poked fun at the newspaper reporters. I remember one incident in particular when he told the newspaper reporters his name was "George Washington." They were writing so fast that they didn't catch his prank until they had already written the name he gave them. About this time, Carlotta chimed in with her name—of course, who else but Martha Washington. Everyone would have a good laugh and begin again. Terrence was sixteen years old in the fall of 1957 and acted with the judgment of a man twice his age. Terrence lived much closer to Central than any of the other eight students. Oftentimes, he played basketball with fellows in his neighborhood—both Negro and white—at the Central High courts. Terrence wasn't able to finish his senior year at Central because of Faubus' order to close the school. As soon as the order came, his parents moved out to Los Angeles with all six children. Terrence was next to the oldest. His sister was going to college at the time. Neither of his parents had attended college, but like so many of the others they were determined for their children to have a chance to learn and better themselves economically. Terrence had an easier time with his studies than the rest of us. We all knew, however, that we had to excel and do as well or better than the average for our classes. For some of us this became a mad race, but I think it boosted the performances of a lot of the white students. Perhaps the key to improving scholastic performances in the South is to allow Negro students to serve as competition. Terrence is now attending school in California and majoring in predentistry.

Jefferson Thomas was a tenth grader and the youngest of the students. He was a thin but well-built person. In junior high, he excelled as a track star. With an eye on science, he hoped to be an engineer. Jefferson came from a large family. Neither his mother nor his father are college graduates, but two of his older brothers are. Although Jefferson was the youngest and the most naive, he always had a comical statement about the day-to-day activities. He was in constant contact with some of the most embittered white students in the school. The tenth graders were the most spirited segregationists. Jefferson spent his first year after Central at Wayne State University in Detroit and is now attending Los Angeles City College and majoring in accounting.

There is one person that I have not mentioned that played one of the most important parts in the crisis, Mrs. Daisy Bates. Mrs. Bates at the time of the crisis was state president of the National Association for the Advancement of Colored People. She was the undisputed leader and the director of events that followed. She and her husband ran a weekly newspaper that didn't have any regrets in calling "a spade a spade." The threats to her life and violence to her home became so great that she was soon immune to them. At the present, Mrs. Bates is still fighting in Little Rock to bring about complete change to the social system.

This brings us face to face with Tuesday morning—the day after Labor Day in 1957.

Tuesday morning I got up bright and early—not fully realizing the importance and anxiety of the day. We were to be driven to the school together. Everyone had been contacted and instructed except Elizabeth. Her family didn't have a phone. Terrence said he would walk to school because he was only a couple of blocks away. This left seven of us assembled at the Bates'. With us were some ministers—Negro and white—who were going to accompany us to Central. The Southern ministers, as a whole, seem more willing to act on their convictions.

On that Tuesday, we got our first taste of newspaper reporters. The publicity was very exciting at the beginning, but after a while it began to become a burden. This was the period when all the legal battles were being fought out. It lasted for about three weeks. During this time, we didn't attend classes, but were given homework by our instructors to keep up with. It was very difficult to study with all the apprehension and excitement in the air.

The segregationists thought that if they could hold us out of school long enough, we would go back to Horace Mann. However, we, of course, weren't prepared to give the other side that concession. If we had returned to Horace Mann, the whole civil rights movement would have been dealt a severe blow. Early in the stages of the crisis, we realized that the situation had further implications than just for Little Rock Central.

At last the waiting came to an end. Our vacation was over. The injunction was granted on a Friday and on the following Monday we went to school.

This was the day of the riots, September 23, the day after my sixteenth birthday. The day before, the president had issued a statement that he had faith in the people of Little Rock to preserve law and order. The police department had stated that it could maintain this. The citizens of Little Rock kept the president's faith. It was people from the outlying rural areas that caused the trouble. It seems ironic to me now that the segregationists call the freedom riders outsiders and most of the real trouble in any area is caused by outside segregationists.

On Monday morning, about 9 o'clock, we entered the school. We went to our homerooms and our teachers and classmates that we were to see for the rest of the year. In my class, no one walked out or attempted to create a disturbance of any kind. In fact, that day was one of the quietest days inside the school for the rest of the year. The reason for this was that all of the avowed segregationists had boycotted school and weren't attending at all. When I went into my physics class, I was greeted very warmly by some of the fellows. In fact, my lab partner became very friendly with me and our friendship lasted the entire year. Many other incidents of this kind happened to all of us in the school. So we couldn't understand why the principal wanted to see us in his office just before noon. When we got to the office, the principal, the assistant principal, and the assistant chief of police told us that there was a mob outside of the school and it looked like they were not going to be able to control it. This seemed very strange to us because conditions in the school were so very quiet and everybody was friendly to us. We thought it was all a joke, but they assured us it was not and that for our own safety it would be best if we went home for the rest of the day. We were each driven home by a policeman—our own Little Rock police bodyguard. It was not until we got home that we realized that there really was trouble outside. My neighbors came over to see if I was all right. It had been reported on the radio that one of the Negro boys had been beaten in the halls and was all bloody. This was very funny because everything that people had heard happening on the outside was just the reverse of what was really going on in the school. I don't think any of us realized that if the mob had broken the police barriers that day, we could have been seriously hurt. People thought that the Negro newsmen who were beaten up at the same time we were entering the school were a decoy to avert attention from our entrance. But we didn't find out about them until after we had returned home.

The next day, Tuesday, something happened that was to change everything. President Eisenhower addressed the country via television. He said that due to the breakdown of local law enforcement bodies and the inability of a state official to uphold a federal court order, he was sending 1,000 men of the 101st airborne division to provide law and order in Little Rock and to enforce the federal ruling. When we heard this it sounded unbelievable. But at the very same time the president was speaking, the troops were flying over Little Rock. They came in about twenty flying boxcars and it sounded like the sky was falling.

As the troops landed and finally "invaded" Little Rock, we knew that we would be going to school Wednesday for the whole day. The 101st came equipped with trucks, food, and bayonets—all to integrate Central—nine Negro students with 2,000 white students. None of us slept Tuesday night. I don't think any of us had ever seen so many soldiers at once.

The army had a station wagon to transport us to the school which was about sixteen blocks away. There was a jeep in front of us and one behind. In each jeep were three men. One man in the back had a rifle with a setup for a machine gun and each of the men was wearing a side arm and equipment for tear gas.

As we came into the school area, we noticed that there were very few people around. We found out later that the army had the area blocked off for three blocks square and nobody—including the residents—could enter without a pass. When the station wagon stopped in front of the school, we were immediately surrounded by a detachment of about twenty soldiers. Meanwhile, the news media were not allowed entrance into the school but had gathered across the street. While the news cameras whirled around, we walked with our guards to the front door. With soldiers' bayonets drawn, in a brisk military march, the "Little Rock Nine" finally integrated Central High School and round one had come to an end.

Once inside the school, we were met by more troops and each of us was assigned a guard. Mine was a rather young fellow from New York.

Imagine carrying on regular classes with 1,000 troops with their equipment all around the school area. But despite all the commotion, classes were getting underway. As I stated before, all of the students in my classes were friendly and the teachers understanding, although some were more genuine than others. Our biggest handicap was in being three weeks behind the other students. Mine seemed bigger in that my courses were all college preparatory.

About one hour before lunch, we had our first bomb scare. The school officials called it a fire drill. The first one was exciting and a novelty but they soon became commonplace—almost routine. When we filed outside, there were two helicopters flying overhead. The football field was being used as a landing strip. There were soldiers everywhere making it look more like a battlefield than a football field. Despite the confusion and the excitement of the troops, school was more relaxed than it would be any day later that year.

I ate my lunch with three of the girls—Carlotta, Gloria, and Melba— the first day. We weren't bothered by anyone. In fact, we got an invitation to eat with some of the other students. The girls were friendlier than the boys. During lunch, the guards were always hovering around us. It reminds me somewhat of the job the secret service agents had in guarding Caroline Kennedy.

The only other interesting thing that happened the first day was in my physical education class. There was no violence, no fear, and little evident hostility. We played volleyball and all got along very well.

As far as we were concerned, the first day of integrated classes had been completed. But there was much more going on outside which we didn't learn about until the evening.

As the days went by, more and more of the segregationists came back to school. Their attempted boycotts had failed. It was at this point that the trouble started for some of us. Some of these boys would follow behind the girls—curse, spit, throw ink and any other degrading thing they could think of. It was not uncommon for us to change lockers about three or four times a week. The other students would always manage to break the locks even though they were combination locks. I don't know how many times our lockers were broken into during the year. We didn't have to pay for any of the books that were stolen.

A funny thing happened early in the year. There was one young lady who ate lunch with us all the time. I had known a friend of hers through my fondness for jazz. The school officials called us in and said we would have to stop eating lunch together because this type of thing was just not done. So a friendly relationship between a group of teenagers was broken up because of the social customs of the South. This seems strange to me when I stop and think that some of these same people would let a Negro nurse their children and cook their food. There is a definite intimacy to these tasks and yet a group of students could not carry on a quiet conversation during the lunch hour.

As the trouble makers started to drift back into the school the cause for racial equality was rougher going. Two girls who had been major instigators from the very beginning were asked to appear on a network radio station panel with Minnie, Melba, and me. So here we were—two of the staunchest defenders of the Southern way of life and three of the prime offenders. While on the air, the two segregationists stated that they had had a change of heart. This seemed to be more surprising to the people of Little Rock than to us. However, their change of heart didn't last once they were thrust back into the old environment.

Around November, things really began to pick up in tempo. There were at least twenty to thirty small incidents happening every day—all by the same core of dedicated segregationists. These small things began to get under our skin. I never had any trouble until I was in the hallway during the change of classes. The teachers did attempt to keep order in their classes no matter what their personal feelings were. In the beginning, the fellows were in separate physical education classes. But, later on, the school decided to put us all in the same class. This really gave the trouble makers opportunity to concentrate their efforts. So concentrate they did. In the physical education classes, we always got along well during the games and exercises. But once we got back to the locker room, all hell would break loose. They would steam up the locker room until you could not see in front of your face. Then they would wet towels, ball them up tight, and throw them at us. This would go on for some time until the instructor almost had to stand right near us to prevent this sort of thing. The kids participating in the incidents would never come out in the open.

I have previously mentioned Minnie Jean Brown and her expulsion from Central High. Well, she wasn't the only student expelled. A few of the white students were expelled for causing trouble. Whenever any of the main trouble makers were out, you could almost feel an air of relief.

By the time Christmas vacation came, we were all anxious to get a rest. But, for the most part, we became immune to all the harassment and didn't really wake up in the morning dreading school and on the other hand didn't derive any real satisfaction from going, although I think we all found pleasure in seeing some of the segregationists boil and fume.

Christmas brought us mail from all over the world. Some of the cards had to be translated from the native languages they were written in. If we had attempted to answer all of the people that wrote to us we would have had to quit school and hire a fulltime secretary. Most of the mail was "fan mail" and it was always refreshing to get encouragement from all over the world after a hectic day at Central. One day, I got a card that was simply addressed: Ernest Green, Central High, U.S.A. It was nice being famous with controversy spinning around us.

Near the middle of March, most of the guards had been removed from the inside of the school. Conditions didn't get much better nor did they get any worse. I guess most of the people were resigned to our presence in the school until the end of the year.

Scholastically, we were all doing fairly well. I was having a lot of trouble with my physics. The course was a tough one to begin with but the instructor's prejudice didn't help me at all. In most of my classes, I was not up to the level of the more advanced students. It was very easy to see that Central was much better equipped than Horace Mann was. It made me wonder how the school officials could sleep at night when they said that the Negro children had the same facilities as the white.

As graduation neared, it was easily observed that some of us were becoming very nervous from the ordeal. I think it remarkable that we all held up as long and as well as we did. On some of the students, the ordeal left a permanent scar. In a lot of cases, I don't think all of the parents realized the shock that the entire situation was to them. Only two families were directly affected economically by the crisis. One father was a brick mason and had a hard time getting work from white contractors when they discovered that his daughter was attending Central High. Melba Patillo's mother was teaching in the North Little Rock public school system. The school board threatened not to renew her teaching contract unless Melba withdrew from Central. All of the families were subjected to a number of prank phone calls.

When I entered Central I was sixteen years old. I was always asked the question why I wanted to spend my senior year at Central. It seemed to me that the whole business about integrated schools was idle chatter unless a few people were actually enrolled and attending classes in them. I like to think that we were a number of years ahead of the freedom riders and lunch-counter demonstrations by testing the right given to each citizen—to attend any public school. With this right proven, the others would follow in natural order. I have, of course, been dismayed since then to see the snail's pace with which these "guaranteed" rights are coming—as is every "second-class citizen" in the United States. Until direct action was initiated in Little Rock, few people stopped to think why they went to the back of the bus or why they were always accepting "second-class citizenship." There was no answer except tradition and "Boss Charlie." This was how I felt upon entering Central High in 1957. My feelings have changed little, but have grown stronger, more sophisticated, and have solidified.

By the time graduation came around, we were all looking forward to the summer. I was the only one not returning to school the following school year. But I had the ordeal of going through graduation. However, I don't think it would have been any different had I finished from an all-Negro high school. It was just a happy feeling to be through with high school. The gifts, cards, and autographs from my Central High classmates proved that the entire year was not in vain. The gifts seemed to pour in from all over the world. I received $100 from a lady in Brooklyn. I don't think I would have earned a scholarship to college as easily had I not gone to Central.

It would be very presumptuous to say that the Little Rock crisis affected the students adversely. Some of the students were withdrawn or very outspoken before they went to Central. Some of them had a difficult time getting along with the other students at Horace Mann and carried this difficulty with them to Central.

Carlotta and Jefferson Thomas went back to Central to finish after the schools had been reopened in 1959–60. I'm certain that at times they may have wished that they could finish their senior years in the usual calm way that their friends were finishing theirs. But giving up the fight when on the verge of victory is a very hard thing to do. When you get involved with something like this, you soon realize that you are never doing this for yourself—because when you "aid the cause" it becomes very difficult. But you really can never get away from the idea that this whole thing is bigger than just you—the individual—and that it has some universal significance.

*Chapter IV*

# SUBCULTURES:
# REFLECTIONS OF THE ADULT WORLD

While some norms, values, and behavior patterns are common to almost all adults in any society, there is also a great amount of variation, depending upon region, residence, status, and the like. Adolescents internalize many adult norms and values, imitate adult behavior patterns, and are socialized primarily within the context of institutions controlled by adults. It would be expected, therefore, that variation in adult subcultures would be reflected in analagous adolescent subcultures. This chapter describes a few of the ways in which these adult subcultures are reflected among adolescents on the American scene.

The effect of social characteristics derived from the adult world doubtless decreases as adolescent society itself becomes more solidified. Subcultures derived primarily from the adolescent world itself will be considered in the next chapter.

## REGIONAL DIFFERENCES

Regions in the United States are represented by large geographical divisions within the country. Usually the regions are defined as the South, Northeast, Midwest, West (or Mountain states), and the West coast. No attempt can be made at exhaustive comparisons of all these regions because there is little research on regional differences. True, studies are available from each of the regions, but differences in methods used, the content of questions, and types of samples prevent anything like a generalized statement of regional differences in adolescents.

One of the most noteworthy differences in behavior which reflects cultural diversity is found with respect to the educational institution. Consistently, Utah is at the top of the list of states on the basis of educational attainment, and other Western states rank high. By contrast, Southern states rate among the lowest both in educational attainment and in the percentage of sixteen- and seventeen-year-old youth in school. (This percentage is usually accepted as a reflection of educational values because most states require attendance until the age of sixteen; any attendance after the sixteenth birthday, therefore, involves a choice between education and work by the adolescent and his or her family.)

Some caution is needed in interpreting these statistics on educational attainment. A higher proportion of the population in the South is in the lower social groupings, and lower status groupings drop out of school more often regardless of region. This limits the type of causal inference that may be made with respect to regional value systems as such, but there is no qualification on the fact of the differences. Similarly, the consistent rating of Utah at the top of the states in educational attainment is doubtlessly influenced by the value the Mormon church places on education, but this does not disqualify the regional rating itself. Still another caution must be made in interpreting the low position of the South in educational ratings. The general case is as stated above, but some of our most brilliant scientists, scholars, and authors have come from the South.

The extent to which regional differences may operate in shaping friendship patterns among adolescents from different parts of the country can be noted in the work of David Gottlieb.[1] In his study of adolescents at a summer camp he found that boys from the South were often stereotyped as socially inadequate but Southern girls were viewed as fulfilling the feminine image of sophistication. Northern boys, unlike their Southern counterparts, were seen as socially adequate and competent task leaders. Northern girls, on the other hand, were viewed by their peers as competent workers but not necessarily feminine in presentation of self. In the election of officers non-South boys nominated other non-South boys and Southern boys nominated boys from their region. The voting appeared to be along regional lines. All the offices except secretary went to non-South boys since the non-Southerners were in the majority. The only office open to girls went to a Southern girl, even though again the persons from this region were outnumbered by persons from the other regions. The election seemed to correspond to the patterns developed in the friendship groupings.

Perhaps the most interesting findings of all with respect to the internalization of regional differences in culture are:[2]

[1] David Gottlieb, "Regional Differences as a Variable in Sociological Research," *Social Problems*, Vol. 10 (1963), pp. 251–56.

[2] *Ibid.*, p. 252.

Figure 1 presents the unfavorable descriptive phrases used most frequently by male respondents. An interesting point here is the tone and quality of the views expressed. A number of the adjectives employed [toward members of the other region] are not unlike those obtained by Katz and Braly [3] and Gilbert [4] in their studies of the traits most frequently attributed to different minority groups.

FIGURE 1

EVALUATIVE PHRASES MOST FREQUENTLY USED BY MALE
RESPONDENTS

| Non-South to South | South to Non-South |
|---|---|
| Lazy | Loud |
| Shiftless | Pushy |
| Dull | Noisy |
| Irresponsible | Aggressive |
| Quiet | Ill-mannered |
| No Initiative | Bossy |
| Slow | Crude |

In both this research and the others noted above, the Jewish stereotype included traits suggesting aggressiveness, self-centeredness, and rudeness, Similarly, the traits attributed to Southern campers by Northern campers are not unlike the traits attributed to Negroes by white respondents. In both cases the phrases imply irresponsibility, a lack of initiative, and a general dullness. This finding suggests, for this group, at any rate, that regional differences may be sufficient to minimize religious homogeneity leading to a situation where the individual reflects the sentiments popular in his community.

It is generally thought that Southern adults are more religious than adults in the North, Midwest, and West coast. This notion itself is a stereotype but it is borne out among college students at least. Rose Goldsen found that Southern college students are more likely to express strong religious feelings than are those from the Northeast.[5]

A large number of studies have shown that anti-Negro feelings are stronger in the South while antisemitism is stronger among adolescents in the Northeast and Midwest. Prejudice in the Western states is more often found directed at persons of Spanish or Latin American origins. In other words, adolescent prejudices do appear to reflect adult prejudices. Adolescent clique groups are frequently exclusive of those minority groups which receive the most prejudice in the region. We may conclude, then, that adolescent subcultures exist with respect to regions of the United States and that these subcultures reflect in large part the more carefully studied adult subcultures in those same regions. It is also apparent that adolescents define regions as a socially significant factor in their relations with others.

[3] Donald Katz and Kenneth Braly, "Racial Stereotypes of 100 College Students," *Journal of Abnormal Social Psychology*, Vol. 28 (1933), pp. 280–90.

[4] G. M. Gilbert, "Stereotyped Persistence and Change Among College Students," *Journal of Abnormal Social Psychology*, Vol. 46 (1951), pp. 245–54.

[5] Rose K. Goldsen, *et. al., What College Students Think*, (Princeton: D. Van Nostrand, 1960).

## RURAL-URBAN DIFFERENCES

The slang of American adolescents, as well as that of adults, reflects the long-standing belief in the differences between rural and urban people; hayseed, hick, city slicker, rube, and even "city boy" and "farmer" are used as invectives. There is much research to indicate that important and fairly large differences have traditionally existed; the farmer appears to have been the more conservative, religious, and quiet, and subscribed more to the "Protestant ethic." Recent research indicates that while rural-urban differences have diminished in many ways and disappeared in others, some differences still exist.[6] Further, these differences are greater within either the rural or the urban group than between them.

One professor, nearing retirement at a land-grant college, summarized the diminishing differences:

> When I first came here, I could walk down the paths of this campus during Farm and Home Week and be able to distinguish the farm boys and girls from the non-farmers just by observing their dress. Now, I cannot. I can even talk to them for a few minutes and usually cannot tell whether or not they are from a farm unless I ask them.

One of the more important long-standing differences between the rural and the urban setting is the much greater frequency of work experience of rural youth. Farm chores and part-time jobs held by youth in small towns are believed to give farm-reared teenagers an advantage in entering the adult work world. The experience is presumed not only to prepare youth to some extent for some jobs, but also to increase their ability to fulfill the work requirements for any position—to foster a favorable attitude toward work.

One recent study finds widespread concern by parents with providing meaningful work role-learning experiences for sons.[7] This concern was present in parents of town as well as fringe (suburban) and farm youth, but the greatest emphasis was among farm parents. It was also found that farm youth were paid less and were less often required to take care of some of their personal expenses from their wages. The greater emphasis on work for adolescents among farm families is usually explained by the closer integration of family and occupational activities in the farm family than in the nonfarm family. This, in turn, is partly dependent upon the proximity of the work to home and partly upon the nature of the work and the tradition of

---

[6] For a summary of the literature on this point see Lowry Nelson, "Rural Life in a Mass-Industrial Society," *Rural Sociology*, Vol. 22 (1957), pp. 20–30.

[7] Murray Strauss, "Work Roles and Financial Responsibility in the Socialization of Farm, Fringe, and Town Boys," *Rural Sociology*, Vol. 27 (1962), pp. 257–74.

using family workers. Farm families seem to retain the virtue of hard work as an important value more than do nonfarm families.

There were also significant differences in the attitudes of the boys toward their work. A higher proportion found the work enjoyable and fewer of them had to be reminded of their duties as compared to nonfarm boys.

Closely associated with work experience and values is the attitude toward various dimensions of occupational rewards. Several researchers have found that, in comparisons of boys and girls from various backgrounds, farm boys consistently rate "income" the most important consideration in choosing an occupation. Nonfarm boys and girls from virtually every other background rate income much lower in comparison with "the good you can do," "creativity," "security," and "liking one's work."

It has also been found that farm boys drop out of school earlier than farm girls, but both drop out earlier than their respective counterparts in towns, cities, and the suburbs. Curricula in high schools favor only a few of the possible occupational groupings in the vocational training courses; one of these groupings is farming. Vocational agriculture courses were initiated at the strong request of farmers, and this aspect of the curriculum available to the teenager is different for farm and nonfarm boys. It is doubtful that farm girls take advantage of home economics courses more than nonfarm girls.

While a large proportion of farm-reared boys hope to enter farming upon leaving high school, almost no boys who are not reared on farms choose farming as a career. The level of occupational aspiration of boys from various residential backgrounds are, then, best judged by eliminating those who plan to farm because the "level" of occupational status of farming is extremely difficult to determine. Aside from farming, occupational status is usually ranked, in summary fashion, on the basis of the following order: professional, proprietary and managerial, clerical, skilled, semiskilled, and unskilled work.

On the basis of the above classifications, urban youth aspire highest in their occupational choices while rural nonfarm, small-town, and farm boys do not seem to differ significantly.[8] The differences in educational aspirations, however, appear greater. In one study approximately four out of every five urban boys planned to attend college

---

[8] Lee G. Burchinal, "Differences in Educational and Occupational Aspirations of Farm, Small-Town, and City Boys," *Rural Sociology*, Vol. 26 (1961), pp. 107–21. See also A. O. Haller, "The Occupational Achievement Process of Farm-Reared Youth in Urban-Industrial Society," *Rural Sociology*, Vol. 25 (1960), pp. 321–33; and A. O. Haller and W. H. Sewell, "The Influence of Planning to Enter Farming on Plans to Attend College," *Rural Sociology*, Vol. 22 (1957), pp. 137–41.

while about two thirds of the small-town boys and less than half of the farm boys had made similar plans. The percentages are somewhat different in other studies but the relationship of residence to aspiration is consistent.

Insofar as achievement is a major value orientation in American society, the higher aspirations among urban boys is of the utmost importance in rural and urban subcultures. Farming is a functionally necessary occupation if a people is to survive, while many urban occupations are not. However, many more boys aspire to farming than can possibly obtain farms. Further, the reduction in the number of farms, the increase in the ability of one farm to produce food and fiber for more and more people, the increasing size of farms, and the increasing capital investment necessary to get started work against the notion that the functional necessity of farming makes it a desirable occupational selection for many of the boys who choose it.

Several authors have shown that the desire to farm has a "depressing" effect on levels of aspiration, especially in educational attainment.[9] However, the lower aspirations of farm youth may not be merely a matter of choosing farming as a career. The degree to which intelligence quotients may be influenced by intellectually stimulating environments has not been determined entirely by psychologists. Also, there is some culture bias in these tests. Nevertheless, some effect may be seen. A very large number of studies of I.Q. and family background show that farm youth have lower I.Q.'s than town or city children and lower than any other occupational groupings other than the sons and daughters of unskilled workers. Some of these studies employed tests which had been standardized on both farm and nonfarm adolescents. If psychologists determine in the future that intellectually stimulating experience significantly increases I.Q., then the lower aspirations of farm youth may take on added cultural meaning.

Many personality tests are divided into various components, some of which reflect values and attitudes of a nonpathological nature. The findings of studies comparing rural and urban youth on the basis of personality tests, therefore, give some insight into subcultural differences. A. O. Haller and Carole Ellis Wolff found urban boys less withdrawn, less submissive, less nervous, and more optimistic about man controlling events than were rural boys.[10] Starke Hathaway, Elie D. Monachesi, and Lawrence A. Young found urban youth to have fewer feelings of shyness and self-depreciation: they were less sus-

---

[9] Burchinal, *op. cit.*; Haller, *op. cit.*; and Haller and Sewell, *op. cit.*
[10] A. O. Haller and Carole Ellis Wolff, "Personality Orientation of Farm, Village, and Urban Boys," *Rural Sociology*, Vol. 27 (1962), pp. 275–93.

picious of the motives of others; and they were more inclined to rebel against authority.[11]

In general, while most of the differences in rural and urban subcultures are either disappearing or diminishing, several continue to exist. Observed rural-urban differences have significance for value themes in the adult culture, especially achievement, and for trends toward urban-industrialization in American society.

## RELIGION

The division of the Christian religion in the United States into over 200 denominations and the presence in the country of non-Christian faiths produce a relatively unique setting for subcultural differences based on religion. Actually, there has been amazingly little research on religion in relation to the adolescent and his behavior. The brevity of the present discussion is much more a function of the amount of research than of the differences which may actually be found once such research has been conducted.

Few attitude studies show differences among the religious faiths. However, one study did find differences among various denominations in grade point average, world-minded attitudes, and misconceptions about human nature.[12] In general, Jewish students had fewer misconceptions about human nature and were more world-minded than Protestants, and Protestants as a whole were slightly more world-minded and had fewer misconceptions about human nature than Catholics. But some Protestant denominations were far below Catholics and some far above.

Some work has been done on the relationship of religious attendance and membership to antisocial behavior. Usually the findings have not indicated a relationship, although one study did show a much smaller proportion of Jewish youth were delinquent.[13] The findings in general suggest church attendance alone is not sufficient to reduce antisocial behavior when taken in the context of other forces. All findings with respect to religion must be scrutinized carefully, because religious affiliation is correlated closely with other factors related to delinquency. Of course, a delinquent is "a delinquent caught and reported," and middle-class adolescents are less likely to be either caught or reported.

---

[11] Starke Hathaway, Elie D. Monachesi, and Lawrence A. Young, "Rural-Urban Adolescent Personality," *Rural Sociology,* Vol. 24 (1959), pp. 331–46.

[12] Carl C. Garrison, "The Relationship of Certain Variables to Church-Sect Typology among College Students," *Journal of Social Psychology,* Vol. 56 (1962), pp. 29–32.

[13] William Kraraceus, "Delinquent Behavior and Church Attendance," *Sociology and Social Research,* Vol. 28 (1944), pp. 284–89. See also Robert A. Denther and Lawrence J. Monroe, "Early Adolescent Thefts," *American Sociological Review,* Vol. 26 (1961).

In a study done in both the Northeast and the South, it was found that children strongly tended to accept the faith of their parents.[14] When one parent was religious and the other parent skeptical, the youth usually was religious. Adolescents who were themselves skeptics scored lower on measures of authoritarianism than did declared Christians.

A more clearly subcultural difference may be found in studies of sects more separated from the major cultural theme in American society. In one such study, Amish children were found to be more submissive and introverted than other children, and obviously less inclined to rebel.[15] The visibility of the differences between adolescents whose parents are Amish, Mennonite, and members of other marginal sects is great. Since adolescents ordinarily strive to conform to the manners and fads of peers, the differences between sectarian adolescents and the other children imply an almost totally different value outlook. The traditional views of Amish and Mennonite parents are more closely adhered to by their children than are the views expressed by other parents to their children. As a result, conformity to the peer-group culture on the part of these relatively isolated children is largely absent.

Sects, more than almost any other organization, protect the young from outside influences. For example, the Amish were able to obtain a favorable Supreme Court decision in a case in which they did not wish their children to salute the flag of the United States. Few groups would dare contest such a notion as respect for the flag, but the case was settled on the basis of the separation of church and state.

Christian denominations differ somewhat in their effect upon adolescents and upon the types of learning affecting future success.[16] A greater difference is noted when we either leave the Christian religion or move to observe sects rather than denominations. The greater difference noted in non-Christian religions and Christian or non-Christian sects doubtlessly results somewhat from the partial participation of these religious groups in the majority society, whether this is by choice or forced upon religious minority groups by others.

Evidence exists to indicate religions are homogenizing. This is clearly true of organizations—witness the merging of large religious denominations at the national level—and of the thousands of small

---

[14] Snell Putney and Russell Middleton, "Rebellion, Conformity, and Parental Religious Ideologies," *Sociometry*, 1941, pp. 125–35.

[15] Elmer Lewis Smith, "Personality Differences between Amish and Non-Amish Children," *Rural Sociology*, 1958, pp. 371–76.

[16] For example, see Russell R. Dynes, "Church-Sect Typology and Socio-Economic Status," *American Sociological Review*, Vol. 20 (1955), pp. 555–60,

communities that cannot afford to maintain separate churches. If this trend involves doctrinal matters and moral precepts, the differences among Protestant churches will likely diminish. However, some differences among Catholics, Protestants, Jews, and sects are likely to remain.

## NEGROES

One in every ten Americans is a Negro. Many Negroes become professionals or proprietors of business, but in the main Negroes are limited to those occupations which receive fewer of the material and nonmaterial rewards whites enjoy. Parents know the opportunities are limited and they communicate this to their children. Further, many Negro parents are too busy scratching out a bare living to give inspiration to their children. The result is that Negro youth aspire to much lower occupational and educational levels than whites. An irony of this situation is that it is now evident the "job calling" for Negroes has been raised but there are few Negroes to accept these positions which require specialized training.

Many schools which are for all practical purposes engaged in the training of Negroes have budgets inferior to those catering to white youth, and often Negro schools are "technical schools" for training in the manual arts. This is true in the North as well as the South, and Negro colleges as well as high schools, the few excellent Negro universities notwithstanding.

The most visible occupation open to adolescents in their consideration of a career in higher education is college professor. Few major universities in the United States have more than one Negro professor, and some have none. Few Negroes have Ph.D's, a requirement for faculty positions in many of the larger universities. School teaching has been open to Negroes for many years, but teaching is, to a large extent, considered a female occupation in the United States and offers little incentive to boys except in certain fields at the high school level.

In the North the restriction on neighborhoods in which Negro families are permitted to live produces a natural schism in the friendship groupings between Negro and white adolescents. In the South the opportunity for mixed clique groups is greater and such groups exist in preadolescent ages. By the time the boy or girl reaches adolescence, however, the racial division so important to adults has produced a socially impossible situation for mixed clique groups. Also, Negroes find it extremely difficult to be involved in leadership positions in the integrated schools in the North, and impossible in the South. As

will be seen in later chapters, such exclusion has tremendous consequences for the acceptance of certain aspects of the adolescent culture; it also works toward lowering educational aspirations. This is
partly due to white exclusiveness, certainly, but not entirely. One
study in the deep South showed that Negroes have no more favorable
attitudes toward white students than whites have toward Negroes.[17]

Negroes have higher delinquency rates than white youth. Certain
factors would seem to explain to some extent this differential. In the
first place, Negroes are mostly from lower-class families and white
children from such families also have higher delinquency rates. Negroes also tend to live in neighborhoods expected to have higher
delinquency rates. It is only natural that more police are stationed
in these areas and, insofar as a delinquent is a "delinquent caught,"
the higher rates are in part due to the self-fulfilling prophecy. Negroes
doubtless resent discrimination, and some theories would hold that
the outlet for such frustration would be delinquency.

It has also been found, however, that Negro youth express equally
favorable attitudes toward religion and morality as do whites.[18] It
appears that, as in the case of adolescents in the majority culture,
Negroes are often judged by unusual and dramatic cases. The large
absolute number of Negroes found to have committed delinquent
acts should not lead one to assess Negroes as " mostly bad." Almost
every adolescent commits at some time or another an act which would
be judged delinquent, but most adolescents, Negro and white, do not
consider such behavior a frequent or usual pasttime.

## CLASS AND STATUS

Sociologists have paid more attention to the effect of parental class
and status on adolescent behavior than to any other factor in the
adult world. Generally, the findings have been rewarding to the student of human behavior who seeks to explain differences in behavior.
Whether adult class and status represent the most important criterion of subcultures in the adolescent world is a moot point, however,
since the comparison with other bases of differences is unequal as to
the amount of research. Further, some evidence appears contradictory as to the present effects of adult status.

Class and status are terms used in the field of stratification. They
apply to inequalities in the rewards our culture defines as desireable.

---

[17] Terry Protho and John Jensen, "Comparison and Some Ethnic and Religious Attitudes of Negro and White College Students in the Deep South," *Social Forces,* Vol.
30 (1952), pp. 426–28.
[18] *Ibid.*

Examples of status differentials are income, educational attainment, level of living, power, authority, prestige, and the like. All these factors are continuous, and the differences are very small at the point where a line may be drawn between two classes. This has led sociologists to believe that social class as a natural, disjunct, and easily identifiable phenomenon is not a valid concept for describing most of the inequalities in the American social structure. Nevertheless, people in a community are willing to "place" people in a class and the result of such classification appears to describe or summarize inequalities very well. Whether "class" represents a socially real phenomenon or merely a shorthand expression used to summarize other, more quantified characteristics, it is a useful concept.

The classic study of class in relation to adolescent subcultures was done in the 1940's by August B. Hollingshead.[19] An intensive case study of only one Midwest community, this research resulted not only in the usual type of data amenable to statistical analysis but also in an unusually large amount of case material and insights into the more subtle features of the operation of the status structure. A critique of the study is offered in Chapter 1.

Hollingshead divided the community into five classes, which we shall call the upper, the upper-middle, and the lower-middle, the upper-lower, and the lower-lower. These names are roughly correct in terms of the characteristics of each class, and they are conventional. Hollingshead characterizes the upper class as based on wealth and lineage.[20] In this community, as in the country as a whole, mobility into this class within one generation is difficult and rare. Rather, membership in the upper class is handed down from one generation to the next. It is also important to recognize that in this class, as in all classes, the status of all family members in the adult community, are assigned on the basis of the parental status, usually the father's. The primary term for judging people is "good blood," and there is a heavy emphasis upon the inheritance of characteristics. The upper class represents only about 2 percent of the community's population and will be referred to only at times in the analysis to follow.

The upper-middle class is a class of "achievers"—almost half of the members of this class moved up from a lower one through efforts primarily connected with education and occupation.[21] Members of this class are oriented toward their career, and they differ from the upper class in this important way. Although they try to minimize it,

[19] August B. Hollingshead, *Elmtown's Youth* (New York: John Wiley & Sons, 1949).
[20] *Ibid.*, pp. 84–90.
[21] *Ibid.*, pp. 90–95.

the difference between the two classes is sharp and easily recognized. In addition to occupation, the prestige of the members of the upper-middle class depends upon their civic participation. These homes are seldom broken by divorce and Hollingshead reports that 85 percent of the children in the class were living with both parents. The occupational orientation of the upper-middle class implies an important value on education. Those who had succeeded without education were somewhat embarrassed by this fact. According to Hollingshead, the members of the upper-middle class give "cavalier" treatment to the lower-middle class and identify with the upper class.

The lower-middle class recognizes two classes are above them and tend to explain their own inability to move any farther upward by the treatment they receive from the upper and upper-middle classes.[22] Members of the lower-middle class believe they have raised themselves to a level of "respectability" from the "common man" in the class below them. There is no embarrassment at the wife supplementing the family income by working. They live with convenience but no surplus, other than a small savings account. They enjoy home ownership, although a few live in apartments. The families are larger in the lower-middle class than in the two classes above them, but still the average size of family was only 3.6 during the time of this study. Education is not nearly so high as in the upper-middle class—only 23 percent of the men had finished high school although the percentage for the women is much higher. Doubtless, comparable classes in the 1960's will have completed high school much more often. Members of the lower-middle class are joiners and participate in a multitude of organizations often organized on the basis of age and sex. However, they seldom are leaders in important community-wide and high-status organizations. The professed moral and religious standards are high but the researcher felt that deviation from the expressed values was somewhat higher than in the upper-middle class.

The upper-lower class is aware of its position and its members are especially prone to point out the differences between themselves and the lowest class of "loafers" and the "criminal class."[23] They are for the most part semi-skilled and unskilled workers, but they do earn a regular wage. They have few comforts but most of the necessities. They purchase many consumer goods through mail-order houses, and during the period of this study this type of purchase was almost exclusively characteristic of this class. During the depression, the members of the upper-lower class were unable to sustain themselves and

[22] *Ibid.*, pp. 95–102.
[23] *Ibid.*, pp. 102–10.

were forced to resort to public relief. Unlike any of the classes above them, the families of the upper-lower class are unstable. Exactly one third had been broken by separation, divorce, or death. This may be compared with the lower-middle class where only 18 percent had been broken by these same factors. Families in the upper-lower class are larger, and they are begun earlier. Unlike the lower-middle class, upper-lower class members are not religious and many attend church seldom or not at all. They are, in the main, excluded from organizational memberships. Those who do belong to organizations and churches find themselves limited to the ones with lower prestige.

Informal relations in friendship groupings are limited to other members of their own class. Members of the lower-middle class shun friendship ties with members of the upper-lower, and the latter in turn shun ties with members of the lower-lower class.

In all respects the lower-lower class occupies the lower rank in the community.[24] Resignation to their lot appears the most important feature of the life of the members of this class. They work in menial and low-paying jobs, often irregularly. They manage, in most cases, the meager necessities. They often purchase their clothing at rummage sales—clothing that once belonged to a member of a higher class. Illness and idleness cut down the dependability of their income. Frequently parents, children, and in-laws all live in two or three rooms. Exploitive sex relations are frequently found between teenage girls from the lower-lower class and boys from one of the higher classes, but such relations almost never end in marriage. Hollingshead reports that physicians and others who are in a position to know estimate 20 to 25 percent of the births are out of wedlock.

Let us now turn to the implications of the class structure for adolescent subculture. The first point is very clear from Hollingshead's data: participation in school affairs and in peer group relations is almost strictly classbound. For example, over two thirds of the boys and girls whose parents were in two upper classes (upper and upper-middle) attended high school dances regularly, while about the same proportion of the youth in the lower-lower class attended either rarely or not at all.[25] A similar finding related high school plays and parties.[26] No members of the lower-lower class were on the student council; the upper-lower class was clearly underrepresented; and the higher three classes were overrepresented.[27] Hollingshead de-

---

[24] *Ibid.*, pp. 110–20.
[25] *Ibid.*, p. 198.
[26] *Ibid.*, p. 199.
[27] *Ibid.*, p. 200.

veloped a participation index summarizing twenty-three extracurricular activities and found a relationship strikingly similar to the findings reported for the student council. For example, none of the members of the upper and upper-middle class were nonparticipants while approximately three fourths of the lower-lower class were.[28] The findings with respect to clique group relations bore out the same relationship between parental status and participation. Most friendship relations were within the same class, and of those that did cross class lines the participants were members of contiguous classes.[29] The same was true of dating. It was also evident that members of one class might name as their best friend a member of the next highe1 class, but the member of the higher class did not reciprocate.

It is clear that at the time of the study this community revealed subcultures based upon parental status. Both groupings and participation were highly correlated with class position. The students themselves accepted such criteria of formal and informal participation, since many of the behavior patterns described were under student control. However, there is more direct evidence.

Work during the summer and after school was clearly related to class position.[30] For example, only girls from the lower classes worked in restaurants as waitresses or in stores as clerks. Leisure activities, therefore, obviously differed according to classes. Dating outside the school was characteristic only of girls in the lower classes, and such behavior downgraded them farther with their schoolmates. Since discipline was handled by the school teachers and administrators on the basis of class position, the necessity of conformity to school demands and the commitment to school norms were different. Tabooed pleasures were found more frequently among adolescents of the lower classes.[31] During this period, roller skating was thought of as a less desirable recreation than bowling. The relationship between class position and this type of recreation was clear, with members of the higher classes more often bowling and members of the lower classes skating. Again the relationship was quite high.[32]

In this study, not only do adolescents accept parental status as a basis of differentiating in formal and informal participation, but a high relationship exists between class position and attitudes toward leisure, school, and tabooed pleasures.

There is some evidence that the effect of the adult classes on adoles-

---

[28] *Ibid.,* p. 201.
[29] *Ibid.,* chap. 9.
[30] *Ibid.,* chap. 11.
[31] *Ibid.,* chap. 12.
[32] *Ibid.,* p. 310.

cent behavior has changed in Elmtown, but the situation in this community in the 1940's is not unlike that found in many communities today.

While a more recent study of one community, using the same methods, comes to essentially the same conclusions,[33] the findings from another famous study on the class structure within the adolescent group indicate that the differentiation was based more upon peer group relations and personal characteristics than upon adult status.[34] This latter study was conducted by James S. Coleman, and Elmtown was included in the sample. The status of boys within the school in the late 1950's seemed to be related more to athletic prowess than to any characteristics of their parents. Further, girls who had any status within the peer group could run with a "fast" crowd, unlike Elmtown as Hollingshead found it or other schools as Coleman found them.

Although the popularity of this variable knows few behavioral-science disciplinary limitations, it probably reaches its maximum coverage in research related to students, teachers, and educational institutions. One has only to review the many readers and textbooks dealing with educational sociology, school and society, and social foundations to see just how strongly the social class factor is emphasized.[35] A more detailed review of this same literature would uncover two consistent patterns. First, there is a high degree of harmony among authors as to the role played by social class in educational experiences. Second, most discussion is based on, or at least has some referent support in, three sociological classics: *Elmtown's Youth*,[36] *Who Shall Be Educated?*[37] and *Middletown: A Study in American Culture*.[38] Each of these classics follows a similar analytical approach and each focuses on social class as the crucial variable. It was noted in chapter one that, in most instances, the authors of the works cited deal with first order (two-variable) correlations. It was also noted that from the two-variable tables presented it is difficult to pinpoint just what causal relationships exist. Generally, these authors fail to consider other factors.

---

[33] Robert J. Havighurst, *et. al.*, *Growing Up in River City* (New York: John Wiley & Sons, 1962).

[34] James S. Coleman, *The Adolescent Society* (New York: The Free Press of Glencoe, 1962), esp. chap. 7.

[35] See Wilbur B. Brookover and David Gottlieb, "Social Class and Education," *The Sociology of Education*, N. L. Gage and W. W. Charters, Jr., eds. (New York: American Book Company, 1964).

[36] Hollingshead, *op. cit.*

[37] W. Lloyd Warner, Robert J. Havighurst, and Martin B. Loeb, *Who Shall be Educated?* (New York: Harper & Bros., 1944).

[38] Robert S. Lynd and Helen Merrill Lynd, *Middletown: A Study in American Culture* (New York: Harcourt, Brace & Co., 1929).

The research presented here attempts to carry the study of social class and education a step further by dealing with a third variable: academic achievement.[39] Selection of this variable was based on the idea that since academic achievement is the business of our schools, it would play a significant role in how students view the total educational experience. We took the view that academic achievement would tend to wash away the impact of social class since it was a variable that would bring together students with a relatively common value system. More specifically, it was our general hypothesis that for college freshmen, at any rate, history of academic achievement would be a better predictor of academic values and attitudes than social class would be.

During the fall of 1960, as part of the first phase of a longitudinal study of changes in academic and career expectations of college students, entering freshmen at three academic institutions were interviewed. For purposes of this discussion we shall restrict ourselves to data dealing with males at two of the sample schools. The third school is included since it differs significantly from the others in academic admission standards, school politics, and student population. Of the two schools discussed here, one is a large Midwestern state university where every fourth entering freshman was selected at random for this investigation. The male sample for the school consisted of 283 respondents. The second school is a smaller, private institution, also in a Midwestern area, where all entering freshman were interviewed. In this school our sample consisted of 115 male students.

A paper-and-pencil questionnaire designed to obtain information pertaining to the experiences, attitudes, expectations, and values of respondents was administered to each student. The material reported here was collected from students prior to any class attendance or participation in school activities.

We begin with an examination of the respondent's social class background as determined by father's occupation. The following divisions were made:

Low: Barbers, postmen, mechanics, bus drivers, clerks in retail stores, etc.
Middle: Plumbers, carpenters, owners of small retail stores, foremen, white-collar supervisors, secondary school teachers, pharmacists, wholesale salesmen, middle management, etc.
High: Major professions, presidents of medium-large firms, high executives in large firms, etc.

Responses to the question, "Who would you say played the most

[39] The material presented here first appeared in David Gottlieb, "Social Class, Achievement, and the College-going Experience," *School Review*, Vol. 70, No. 3 (Fall, 1962).

important role in helping you to decide to attend college?" were also considered. Possible choices included parents, teachers, guidance counselors, friends, clergy, relatives, and "no one." The distribution of parental choices went in the expected direction with middle-class and upper-class boys more likely to mark this category than lower-class boys. Selection of adults within the school system as perceived influencers went in the opposite direction with lower-class boys naming teachers and guidance counselors more frequently than did respondents from the more affluent class groups. The results, while meeting directional expectations, were somewhat dazzling in the degree of differences among the three class groups. For example, in middle-class and upper-class families it is usually assumed the children will attend college. It seems reasonable, then, to expect that boys from these class groups would be less likely to mention nonfamily influences, if they mention outside sources at all. In contrast, college attendance may not be taken for granted by lower-class families. Thus, the lower-class boys would be more vulnerable to nonfamilial sources of support and encouragement than the respondents from the middle and upper classes. At the same time, it was surprising to find that only a third of the lower-class boys mentioned parents, since other investigators have shown parental influence plays a significant part in the lower-class child's educational and occupational aspirations.[40] Evidence of support for lower-class children from adults within the school system was not in harmony with the classic work of W. Lloyd Warner, August Hollingshead, and Robert J. Havinghurst, who report middle-class school personnel do little to enhance the upward mobility of lower-class children.[41]

The fact that these lower-class students who have obtained encouragement from school personnel are in college despite limited parental support suggests they are a highly selected group. Indeed, when a comparison is made of students in each of the socioeconomic groups one finds the lower-class student group contains the highest proportion of those who have graduated in the top third of their high school class. This finding makes sense since it would be anticipated that for the most part only the very best of the lower-class students would go on to college. In addition, we see that social class alone is not sufficient to explain variations in the attitudes, values, and behavior patterns of college students.

Table 4–1 shows that regardless of achievement level, middle- and

---

[40] Joseph A. Kahl, "Educational and Occupational Aspirations of 'Common Man' Boys," *Harvard Educational Review*, XXIII (Summer, 1953), pp. 186–203.
[41] Warner, Havighurst, Leob, *op. cit.*; Hollingshead, *op. cit.*

upper-class boys are more likely to report parents as influencers than are respondents from the lower class. Students who graduated in the top third of their high school class are here considered high achievers, while all others are considered low achievers. In each case the high achievers report the greater parental encouragement.

TABLE 4–1

SOCIAL CLASS, ACHIEVEMENT, AND SIGNIFICANT INFLUENCES*

Expressed as Percentages

| Social Class | Parents | School Personnel | Other | N |
|---|---|---|---|---|
| High Achievers | | | | |
| High .....................50 | 8 | 42 | 66 |
| Middle ..................45 | 20 | 35 | 110 |
| Low ......................34 | 38 | 28 | 61 |
| Low Achievers | | | | |
| High .....................43 | 13 | 44 | 47 |
| Middle ..................39 | 11 | 50 | 85 |
| Low ......................26 | 5 | 69 | 29 |

* Not significant at .05 level.

While there is a positive correlation between social class and parental encouragement at each achievement level, a somewhat different picture is seen when the patterns of influence of teachers and guidance counselors are examined. With the exception of the upper-class boys (and the difference is not great), support from adults in the school system is given to high achievers and reaches its maximum point with the lower-class students in this group. The class factor seems to operate in the performance expectations teachers may hold for students from the different social-class groups. In other words, students who most depart from expected patterns—lower-class high achievers and upper-class low achievers—receive the greatest support from teachers and guidance counselors.

It can also be seen from Table 4–1 that many students have listed sources of personal support that fall in the "other" category. While there were no significant differences between class and achievement groups in respect to items in this category, the "no one" response was most frequently selected by upper-class high achievers and lower-class low achievers. As noted earlier, this finding might have been predicted since college attendance is so much a part of the value system of the upper class that encouragement from others seems hardly necessary. What, then, can be said about the lower-class low achievers? At this point, very little that is founded on empirical evidence. We might speculate, however, that here youth know what they do not want, that is, occupations similar to those held by their fathers. Without the benefit of parental encouragement, support from school personnel, or a value climate conducive to college attendance, they have made it this far and by their own admission they not only would like to complete college but anticipate doing so.

In response to the question of why they come to college, most students in each class and achievement group stated for "a broad education" or for "vocational training." Again, interesting differences are found when the total picture is studied in terms of class and achievement.

Table 4–2 shows that in each case, no matter what the achievement level, selection of the occupational-training item correlates with social-class background. However, differences are not too great; and when achievement level is controlled the impact of class tends to be washed away. Finally, it can be seen that the lower-class low achiever is most likely to mention occupational training as his main reason for being in college—a finding that lends some support to the earlier interpretation that a desire to move away from the father's occupational position urges these boys along the academic path.

TABLE 4–2

SOCIAL CLASS, ACHIEVEMENT, AND REASON FOR COLLEGE[*]

Expressed as Percentages

| Social Class | High Achievers | | | | Low Achievers | | | |
| | Broad Education | Vocational Training | Other | N | Broad Education | Vocational Training | Other | N |
| --- | --- | --- | --- | --- | --- | --- | --- | --- |
| High ....... | 43 | 48 | 9 | 66 | 38 | 53 | 9 | 47 |
| Middle ..... | 47 | 46 | 7 | 110 | 40 | 52 | 8 | 85 |
| Low ........ | 34 | 57 | 9 | 61 | 26 | 68 | 6 | 29 |

[*] Not significant at .05 level.

Given this information as to why they say they came to college and perceptions as to who has encouraged or influenced them, how do these students differ in their view of the ideal college professor and what it takes to attain high prestige with him? Each respondent was asked to select which of fifteen items he considered the most important characteristic of a good college teacher. The items and distribution of responses by social class and achievement level are presented in Table 4–3.

The students show a fair degree of consensus as to the ideal college professor. He should be an entertaining teacher; he should know his field; and he should make his students produce. Participation in civic, religious, and campus affairs is not considered too important. He

TABLE 4–3

SOCIAL CLASS, ACHIEVEMENT, AND THE IDEAL COLLEGE PROFESSOR

Expressed as Percentages

| Characteristic | High Achievers | | | Low Achievers | | |
|---|---|---|---|---|---|---|
| | High | Middle | Low | High | Middle | Low |
| A. Active in civic affairs............... | 5 | 1 | 3 | 2 | 0 | 0 |
| B. Active in campus affairs............. | 2 | 0 | 0 | 2 | 0 | 0 |
| C. Will discuss student's career plans..... | 3 | 3 | 5 | 4 | 5 | 24 |
| D. Will discuss student's personal problems ......................... | 2 | 1 | 3 | 2 | 6 | 0 |
| E. Is an entertaining teacher............ | 22 | 18 | 11 | 23 | 19 | 14 |
| F. Not a "buddy" to students............ | 2 | 3 | 3 | 0 | 0 | 14 |
| G. Active in religious affairs............ | 5 | 0 | 2 | 0 | 0 | 7 |
| H. Knows his field.................... | 39 | 35 | 36 | 26 | 27 | 21° |
| I. Does not give many reading assignments ..................... | 0 | 0 | 0 | 0 | 0 | 3 |
| J. Helps students decide on religious and political stand................. | 0 | 0 | 0 | 0 | 0 | 0 |
| K. Judges students on work, not dress.... | 0 | 6 | 0 | 4 | 6 | 3 |
| L. Makes students produce............. | 15 | 16 | 29 | 27 | 20 | 12° |
| M. Gives students a break.............. | 2 | 5 | 2 | 2 | 10 | 3 |
| N. Allows student participation in class objectives.................... | 0 | 2 | 3 | 2 | 2 | 0 |
| O. Does not indoctrinate students........ | 2 | 8 | 3 | 6 | 5 | 0 |
| | $N = (66)$ | (110) | (61) | (47) | (83) | (29) |

° Not significant at .05 level.

should not indoctrinate his students nor become too involved in their internal dynamics. All in all, there is a desire for a person who is competent and will keep students going without making it too personal or painful an experience.

While this general agreement exists, some differences are found when students are compared at the various class and achievement levels. Regardless of achievement, students from the lower-class are the least enthusiastic in stating a preference for an entertaining teacher. This is not so much an expression of preference for the cold, sober type as it is a reflection of the lower-class view of educational institutions as places where, at least in the classroom, affairs are conducted in a businesslike manner. Achievement level, however, is tied in with preferences for a college professor who knows his field. In this case the high achievers in each class group are the strongest in expressing a desire for a professionally competent instructor.

Both variables appear to operate in the selection of a teacher who will make students produce. Among the high achievers it is the lower-class boy who seeks the faculty push, while among the lower achievers it is more likely to be the student from the middle or upper class.

As for the lower-class low achiever, he continues to behave in a unique fashion. He wants a man who will help him with his career plans but makes it clear he does not wish to become involved on a more personal level. He is not particularly concerned with the quality of his training. He continues to operate as he did in the past, without adult support and quite self-reliantly as he goes about the business of moving up the occupational ladder.

Behavior patterns and attitudes learned and applied in earlier educational experiences will, of course, play some part in the student's total view of his college and ideal professor. The lower-class high achiever, for example, continues to depend on adults in the school system for support. In high school, the encouragement and press of teachers led to success; now, in college, he looks to the faculty for the push which will keep him producing at a high level. The low achievers in the upper and middle class see the faculty as the group that can, by continued pressure and pace setting, bring out the potential they have been told they possess and finally move them into closer harmony with the academic expectations held for members of their social class.

Students from the middle and upper class who are high achievers express little need for faculty press or assistance with career plans. Knowing they have done well in the past, and having had few difficulties in making the move to college, they can afford to hold the less rigid view of the total academic picture. These young people are not particularly intimidated or awed by the many reading lists, classes, and rituals of college life. They are the elite with greater social sophistication and know-how when it comes to manipulating people and things in the educational bureaucracy. As will be shown in the final portion of this analysis, the high achiever in the middle and upper class believes there is more than one way to win prestige and status with the faculty.

Each respondent was asked to indicate among nine items those factors they felt would give a student prestige with the faculty. The prestige items and distribution of responses are shown in Table 4–4.

Clearly, three items were not considered important by the entering freshmen: coming from the right social background, being active in intercollegiate athletics, and being a member of a sorority or fraternity. Of the six remaining items, "demonstrating scholarly capacity" was mentioned most frequently, followed by "being original and creative" and "dedication to studies."

Of the three academic-centered items (A, C, and E), the different class groups varied little in response to "demonstrating scholarly capacity," but the high achievers in each group tended to place

TABLE 4–4

SOCIAL CLASS, ACHIEVEMENT, AND PRESTIGE WITH THE FACULTY [*]

(Expressed as Percentages)

| | High Achievers | | | Low Achievers | | |
|---|---|---|---|---|---|---|
| Factors | High | Middle | Low | High | Middle | Low |
| A. Being original and creative............47 | 51 | 59 | 40 | 40 | 38 |
| B. Having a pleasing personality............41 | 36 | 25 | 28 | 29 | 24 |
| C. Demonstrating scholarly capacity........76 | 68 | 66 | 70 | 68 | 69 |
| D. Active in campus affairs................32 | 25 | 13 | 28 | 19 | 17 |
| E. Dedication to studies..................41 | 36 | 49 | 34 | 31 | 38 |
| F. Not being too critical..................27 | 25 | 17 | 7 | 1 | 0 |
| G. Coming from the right social background.. 0 | 0 | 2 | 0 | 6 | 0 |
| H. Active in intercollegiate athletics........ 5 | 2 | 2 | 0 | 2 | 0 |
| I. Being a member of a sorority or fraternity.. 0 | 2 | 2 | 0 | 2 | 0 |
| N = (66) | (110) | (61) | (47) | (85) | (29) |

[*] Base N's are the same for each column.
Not significant at 0.5 level.

greater emphasis on originality and creativity as well as on dedication to studies.

The three more socially-oriented items showed some differences on both the class and achievement level. It is quite apparent the high achievers, and the middle and upper classes especially, felt that not being too critical is one means by which a student gains prestige with the faculty. It might also be noted that the personality item most frequently chosen by high achievers in the middle and upper classes was participating in campus affairs. While the differences are not too great, the directional consistency suggests the most successful middle-class and upper-class student feels that, though academic performance is certainly important, application of the proper social skills has its place.

### Summary and Conclusions

This section has dealt with three variables: social class, academic achievement, and the college-going experience. We began with the notion that perhaps too much emphasis had been placed on the class factor at the expense of certain intervening variables which could be valuable predictors of academic expectations and attitudes. Selection of the "academic achievement" factor was deliberate in that we saw this item as one which might cut across class lines, bringing together students with a more serious academic outlook. A second reason for use of this variable was suggested by James S. Coleman's research on high school student value systems.[42] Coleman conducted a study of the "climate of values" existing among students in a number of public

[42] Coleman, *op. cit.*

schools. He proposes that adolescents have their own set of values and norms, and these may differ from the ones held by adult members of the society. As a result, adolescents involved in the different climate systems may find themselves in situations where peer-held values play an important role in academic and career divisions.

Of particular concern to our research are Coleman's findings on the kinds of academic value systems that might exist both between schools and among students in the same school. Briefly, his research indicates that students may be part of different subsystems in the school. Some of these are built around academic interests and achievement; others center more on the social events and functions of the school. As a result, identifiable student subcultures are formed where interests and activities may differ significantly. These groups are not necessarily homogeneous in socioeconomic background. On the contrary, as Coleman's research makes clear, social class may be less salient than skill and ability in certain school systems. The football player, for instance, although of lower socioeconomic origin, has access to the middle-class student group since he is proficient in a status or prestige-giving activity.

Moving a step further with the Coleman analysis, we proposed that the factor of academic achievement would bring together students with a common value outlook. In other words, regardless of socio-economic background the students who perform well would experience certain types of rewards and influences and could be viewed as being part of the same student subculture. (In this instance, "part of the same student subculture" may mean either direct face-to-face contact with similar peers or through some reference group indentification.) Given the kind of prevailing value system which Coleman attributes to adolescents in our high schools, it seems quite feasible that high achievers might well become a unique group. Homogeneity of values and attitudes among similar achievement groups would be expected, given school systems which encourage a variety of activities and student groupings.

This research does not deny the importance of the social class variable, as the data presented in the tables clearly show. Each table indicates a similarity among members of the same social class group when educational experiences and expectations are examined. Still, the research does indicate that social class impact may vary when correlated with academic achievement.

The findings of this investigation have certain important implications for a sociology of adolescence and for further research in youth socialization. We have observed that the work of Warner and his associates, of Hollingshead, and of the Lynds has had and continues to have a great impact on how one views adolescent behavior. This continued dependency is somewhat surprising when we recognize the methodological shortcomings of these investigations as well as the changes which have occurred in our schools since the studies were published.

*Chapter V*

# SUBCULTURES:
# RELATING TO THE ADULT WORLD

Adolescents differ greatly in the way they relate to parents, the school, and the adult community in general. In this chapter, we suggest a typology of these different relationships. It is clear that this typology represents differences found currently among adolescents. It also appears that the three types suggested represent stages which characterize the majority of adolescents at different periods in our history. (It is important to understand that in no period of our history have all adolescents behaved in a manner resembling any of these three types.) The three types of relations with the adult world are, in turn, the apprenticeship eras, the adolescent rebellion, and the cool generation.

## THE APPRENTICESHIP ERA

In folk societies and in the early part of the history of the United States, child training, especially the occupational preparation of both boys and girls, took place almost exclusively within the home. Adults determined the time at which youth were ready to move from one age-grade status to another. Parents usually determined nature of occupational choice. It must be remembered that in such societies status mobility depended much more on the occupation ascribed to the person by his family background than on talents and achievement he as an individual was able to exhibit.

Perhaps our most accurate data come from the anthropological studies of "primitive" and "peasant" societies. The family situations in these societies differ greatly from present-day American society. In our society, the young grow up with decreasing involvement in the family; they marry; and they establish their own nuclear family. In the primitive and peasant societies the lines of kinship are extensive. Further, the presence of grandparents, uncles, and aunts in the home is not uncommon. Marriage means bringing another person (usually the new wife, but sometimes the new husband) into the home rather than establishing a separate domicile. In these "folk" societies, learning by the young is highly limited and includes a strong emphasis on moral codes or tribal lore. Malinowski points out, for example, that while there is technical knowledge of how crops will best grow or the proper dimensions of canoe building, there is also a strong belief that certain magical qualities are essential to successful crops and good fishing. In other words, religion, magic, and symbolic rites are very much integrated into the total training for occupational competence. Teaching of rites and magic is in the hands of parents, uncles and aunts, grandparents, and, to some extent, local villagers. There is little reason to send the young beyond the village, especially since another village may vary in its magical beliefs.

Moving to the broader context of the general apprenticeship type of relations between adolescent and adult, it may be observed that skills are passed down from father to son and from mother to daughter. Despite any actions and influences from outsiders, traditional ways are maintained. Frequently there is a heavy emphasis on the institutionalization of age-grade passage. The term "rites of passage" refers to the formal and highly ritualized procedure by which the young move into adult positions. In many primitive societies these rites are quite elaborate and involve many days of tests and proof-giving on the part of the young. Within the structure of these rites, the young show they are ready to be accepted as full members of the community.

The emphasis on total community identity is particularly strong in these societies. The young look to adults for status confirmation— that is, for the general social recognition that the boy has become a man. The individual is heavily dependent for both practical reasons and social solidarity on the immediate group in which he interacts. Religion, for example, is a part of the community and not so much an individual act. These are total social acts in which the young again and again show their identification with the tribe and the elders.

This procedure stands in contrast to modern or highly industrialized societies where traditions are moved aside by social change. In our own society, mobility is accepted and often encouraged to the extent that parents give "real" assistance to their offspring to move to another community or another job at the time of high school graduation. The notion of being independent, of striking out on your own, of getting away from the old folks, is emphasized. In primitive societies this outward mobility is limited to a brief period in which the young may move out in order to show they are capable of making it on their own. When, however, the rites are complete and adult recognition is given, the new man returns to the village and plays a vital role in maintaining family and community solidarity. The importance of the community is reflected in the fact that in many primitive societies the most severe social sanction is banishment. To some extent, these traditional ties are found in subgroups within present-day American society. Certain ethnic and religious groups maintain strong integrative bonds and the individual who violates these may be moved, isolated, or excommunicated. The American boy of Greek origin who marries a girl outside of the veil of the family may be rejected by the Greek community. The Catholic or the Quaker who violates the acceptable marital procedures may find certain limitations imposed upon him. In the case of the Catholic church, there is a strong effort to be sure that the spouse and especially the children will belong to the group. In the case of the Quakers, intermarriage often results in the member leaving the church at the suggestion of the church. Doubtlessly, some rural families, especially those in relatively geographically isolated areas, still exercise many characteristics of so-called primitive societies.

Returning now to the earlier apprenticeship era as it was found in American society, many more of the characteristics described above in connection with the primitive society were characteristic of this period than is usually thought. However, the most important aspects of our own history are the occupation skills which were learned, the limited number of skills which were passed on, and the taboos against the expression of conflict between parent and child.

The extreme limitation upon mobility from the community or from the occupation of the parent both required and permitted extensive apprenticeship experience on the part of the adolescent. Since the son was going to enter the father's occupation, and since the father needed cheap labor on the farm or in his business, it was quite natural for the son to begin work very early in life. (Chores on the farm are still a part of apprenticeship although they may be relatively narrowly defined and, according to one author, appear to be viewed by the adolescent as training rather than control.[1] The essential nature of the relations was the learning of occupational skills and attitudes of craftsmanship. All else was subjugated to the requirements of this learning. Therefore, to the extent that the teacher-learner character-

---

[1] Murray A. Strauss, "Work Roles and Financial Responsibility in the Socialization of Farm, Fringe, and Town Boys," *Rural Sociology*, Vol. 27 (1962), pp. 257–75.

istics of the father-son or mother-daughter relation may have aroused some feeling of conflict, the objective nature of the things to be learned and the obvious superiority of the father kept expressions of conflict at a minimum. Further, the quiet patience with antagonism or feelings of hostility was reinforced by the high value placed on the "quiet man."

Everything that has been said of the father-son relation could also be said of the mother-daughter relation. Heavy emphasis was put on the girl learning to take over household responsibilities early in her life. Certainly, with very large families and very few appliances the mother needed a great deal of assistance in her work. In the earlier days, the baking of bread and milking of cows fell often upon young daughters.

Talcott Parsons has pointed out that in the urban middle class it is impossible for the boy to emulate his father because the father does not work in the home.[2] Many masculine traits which must be learned by emulating an adult male, therefore, must be picked up by mere haphazard methods. He points out that an important test of the hypothesis with respect to morals and masculine roles would be the comparison of rural and urban boys in terms of their ability either to conform to morals or to assume masculine roles. He says, "It is my impression that farm boys tend to be 'good' in a sense in which that is not typical of their urban brothers."[3]

Another important aspect of the apprenticeship era in American society was that the adolescent was not in frequent contact with other adolescents his own age. Centralized schools did not begin until about the turn of the century, and even after that many adolescents still attended one-room schools. The contact was lessened, as compared to present-day school systems, by several factors: a shorter school year, a more austere approach to study and recess, and a very early dropout of most adolescents from school in order to work in the father's farm or business. Therefore, whatever reinforcement is needed from peers for conflict with the parent or the general adult generation may have been absent from the scene during this era.

Charles Horton Cooley described society as a function of the primary group, by which he meant frequent intimate and face-to-face contact. It is in these groups that ideals were formed. Doubtless, many of Cooley's generalizations still apply in some varied form to-

    [2] Talcott Parsons, "Age and Sex in the Social Structure of the United States," *American Sociological Review*, Vol. 7 (1942), pp. 604–17.
    [3] *Ibid.*, p. 605.

day. But they certainly describe the family in the apprenticeship era.[4] It is most interesting that Cooley, as well as other writers, never mentioned that the people involved in these groups liked each other. Love obviously was present, but the mutual interests and desire to be with each other are questions which will always remain unanswered.

## THE ADOLESCENT REBELLION

Practically everyone who currently writes on the subject of adolescence, be he psychologist, sociologist, physician, psychiatrist, has noted the agonies of the period—the preoccupation with self-identity and the ambivalent feelings toward becoming an adult. Whether such stresses were experienced by adolescents during the apprenticeship era is not known, but during the last three or four decades the emphasis on personal stress has been emphasized in the literature on adolescence.

Perhaps many factors might produce such a difficulty, but the widespread phenomenon implies that generational conflict is in the cultural and social milieux of our society. This is true because it has been found that in some primitive societies there is not only an absence of the period we call adolescence (there is only a boy and a man), but there also is an absence of the conflict and strife recognized generally as an important part of adolescence in our society. During the time at which adolescent relations with the adult world generally, and parents in particular, moved from the, at least overtly, smooth relations found in the apprenticeship era to the period we call the adolescent rebellion, there were many changes in social conditions which might separate youth from adults. The great increase in mobility from the family, from the community, and especially from the father's occupation tend to be characteristic of contemporary society. More and more people follow an occupation different from that of their fathers. Furthermore, as the occupational world became more specialized there was less opportunity for apprenticeship. Certainly it would be most difficult to conceive a social structure in which sons worked with their fathers on the assembly line to gain experience and knowledge of the future adult acceptance of occupational roles.

A second factor which may have brought about a change in relations is the increased periods spent in school and the less austere approach taken to school subjects. The greater amount of time spent with peers lends reinforcement and strength to a rebel. Peers also furnish a source of intimate relationships to which the adolescent may

[4] Charles H. Cooley, *Social Organization* (New York: Charles Scribner's Sons, 1920), chap. III and IV.

turn when the situation becomes unbearable in the family. A girl, reflecting on her adolescence, says:

I began dating a boy my parents disapproved of, but I kept dating him. We dated very steadily and in about three months we were engaged. My parents were very much against it, insisting that I was too young, that I didn't really know him very well, that we would not have enough money to live on comfortably, and that I would be very unhappy with him in the future. I didn't want to hear any of these things, much less believe them. So I directed my antagonism mainly at my father. He always represented the strength, stability and intelligence of the family to me, and I wanted to hurt him, indirectly hurting the family, because of their strong disapproval of my marriage plans. My father used to have to drive me to high school every morning and there were mornings when I didn't even talk to him. But he never gave up trying to show me that I was making a mistake. He would constantly point out the fact that we would have no money to live on and that if we waited, we would have the money, and we would be sure of what we were doing. Well, I already thought I was as sure as I could ever be. I also thought that he was being too cynical about marriage, which made me even angrier. I had a conception of marriage as being all love and roses and money problems barely, if ever, entered my picture.

I think the main thing that helped me realize that my parents were correct in their views about my engagement was a somewhat long period of separation from my fiance. It gave me time to re-evaluate my feelings and the whole situation. The separation came just after I graduated from high school and since I wanted to get married right away after the separation was over, I got a job working in a business office. I think I learned a lot about what life really means through the job. It was a completely new experience. I was surrounded by older married men and women, and I was the youngest employee. I was able to see my situation in a new and different perspective, which was what I needed then.

Any improved relations with my father during this time did not occur suddenly or spontaneously. Somehow things just gradually started to improve. There was no definite turning point in our ideas and reactions to things. Now I think we are closer than we ever were. I respect him for his actions during my engagement and I think he respects me and my decisions more, especially since I decided that I wanted to attend college. It felt strange for me to desire to go, because I fought against it for so long. Both my father and my brother were college graduates, so I think I was just fighting against conforming to their expectations, and against following even this much of their lives. I didn't want to be like they were. I wanted to be different, never realizing that I didn't have to prove myself to be an individual.

The situation with my mother during my engagement was a little different than with my father. My mother and I had always been very close in almost everything. So during this time, we had to get used to being at opposite sides of a very important problem. One of the most difficult things for me to accept was that my mother said that she could not attend my wedding if I married against their wishes. I wanted both their support so badly because I was afraid of making all the preparations and of going through the actual ceremony by myself, with no moral support. I think I suspected that she was right all along, but I didn't want to face it. I figured that I was old enough to make my own decisions and even if I felt that they were right, I could not back down on such a big decision. I had to prove myself and I thought that this was one way to do it.

My mother sensed the growing doubt that appeared after I started working, and she began to feel reassured about my future. We gradually began to get along better and better. It was wonderful to feel close to my mother again.

My friends influenced me greatly. For instance, when I was engaged, I got to know a girl who also was fighting to get married against her parents' wishes. She displayed an extremely large amount of independence from them and I admired this very much. The only thing that stopped her from marrying was that she was below the legal age in Colorado when you can get married without parental consent. Her independence influenced me insofar as my actions were concerned. It gave me self-confidence to be able to act independently of adults.

Indeed, it would appear from autobiographical data that the selection in dating is a most important aspect of the conflict in adolescents' relations with their parents. Another girl says:

Dating behavior was never a real problem between my parents and I until I became a sophomore. I had casual chaperoned dates (parents drove us to movies, etc.). Then, I became very attached to a boy at age fifteen and tried to conform to the "going steady" norm in our high school. By the end of my junior year, I was still going steady. My parents then stepped in. This was my only problem from then on. The boy involved was a very religious, mannerly and intelligent boy who also was having trouble with his parents. Both parents tried formal talks, punishment, and just about everything to stop our dating. Finally, both his parents and mine decided to quit riding us about our dating. The boy and I did break up not more than six months later after we found out that we were only fighting our parents.

The fact of dating in itself, then, is apparently not of great significance, but rather the source of the decision. The following autobiography makes this more explicit:

I believe that my parents turned out to be my chief source of frustration in my adolescent period. Being an only child, I was greatly over-protected and they guided my every move. I greatly resented this overbearing authority, but accepted it until the middle of my high school period. Rebellion against this authority finally broke loose in my dating behavior. I first dated a "wild senior boy," not a "chuke" in high school terminology, but one who had a great lover boy reputation. As far as my behavior with him, the greatest amount of "loving" we did was a short goodnight kiss on my front door step. My parent's values about sex were greatly imbedded in me, although I went against their authority in dating selection.

The general phenomenon we refer to as the adolescent rebellion probably was well underway in the 1920's, flourished fully in the 1930's and 1940's, but was apparently beginning to wane by the end of the 1950's. It has been variously analyzed and named. Many authors refer to it as conflict between the generations, some as withdrawal from the adult culture, and some as dual ambivalence. All these features are present.

In a brilliant analysis, L. Joseph Stone and Joseph Church[5] say that if the adolescent must find self-identity and become an independent man, he must "break numberless familial ties based on authority,

---

[5] L. Joseph Stone and Joseph Church, *Childhood and Adolescence* (New York: Random House, 1957), pp. 275–78.

affection, responsibility, respect, intimacy, and possessiveness—not to mention force of habit." [6]

The child has enjoyed the company of his parents, especially his mother, and has learned to depend upon his parents for teaching him right from wrong, for security against trouble, and for affection. As he enters the adolescent period the young person increasingly sees the need for becoming an independent adult. He "tries on" different personalities, different faces before the mirror, and different degrees of self-determination. Because of the habitual dependence upon parents, the adolescent moves toward independence by degrees, but these changes are not smooth and even. Rather, he is now a man and now a child, both in his own view and in the behavior he exhibits to others. The security inherent in parent-child relationships is not easily surrendered by the adolescent. He is, in other words, ambivalent toward his manhood.

A second aspect of this development is that the norms (codes of conduct) for gradual development are neither clear nor agreed upon. At any given age we are likely to disagree among ourselves as to the level of independence appropriate to that age. This ambiguity of the roles and norms for development may be found within the same person at different times. Adolescent development is therefore characterized as ambivalence on the part of the adolescent toward a set of norms which are ambiguous.

However, a third aspect of the social situation of the adolescent further confounds the ability to develop steadily and without frustration. Parents wish their adolescents to become adult men and women, but they also regret losing their little children. There is the desire for adolescents to learn to make their own decisions, but also there is the desire for the adolescent to learn from the adult's mistakes and experience. If the adolescent is to learn from the adult's experience, the only choice in relationship is between advice and control. Doubtless, a major part of becoming an adult is learning from one's own experience and failures. However, parents are understandably impatient with the tedious learning by trial and error. Further, adolescents can easily make serious mistakes, even to the extent of influencing their whole lives. Parents quite naturally wish to avoid such mistakes on the part of their own offspring. Therefore, an ambivalent adolescent is fighting an ambivalent parent. This is referred to as "dual ambivalence" by Stone and Church. [7]

Parental assistance is considered by adolescents less in terms of the

[6] *Ibid.*, p. 275.
[7] *Ibid.*, p. 278.

wisdom of the advice or the demands and more in terms of impositions upon a subordinate. Such assistance, especially when it takes the form of frequent advice and "nagging" on minor points, appears to be degrading and burdensome. Many observers of adolescent behavior believe there is anxiety on the part of some adoloscents to achieve complete independence and a secret relief when the parent steps in with the exercise of some control. The ambivalence is evident from contradictory statements from the same person in the same situation. A high school student will say that parents should treat adolescents more like adults and at the same time complain about parents not forcing their sons and daughters to do their homework.

Within the confusing complexity of the developmental situation the adolescent often comes up with solutions to his problems which, to the parent, are silly. Further, the adolescent appears to the parent not to want to accept the responsibility for his independence. This irresponsibility concerns the parent greatly, leading to further, but intermittent, control. Actually, the early physical maturity in early adolescence may lead the parent to expect too much responsibility.

A great amount of emotion can be generated on relatively minor problems and the mutual affection and love may be temporarily forgotten. The minor nature of the surface problem is misleading. The use of the automobile, the date, the wearing of certain clothes, the trip to another town with friends, and such similar subjects are not the essence of the problem situation. Rather, the essential nature is the source of the decision—who has the right, or who has the maturity, to make the decision? The source of conflict between the generations is not, then, in the many lists of "types of adolescents' problems" which abound in the popular and professional literature. The source of conflict is in the ambivalent feeling and the ambiguous codes of conduct concerning adolescence.

The child is taught that right and wrong are clear-cut categories. Rigid rules and rigid discipline are the major characteristics of moral teaching. The child learns from his parents and other adults that the world is orderly and well-organized. He enters adolescence to find that right and wrong are not categorical and that what people say and what they do are different. The adolescent is embarrassed to find that even those who have taught him right and wrong often see shades of morality, extenuating circumstances, and the like. The adolescent further sees that his peers, who are so important to him and who have the same rigid idealism he has, will think less of him if they see his parents violating these idealistic expectations.

Parents are nonplused. In the immediate situation, they do not understand the dynamics involved. However, the trauma of the experience makes information seekers of parents. A review of the popular literature available to parents reveals that increased clarity is not to be expected as a result of a thorough reading. Indeed, if any effect is to be hypothesized it may well be that ambiguity is reinforced by the constant reading of conflicting media. This ambiguity or apprehension may well result from the heavy emphasis on antisocial behavior found in the popular literature.

The adolescent "rebellion" takes many forms and the content of the issues also changes. One study shows that present-day college students seem to have shifted greatly, moving from identification to parental preferences toward independent ideologies.[8] This is an important area of change because youth have traditionally been alienated from the political process. The beat, silent, apolitical generation of college students in the 1950's appears to have been succeeded by a generation in which two fifths of the students have rebelled from what they believe are their parents' views. The rebellion itself is overwhelmingly to the left and away from the right. Further, those students who have rebelled are those who are most interested in the political process. It is interesting that the students in this study were high school students in the late 1950's. We hypothesize that at the end of the 1950's (around 1960) a new type of relationship began among middle-class high school students.

Kingsley Davis attempts to explain why there is an unusual amount of conflict between parents and adolescents in Western societies.[9] Part of this explanation rests upon the following interrelated propositions:

1. Each generation learns the culture early, and as age progresses there is greater difficulty in changing views of right and wrong.
2. The cultural content in American society is changing rapidly.
3. The culture learned by the parental generation was much different than that learned by the offspring, insofar as the adolescent learns from peers and from adults who are more current in their thinking.
4. Therefore, there is a culture conflict experienced by parents and their offspring.

The third proposition needs some elaboration. The adults other than parents from whom the adolescent learns the culture also were socialized in an earlier era. However, adults are likely to be more conservative with their own children than they are in places where

[8] Russell Middleton and Snell Putney, "Student Rebellion Against Parental Political Beliefs," *Social Forces*, Vol. 41 (1963), pp. 377–84.

[9] Kingsley Davis, "The Sociology of Parent-Youth Conflict," *American Sociological Review*, Vol. 5 (1940), pp. 523–36.

they may come into contact with adolescents through their work.[10]

## THE COOL GENERATION

Around 1960, certain segments of the high school age groups appear to have changed in their reactions to the adult world. This relationship became less rebellious and is characterized by various slogans and slang which may be summarized by the expression, "Don't fight it." We still have our "hoods," "finks," and whatever other names are applied to antisocial gangs by more conforming peers. We hypothesize that the new relationship is characteristic of increasing proportions of the middle-class high school student.

The location of the "cool generation" in the class structure is doubtlessly due to the social dynamics which we believe produced the cool generation in the first place. We would submit the following hypotheses concerning the development of the new reaction to the adult world. As the veterans of World War II returned, they were fed up with international relations and political problems and were interested only in settling down to the quiet life. Family and home was of paramount importance. These veterans had been reared during the adolescent rebellion and their army experience further alienated them from their parents in terms of interests and beliefs. They turned rather to their own nuclear families.

With this orientation toward the nuclear family, the affluent society was a condition in which the parent could give a great deal of aid and comfort to the enemy of the adolescent rebellion. Christmas could become a time to shower gifts even beyond every wish of the child, and, with at least one car in every garage and sometimes two, the mother could assume a new role—that of chauffeur to the young in the home. Since these characteristics were found in the middle class, we may add the factor of the absence of any serious economic, social, and political problems which entered the field of perception of the young. The child had everything he wanted. He was pampered; discipline was limited; and attention was showered upon him. Nor did things change for him at puberty. The parent seemed almost overly anxious to please, in areas from learning to drive to dating and buying records.

In discussing the adolescent rebellion, Stone and Church recognized a trend in the direction toward the cool generation.[11] They were reluctant to generalize about it, because they were writing when it

---

[10] Talcott Parsons, "Youth in the Context of American Society," *Daedalus*, Winter, 1962, pp. 97–123.

[11] Stone and Church, *op. cit.*, pp. 194–95.

was only beginning. Nevertheless, they indicated at the end of their chapter on adolescence that there was already evidence in 1957 of the characteristics which we call the "cool generation," a term suggested by Gallup and Hill.[12]

Still further support for the viewpoint of the cool generation is given by Talcott Parsons with an entirely different approach to the problem.[13] In writing on a volume on youth, Parsons indicates that in general American youth are accepting our institutions and are operating without rebellion.

In order to understand Parsons' point, it is first necessary to see his view of the main theme in American culture. This main theme he calls "institutionalized activism." By activism he means that the cultural theme in America orients the person toward attacking problems rather than resigning oneself to the unsolvability of the problem. However, this optimism and work in the face of adversity is taken within a limited range of means of solving the problem. In other words, we severely limit ourselves through our taboos in the ways in which we may solve a problem. In this way the means of problem solving become institutionalized. Thus, the term "institutionalized activism."

Parsons contends the standards of educational achievement have been raised considerably; the quantity of material is greater and the quality of educational content is higher. Furthermore, to achieve certain occupational levels in our social structure, it is necessary to attain higher formal educational degrees than in the past. Parsons feels the willingness of youth to accept these higher standards indicates their full acceptance of the major cultural theme of American society, institutionalized activism. But there are further considerations. Parsons also contends that youth are given much more autonomy both in school, through progressive education, and in the family, through more democratic orientation toward child rearing. The combination of higher standards and more freedom indicate that youth both as individuals and as a group have accepted the goals and means provided by our normative structure. The impatience with the long period of training for adulthood is, in Parson's view, evidence of the acceptance of the activistic component of our culture. Youths are anxious to become participating members of our institutional processes, thereby giving them the opportunity to attack their problems. Alienation is not for them.

---

[12] George Gallup and Evan Hill, "The Cool Generation," *Saturday Evening Post,* December, 1961.

[13] Parsons, "Youth in the Context of American Society," *op. cit.*

There is only a small amount of empirical support for the notion of the cool generation. The most extensive study, and the only work which bears directly upon the problem, is the survey by Gallup and Hill.[14] This study was commissioned by the *Saturday Evening Post* and involved interviews with some 3,000 adolescents ranging in age from fourteen through twenty-two. The sample included 648 high school sophomores, 641 high school seniors, 1,020 juniors and seniors from seventy-eight American colleges across the country, and 744 young adults under twenty-three who had quit school and were in the labor force at the time of the study. The interview schedule included more than 200 questions. A considerable amount of open-ended data were included and were quoted in the article to give the reader a "feel" for the findings. This report in the *Post* compared youth more to hothouse plants than to beatniks and delinquents. The analysis was based less on a statistical array of attributes in youth than upon a composite picture of a typical American youth, thus losing something in precision.

One of the primary findings was that the typical youth of today is willing to settle for low aspirations and few successes rather than aspire highly and risk big failures. Anticipation of adulthood is in terms of a nice family and a wife who is "affectionate, sympathetic, considerate, and moral." The adolescent is not especially concerned with intelligence and achievement. The general tone of attitudes toward international relations and the like is one of compromise rather than risk. The cool generation is religious, but is willing to accept a small amount of dishonesty on minor issues.

There is little rebellion among the cool generation although there is a critical attitude toward both education and religion. Nevertheless, the criticism is directed at effectiveness, not at the basic notions involved in these institutions. That is, the cool generation does not wish to overthrow our institutions but to increase their effectiveness. While the affluent society has produced the cool generation, where youth have everything they want (with no need to fight), adolescents are generally unaware of the economic system, how it operates, what its problems are, and what job alternatives are available to them.

The primary worries of the cool generation concern the future. This fear for the future is in terms of failure of social security. The percentage of the college group concerned with world instability is twice as high as that found in other groups. When asked what should be done if we entered another limited war such as Korea, the answer was

---

[14] Gallup and Hill, *op. cit.*

often, "A compromise." Well over a numerical majority of the youth said they were unwilling to risk war. The notion of compromise is most consistent with their philosophy of life generally. One girl was quoted as saying that our country had been built on compromise and there was no reason for changing the method of development at this point.

Several of the youth apparently indicated an awareness of the way in which American adults guard adolescents from knowledge of real problems. One boy indicated he had always been told things were "peachy fine." Now, he knew things were not all "peachy fine," but he had not been taught what to do in the face of imperfection. Such a manner of teaching adolescents results in confusion when the adolescent learns something of the real world. According to Gallup and Hill, "It is not easy to be secure in a world of contradiction, disillusion and controversy, but our youth seem to have succeeded." They do this by turning to religion, by turning inward, and by ignoring the problems surrounding them. The authors indicate 84 per cent of the cool generation are church members and more than half attend church regularly. Approximately three fourths of the cool generation firmly believe in God, think of God as an omnipresent judge, and believe in a hereafter. Only a slightly smaller percentage believe the Bible is "completely true." It appears that the persons most religious are also most critical of the religious institution. Criticism primarily is in terms of the ineffectiveness of the church, rather than in the doctrinal aspects. They accept the rigged television quiz show and payola as facts of life, and do not connect this type of dishonesty with religion. They admit that there is a lot of cheating, but about 80 per cent of the high school youth and about 70 per cent of the college group would not report cheating when they themselves discovered it. They just don't want to be involved.

About 85 per cent of the high school youth would like to go to college; over half expect to go. Of those who actually expect to go, approximately half of the high school seniors have already saved some money for college and—what is more indicative of the cool generation —so have about one third of the high school sophomores. In terms of their general perspective on life, they underestimate the costs of college. They view education in terms of the diploma it produces and the effects which accrue to receiving the diploma. They recognize that a secure life with material comforts is gained by a college diploma, not by how much one learns. Nevertheless, they are highly critical of education for being too easy. They indicate one can get through high school without intensive study.

Unlike the youth of a few years ago, today's adolescent rarely uses slang. Occasionally they do slip into what the authors call the "tribal tongue." Much of this is used in an imaginative and perceptive way and is based upon recent political and scientific achievements.

College youth generally have a colder and less moralistic view of honesty than others. They recognize that to "succeed" one may "need" to cheat once in a while. About one third of the college members of the sample, compared to two thirds of the high school group, think honesty is extremely important to success. For the total sample less than one half would report it if they observed someone in illegal hunting, under-age drinking in a bar, and carrying a concealed weapon. More than one half would report wife beating, and about three fourths would report stealing a coat. Almost all the youth would report stealing a car, dope peddling, and hit-and-run driving.

The income aspirations are not to be rich but to be above average. This is consistent with the security orientation of the cool generation and with their inclination to aspire to relatively easy goals to assure success.

Almost 90 per cent of the youth like themselves and feel life is exciting. A similar percentage feel satisfied with the kind of person they are. They are not arrogant; they are self-satisfied. They feel that today is the happiest time of their lives.

The authors of this survey conclude that happiness is the main objective of the cool generation. However, the evidence and quoted statements indicate happiness is narrowly defined, primarily in terms of security. Their notion is qualified also in the sense that it is family oriented with little concern for the outside world. Family, home, and a secure job seem to be the characteristics they feel would make for happiness.

Practically all of the cool generation read newspapers, but extremely few read books. Movies, dancing, television, and activity with the opposite sex are the primary forms of recreation.

More than half of the college upperclassmen and working youth smoke and drink. This is true of both males and females. In college, more students drink than smoke. Less than half of the high school seniors either drink or smoke and only a fifth or less of the high school sophomores drink and smoke. In all cases, the percentage of boys exceeds the percentage of girls in these kinds of behavior.

Over 80 per cent of our young people do not intend to enter politics and many consider it in the light of the past stereotype—it is a "dirty, selfish game." Only about one third of the youth want to vote at the age of eighteen. They are inclined to say they are too immature or uninformed to cast an intelligent ballot. About half of the American youth admit they have no concept of the platforms or policies of either political party; those who do, hold to the old stereotypes with the Republicans as rich men opposed to change and the Democrats as uncouth men interested in the common man and agreeable to change. For the most part they reflect the political values of their parents as to party. While youth are very conservative with respect to their own behavior, there is no surge of political conservatism in American colleges nor in the other segments of the sample. For example, Richard Nixon and Nelson Rockefeller far outdistanced Barry Goldwater at the time of the study. Goldwater attracted only about one eighth of the sample.

Except for Southern youth, about two thirds of the cool generation approve of school integration.

The cool generation is fairly close to parents. Adolescents need advice and 70 per cent of them turn first to their parents. It is still true, as in the adolescent rebellion, that many parents embarrass their children. This is especially so of the younger members of the sample. Two types of parental behavior in particular embarrass adolescents: when the parent puts the adolescent on display in front of adult friends, and when the parent tries too much to win the friendship of the adolescent's friends of his own age.

The cool generation recognizes the adult world is giving it everything it wants. Parents are effusive in social efforts and economic resources. The parent is a chauffeur and hauls the adolescent around. They are a pampered generation both by their own view and from the results of this study. Two quotations from the article, one from a member of the sample and one from the authors, will perhaps summarize the general view of the cool generation.

"What my generation lacks is necessity. You didn't lack it. You had a war. You had a depression. I really think if we were faced with the necessity, we would respond."

"Will they do as well as their fathers did under the pressures of war and economic slump? . . . The older generation wonders. In the meantime American parents candidly admit they are spoiling and pampering this new generation. They admit it, cluck their tongues and keep on pampering."

## SUMMARY AND CONCLUSIONS

Adolescence in American society is hypothesized as going through three stages.

In the apprenticeship era occupational apprenticeship allowed a great amount of contact between sons and their fathers and daughters and their mothers. Not only were occupational skills learned but the adolescent could emulate his parent in terms of approaches to other problems of life. Within the family little conflict was allowed to become overt.

The adolescent rebellion came about as a result of the greatly decreased contact between parent and offspring, especially in terms of work. Reinforcement for whatever feelings of resentment were experienced came through greatly increased contact between adolescents. Much of the difficulty in parent-youth relations resulted from a dual ambivalence: the youth wished to become an adult but did not wish to leave the security of control by the parent while the parent wanted the adolescent to become an adult but did not wish to lose his child.

Although the cool generation began sometime around 1960 there is yet little or no rigorous evidence on which to base an analysis of the nature of this youth relationship to the adult world. The little research available indicates the new generation of adolescents has been given much pampering and has no great "causes" to fight. These youth aspire to low degrees of achievement, primarily because they fear failure. They are oriented toward compromise rather than fighting, whether they are discussing relations with parents or with Russia. Their main orientation is toward security.

None of these relations to the adult world characterizes all adolescents at any time in our history. It is suggested that the dominant theme up until the 1920's was that of the apprenticeship era; that the dominant theme from the 1920's until around 1960 was that of the adolescent rebellion; and that the cool generation is increasingly a middle-class phenomenon in the present decade.

# Chapter VI

# DEVELOPMENTAL TASKS

In American society adolescence is a period during which the individual is expected to change from a child to an adult. This expectation, on the part of adults, is general and abstract. It is expressed in numerous ways in day-to-day relations between the parent and the child, and through the age concept, especially, "You are too young to do that" and "You are too old to do this." The expectations are neither well-defined nor uniform from one family to another. The verbal expressions are often inconsistent from one time to another and from one type of development to another. The verbal expressions are, therefore, often strongly influenced by the immediate situation, the mood of the parent at the time. "Advice" is probably, in general, much more a function of annoyance at adolescent behavior than it is a function of a genuine plan for helping the adolescent develop from one stage to another.

Nevertheless, the adolescent who fails to meet certain implicit developmental tasks finds himself in trouble during early adulthood. The trouble results from certain social conditions which present themselves to him as he enters the labor force, as he marries, or as he attempts to become accepted by others as an adult. The difficulty for the adolescent, as well as for the parent, rests upon several conditions:

1. Parents do not clearly understand all the tasks to be achieved.
2. Parents feel that such tasks must be achieved, so they "lead" the adolescent toward goals which they, the parents, do not understand.
3. Society enforces the goals but does not provide clear-cut norms to guide the behavior of the adolescent toward them.
4. Adolescents are influenced at least as much by other adolescents as by parents, and the other adolescents understand neither the tasks to be achieved nor the processes by which the achievement is to occur.
5. Schools are limited by taboo in helping the adolescent in certain of the tasks.

Since both the goals for development in adolescence as well as the means or processes by which the goals are to be achieved are vaguely defined and generally not well understood, we must turn to other sources than the observation of adolescent behavior and parental actions to infer the kinds of tasks adolescents must accomplish. Several efforts in this direction have been made. The goals of the public school have been listed in a variety of ways (the most famous is the "Seven Cardinal Principles"[1]), and practically all of these are in terms close to developmental tasks.

Perhaps the best manner in which developmental tasks may be described is to infer them from the frustrations, failures, and successes of adults. The inferences may be made in terms of the causes of failure which lie in behavior during the adolescent years. The most widely accepted and perhaps the best list of developmental tasks currently available was well presented by Robert J. Havinghurst.[2] This list is framed much in terms of the process by which the tasks must be achieved during adolescence. In this way, they become more easily understandable to parents and to adolescents alike, and may, therefore, be interpreted into action more easily. The list also corresponds to the kinds of problems the adolescent will face if he fails to make some progress during the time from, say, the twelfth year until he enters the labor force and marries. This chapter is organized around a modification of the list of developmental tasks suggested in Havinghurst's monograph.

## ACCEPTING ONE'S PHYSIQUE

Havighurst indicates that the nature of this task is to become either proud or at least tolerant of one's physical characteristics. Adolescents are most interested in the development of their physique. Part of this, of course, is an attempt to determine how close they are to adulthood; another part appears to be worries and concerns with physical defects. Acne, obesity, and late or early maturation play especially important parts in giving rise to emotional problems. The young boy or girl may spend hours in front of the mirror making faces, testing personalities, and inspecting most closely his physical characteristics. It would appear from autobiographical material (submitted by both high school and college-age youth) that the adolescent not only is acutely aware of every physical variation from his concept of what is normal or beautiful or handsome, but that this is perhaps his most frequent frustration. A boy writes:

Retrospectively, I can see that I was late in developing secondary sexual,

---

[1] N.E.A., Commission of the Reorganization of Secondary Education, *Cardinal Principles of Education* (Washington, D.C.: U.S. Government Printing Office, 1918).
[2] Robert J. Havighurst, *Human Development and Education* (New York: Longmans, Green & Co., 1953). Courtesy of David McKay Company.

physical characteristics and this was often an embarrassing point. I seldom shaved in earnest until I was nineteen years old and was often kidded about this. I can remember in high school where I was on the wrestling team, I would try to wrestle as much as possible with my arms to my side as I had no hair under my arms. I may laugh at this now, but I considered it a serious problem then.

A girl writes:

When we, as seventh graders, began to date, I felt most unsure of myself. I was as tall as I am now during that year. The boys were much, much shorter so I despised wearing high heels. I distinctly recall one high school dance I attended while still in junior high. My date was at least six inches shorter than I, even when he danced on his tiptoes. As we were dancing around the room, I glanced at our shadows on the wall. It made me feel terrible—all I wanted to do was sit down somewhere so people would not notice our comparable heights. I was further embarrassed because I could not follow my date's dancing pattern; we were constantly apologizing for stepping on each other's feet. I must have been an exception to the rule that girls are not usually embarrassed by clumsiness in adolescence because of their earlier development. I was all arms and legs.

I was exceptionally embarrassed about the facial hair, especially a mustache, that was starting to show. I wanted to shave it off so badly, but knew the consequences of doing so. Instead I tried to remain away from close contact with others as much as possible.

Gradually, I gained weight until in high school; I was a 140 pound failure. I never wanted to take off my coat because I was ashamed of the way I looked. I dieted in a ridiculous manner, starving myself for three days and gorging myself for the next six. The fact of my being overweight caused many conflicts between my family and me. I was tormented by cutting remarks from my brother and sister and hounded by mother to eat more balanced meals and to cut out eating all the "junk" I had developed a craving for.

One exciting incident did happen which helped to boost my spirits during my early teens. The braces were taken off my teeth when I was in the eighth grade and false teeth replaced the "gaping holes" in the front of my mouth. My ego was elevated, and I was not afraid to smile at people anymore. Compliments from and acceptance by others were two important factors here. I was gaining self-confidence. I even began to run for school offices, although I was defeated most of the time.

Our society places a high value upon physical appearance. In the adult world as well as in high school the beautiful girl enjoys many advantages which logically have nothing directly to do with beauty. Boys who are handsome have traditionally received "breaks" from peers and adults alike. Extreme physical malformations are definite disadvantages even in the kinds of situations in which physical appearance is actually irrelevant. In many positions, such as airplane stewardess and receptionist, physical attributes are a criterion for employment. The orientation toward movies and television enhances the cultural values on physical appearance. It is, then, small wonder that youth are concerned with such malformities as close inspection may reveal. Their relations with persons of the opposite sex, so important to them, may depend almost entirely upon their physical appearance.

The actress and actor (at least until recently) who appear in two dimensions on the screen are selected partly because they are photogenic. The standard of beauty set by their appearance on the screen may well be higher than they themselves can meet in real life. Certainly the movie and television industries have techniques to further beautify persons picked because they were photogenic to start. Yet these are the standards by which youth often judge themselves and the standards by which they know they are judged by others.

Few people have not experienced the difficulties of overcoming physical handicaps. It is often obvious how certain kinds of reactions to others may be traced to embarrassment and physical handicaps. The person who looks down because of crossed eyes, and the tight-lipped smile because of uneven or parted teeth, are only two examples of the types of permanent reactions to embarrassment at physical malformation. One boy reports in an autobiography that he reached puberty very late compared to the other boys in his class. He commented that he would be late for gym and for his next class because he wished neither to undress nor to dress in front of the other boys. It is also characteristic of younger children to pick out physical handicaps as sources of ridicule. Nicknames follow along these lines: "fat," "slim," "bucky," "foureyes," "longshanks," "gimpy," "limpy," and the like. Tormenting one with such handicaps is a favorite pasttime in the prepuberty and early-childhood stages of life.

This setting fosters worry about physical handicaps as the adolescent enters the period when relations with the other sex are so important.

Physical defects need not be obvious or even real to have adverse effects on adolescents. Such close inspection as they give themselves usually will render at least one source of worry. Neither does it need to be unusual. Note the comments written by a beautiful girl (the italics are ours):

One of the first problems of my adolescent period which I can remember was due to ignorance. I was thirteen and in junior high school when some of my friends started talking about menstruation. I knew nothing of this and neither did they, for my introduction to menstruation was one of fear and mystery. I did not know why this process took place, if it did at all, and did not know where to go to find out. Too embarrassed to ask my mother or any adult, I pushed it as well as I could to the back of my mind and let it ride for awhile. About this time an educational movie concerning the subject was being shown at the high school by the sponsors of the Girl Scouts, and a friend's mother asked mine if I could go with her daughter to see it. Of course I went, as my mother was quite relieved that she wouldn't have to start the explanation. If this movie had not come up, Mom said that she was going to take me to the family doctor and have him explain it. At thirteen this would have been a traumatic experience for me and I am very glad it happened the other way.

I can remember sitting in class with my hand on the side of my face so that the boy to my right or left could not see my nose. Here we were beginning to date and it was the big thing to be asked out by boys from the "right group." This, of course, multiplied my feelings about my "crocked" nose. Another time my best girl friend and I had our picture painted at the stock show and to add to it, he would only paint profiles. I couldn't say no very well, but wished with all my heart that I could. The painting called many an unhappy day for me, for it magnified (to me) my supposed fault. Then one night at a basketball game one of my friends who was in a different and a little higher clique, made a remark that was somewhat the stopping point for my increasing anxiety. She said that I would not be me without my nose and she liked it. I don't know how many times I have repeated that to myself. Then slowly I began to get over my self-consciousness and my behavior was no longer guided by it. However, in college as a sophomore, it came to my mind, but did not hurt as it did before. *The night I was crowned "Miss University," one of my first thoughts was "even with my nose, it can't be true."* The self-consciousness is gone and with it the hurt, but it took years and a series of events to show me that my nose did not make the difference as to whether I was going to be accepted, but there were many other important attributes to work on. As I look back now, the self-consciousness about my nose was probably the cause of a lot of my behavior—the manner I would go about trying to be accepted by my peers.

## ACCEPTING A MASCULINE OR FEMININE ROLE AND PROPER RELATIONS WITH BOTH SEXES

Societies the world over approve much different roles for males and for females. The inability or unwillingness to accept the approved role has dire consequences to the individual. There is perhaps no greater ridicule than that found for the homosexual, and even the effeminate man or the tomboy in early adulthood receives his or her share. Note the following report by a girl:

Our neighborhood was entirely composed of boys. Then the fact that I have two brothers and no sisters added to the problem. As a result of this environment, I was always considered "one of the fellas." One excursion was planned in which we were going to run away from home—three boys and I. The wagon was packed with our supplies and we were set. The fellows did recognize my femininity in the fact that I was going to do the cooking, but this was a "man's trip." I was also considered one of the fighters in the neighborhood. I received excellent training from the gang. As a result, I had one slight concussion, one broken tooth, and several black eyes to my credit—all given to boys, of course.

Thus, when it came time to don high heels, earrings, and the usual female finery, I felt out of place. My mother, of course, was very anxious for her only daughter to be recognized as her "feminine" offspring. It was only after considerable effort on her part that I accepted my sex with its advantages and welcomed my social role.

Upon entrance into adolescence, the physiological differences between males and females become of paramount importance. There is again a setting which produces some anxiety. Menstruation appears to be an especially embarrassing, mysterious, and frustration-producing phenomenon for girls. Boys experience impulses and feelings they have neither had before nor been prepared to expect or handle. Long after boys and girls are capable of sexual intercourse and reproduction, they may be most embarrassed at expressing any interest in the other sex. Actual interest in members of the opposite sex is often delayed far beyond the point at which adolescents are physically capable of sexual intercourse.

A factor that I have been greatly worried about in my adolescence was my popularity with the opposite sex. I am basically inhibited, and it was difficult to flirt with those strange new creatures called boys. In my relations with members of the same sex, I have had to achieve a more mature relationship also. I learned with difficulty to accept the fact that my girl friends were interested in dating, and that being with boys took precedence over a get-together with the girls.

I can see now that these problems, that at the time seemed so major and unusual, coincide in many ways with the things that all adolescents must pass through. At the time I felt that I was alone with these problems.

Girls apparently have an easier time of accepting their role than boys have of theirs, although this is still open to some disagreement. Girls have in their home a person to emulate, and since most schoolteachers are women, the girls' adjustment is reinforced in their other major activity. However, in modern society a large proportion of fathers is away from the home much of the time and the boys are therefore deprived both of frequent contact with the parent and of male teachers, in finding someone to emulate. The greater difficulty boys experience is borne out by their erratic behavior, as evidenced by delinquency rates and referrals to counseling. It is obvious that they wish to become men very soon but that they do not know how to do so.

During childhood the relations between the child and adults generally are well prescribed and in fairly complete control of the adult. Adults also oversee the relations between people of the same age. The beginning of adolescence, however, uncovers an aptitude for a much different relation with members of the opposite sex, and this may in some ways result in social pressure for different types of relations with members of the same sex.

Very small children play with each other without distinction as to sex, although they "marry," plan to marry, and often refer to "boy friends" and "girl friends." Later, with their changing interests and the distinctions adults continually make, an exaggerated separation occurs that almost amounts to scorn of each sex by the other. They do tease each other and even early in childhood girls, especially, discuss their boy friends. It is more of a mock dislike. In images of himself as a growing man, the boy is doubtlessly embarrassed to be shorter and lighter in weight than most of the girls in school. His masculinity is outraged by this inferior position. Because of the later physical maturation of boys, girls are frequently more attracted to boys in more advanced school classes. Indeed, the pattern of our culture even is for the husband to be older than the wife, and certainly for girls to date frequently boys who are older.

The awareness of adolescents of this developmental task (adjustment to the opposite sex) is evident in all the research on adolescent society. The orientation toward members of the opposite sex in high school and college is a continuous phenomenon with which teachers, counselors, and parents must deal. Most observers of youth believe boys and girls in association with each other in schools and in families learn to make the new adjustments required in their relations with members of the same sex and with members of the opposite sex better than those who are more isolated. However, there is no rigorous evidence on this point. The implications of this developmental task for both marriage and friends in terms of the ability to adjust in later life are of considerable consequence.

## EMOTIONAL INDEPENDENCE OF PARENTS AND OTHER ADULTS

The childish dependence upon parents must gradually be relinquished as adolescence proceeds. Emotional ties with members of the same age of course are strong, but the extreme attachment and dependence placed upon parents and other adults are a deterrent to the development to adulthood.

Both girls and boys love their father and their mother in different ways. Most children have a more affectionate and intimate relationship with the mother which seems to be a natural outgrowth of continued frequent contact during early childhood.

Boys begin by having the closest affection to a member of the opposite sex. It is entirely possible that the effect of this is to facilitate an easier transition from the almost-singular affectional attachment to parents, to the girl friend or wife. However, it can also have a disadvantage in that if the mother has taken advantage of the affection and encouraged the boy to hold on to the apron strings, he frequently will, as a young man, have difficulty in adjusting to a girl friend or wife as an individual in her own right. Many marriages are cursed with the invidious comparison of the wife with the husband's mother.

As we mentioned before, on the one hand adults want their children to reach manhood and womanhood; on the other, they are most reluctant to "lose their little boy" (or girl). Adolescents themselves are also ambivalent toward achieving independence. On the one hand, they frequently rebel against parents. When they are called upon to accept the responsibility which must necessarily go with freedom, however, they often find themselves frustrated and insecure. The ambivalence of an adolescent is exhibited in the following autobiography.

I was never particularly close to my mother, mainly because I rejected her untactful attempts to help me. I always felt my mother was much too critical and she had a natural tendency to nag. Again looking back, I can now understand her position and I realize I made an issue out of relatively unimportant things. I was trying so hard to be a part of the crowd, especially during my first year in high school. Everything I did was related to making sure I was doing the accepted thing in the eyes of my peer group. My mother was constantly criticizing the way I dressed, the things I did, and especially the way I wore my hair. As a result, I developed a strong negative attitude toward her suggestions which made me even more determined to do exactly the opposite from what she wanted. I considered her interest in helping me as direct insults rather than helpful advice. I would let little things get the best of me until it got to the point where I wanted to run away from home every time she'd offer her advice. The more she complained, the more the problem affected my relationship. I felt she should help me more than she did in meeting the demands of the school and of my friends.

Both parents and adolescents doubtlessly feel that independent decisions on the part of the young and inexperienced youth may lead to serious consequences. This feeling often results in an overprotected youth who will depend upon his parents far into young adulthood. Although the value may be changing, the man who searches for independence and does so in a stable and mature manner is still respected in our society. The person who is incapable of making decisions or who depends too much upon his parents after late adolescence is often the subject of ridicule. The value on initiative in employment and leadership positions is almost as important as the value on hard work. Despite this value on independence, however, the process for most adolescence is not easy. Witness the differing patterns in the following three cases.

### I

When I began to be interested in boys, about fourteen, I envied my mother's ability to charm the young neighborhood boys. I felt inferior. Nor did I appreciate these boys' rabid attention to my sister who, realistically, is beautiful. As a result I have felt socially insecure and inadequate. It has taken much serious effort and concentration but I feel that I have gained some self-confidence in social situations.

This feeling of resentment against and competition with my mother drastically affected my relations with her. She is still an extremely attractive woman and is often taken to be my sister rather than my mother. She perpetuates this appearance and as a result has not inspired in me a desire to confide in her and trust in her values and opinions and advice. I have developed values and principles opposite from hers in many cases and have hated any traits of hers that I found in myself. Needless to say, my antagonistic feelings were not hidden from her and the gulf of misunderstanding widened between us. It became a habit to reject her values and advice and I looked elsewhere for these guiding principles.

Perhaps in this respect I found my individuality earlier than usual. Seemingly it was forced individuality but, nevertheless, I was a separate individual from my mother. I have incorporated into myself only those ideas of hers which did not appear inconsistent with what I had learned to believe in and stand for.

My early mental independence only made my physical and social dependence more difficult to accept. My sister's almost total dependence on the family, especially mother, also made it difficult for them to accept my desire for independence. Mother saw me only as an extension of herself, which my sister was, rather than a separate individual. When all through high school my sister continued to seek mother's opinion and consent in all of her activities, my refusal to seek or to accept her advice was even harder for her to understand or accept. Early in junior high school I had stopped asking her to help me decide what to buy or what to wear. I was master of my own time schedule and did well by myself.

I did not begin dating until I was sixteen, a sophomore in high school. Within the first month I had a "steady" boy friend. This relationship with the boy strained the relations with my family. They did not approve of my dating only one and mother repeatedly expressed her wish that I be a "social butterfly." Several other "steadies" followed with a sprinkling of casual dates intermixed. Although I had respected my family's wishes and not gone "steady officially" they resented my spending so much time with and thought on my boy friend. As a result, I drew closer to the boy friend and farther from the family. The family had not respected my ability or need for making my own decisions in my choice of social life.

## II

My father was very broad-minded and permissive as I grew up. He was very willing to realize that his daughter was approaching the age when she should make her own decisions, with some supervision, of course. My mother, on the other hand, is an extremely dominant person. Her high school record is very outstanding scholastically, she is very adept at anything she tries to do, and she has a multitude of friends who respect her. She is also a very nervous person and a perfectionist.

When I thought I should make my own decisions as to clothes, she had her very definite opinions. She had an intense desire to have perfection personified in me. However, her ideas to me were old-fashioned. I knew what the fads were, what the "crowd" was wearing, and how I wanted to look. This, I believe, was the greatest source of conflict in my entire adolescence. I wouldn't wear the things she bought for me because I didn't like them, and she in turn was not about to change her mind on what I should wear. This one point was the source of many heated arguments within our household.

Not only did these arguments involve the two of us. After an argument, I would retire to my room and mom somewhere else in the house. My dad was caught in the middle. His love for his wife threw him into turmoil because he had foresight to understand my desires and position. Also this involved my brothers. They felt they should stick up for their cohort and sister; yet they were not at the stage yet where things like clothes made any difference to them. As a result of our quarrels, the family was virtually separated.

III

Problems in puberty began for me at home. I was very embarrassed by my low economic status and tried to cover it up by inviting to my home only those whom I knew very well and who were no higher up the social scale than I. I also was ashamed to bring any of my friends from school home without giving them many warnings about the treatment they would receive from my mother. She always managed to make many snide, insulting remarks about anyone I invited into the house and she made all of us feel very uncomfortable. This led to many arguments about my choice of friends, since my parents sided with each other against me on my choice most of the time. That they were probably correct in their evaluations of my friends' characters was overshadowed by my desire to make the choice myself. The free choice of my friends was something I was not actually allowed until I was about twenty-one. Until that time, I just left the house and stayed away as long as possible to avoid contact with my parents over the matter.

Other arguments vivid in my memory are ones over how I should dress, what I should eat, what I should spend my money on, and how late I should be allowed to stay out at night. There were loud arguments and quiet ones, none of them bringing about any result other than helping to destroy happy family life. The strict discipline of younger days had set my thinking into such a pattern as to consider everything in the world as subject to some prearranged master plan. I couldn't change my way of thinking and neither could they.

It is evident from autobiographical material as well as from more rigorous research that the peer group is a strong influence in the process of achieving independence.[3] In addition, the schools probably play considerable part in the achievement of this developmental task. Teachers help to some extent, but the burden of passing courses and of getting grades still rests with the student. Although large classes force the teacher to put the responsibility on the student, yet another factor may enter in. Teachers are perhaps less prone to be fearful of leaving the student alone to solve his own problems because the teacher's affection for each child necessarily cannot equal that of the parents'. Certainly teachers do not feel the ambivalence toward the adulthood of the adolescent based on the reluctance to lose the affection of the child.

## ACHIEVING ASSURANCE OF ECONOMIC INDEPENDENCE IN SELECTING AND PREPARING FOR AN OCCUPATION

Several aspects of occupational choice may be viewed as demands made by society. Traditionally, a person in our society who failed to prepare himself for economic independence could expect to go hungry and live in poverty. The situation has changed a great deal

---

[3] This is a major theme running throughout the work by James S. Coleman, *The Adolescent Society* (New York: The Free Press of Glencoe, 1962). A similar position is taken in Ernest A. Smith, *American Youth Culture*, (New York: The Free Press of Glencoe, 1962). See also Cloy V. Brittain, "Adolescent Choices and Parent-Peer Cross Pressures," *American Sociological Review*, Vol. 28 (1963), pp. 385–91.

since the early 1930's, with welfare payments and other kinds of economic aid to the poor. Our labor force is moving from semiskilled, unskilled, and farming jobs toward the types of jobs which require higher levels of educational attainment. These trends increase the importance of the selecting and sorting function of the schools. Youth who leave school before high school graduation eliminate themselves from many types of jobs, unless they later return to complete the requirements for the diploma. Further, those adolescents who complete high school with low grade averages likewise are disadvantaged in that college graduation is increasingly a prerequisite for many jobs.

Adolescents who leave school or complete high school work with low grade averages because they do not have the brain power to compete are merely casualties of the social order. However, the research shows that many school dropouts and many who finish high school with grades too poor to enter college are among the students with higher intelligence quotients. In such cases, the more idealistic side of our value system tells us the school is somehow failing in its function of allocating human resources.

The same factors which produce this "underachievement" on the part of students also make it more difficult for the school counselors and teachers to convince the students of the trends in the labor force. Similarly, the parents of underachievers are also the parents least likely to understand the trends of the labor force and probably often the least likely to be able to influence their offspring to remain in school.

The adolescent, in making an occupational choice, must anticipate the labor-force trends over a period of approximately forty-five years. The need for such long-range prediction is dramatically demonstrated by the unemployment due to automation.

## DEVELOPING INTELLECTUAL SKILLS AND CONCEPTS
## NECESSARY FOR CIVIC COMPETENCE

Havighurst defines the nature of this task as the ability to develop concepts of law, government, human nature, and the social institutions which will help the person adjust to the modern world. Many factors affect the ability of youth to develop civic competence. One of the most basic is the confusion in the adult world over whether we wish the schools to foster conforming citizens or creative and critical ones. The person who gains high prestige often conforms on all but one or two major issues, and to these he applies his creativity. However, even citizens who are able to focus their efforts toward social change in such a manner are not universally respected; respect depends in large part on the particular areas of life in which they are "progressive." More at issue, however, is the probability that the adolescent, and the school as well, find it difficult to focus creativity and critical reasoning so narrowly. The person capable of critical attitudes toward a small part of our social organization is likely to be critical of other parts as well. More generalized nonconformity is less apt to be appreciated by those who control the policies of schools. Further, families which produce nonconformists often suffer pressures and loss of respect in the community. It appears that, with notable exceptions, the school and the family are oriented more toward conformity than toward creative and critical citizens.

While adult agencies directly concerned with adolescent development are oriented toward conformity the peer group is even more so. The expression of individualism in such detailed areas of decision making as dress, speech, and the like often results in sanctions far more serious in the immediate environment of the adolescent than those imposed by adult agencies. Ostracism is not an uncommon punishment for nonconformity, and ridicule is used extensively. It is true the peer group itself may adopt nonconforming modes of action, but even these modes are applied to each member of the group with inflexibility.

Conformity to adult norms is not as easy as it may appear. The adolescent is faced with cultural dualisms—the difference between what we say and what we do. The presentation of a few of these cultural dualisms, developed by Robert S. Lynd, will indicate the dilemma the idealistic adolescent is faced with in developing his own code of ethics:

Democracy, as discovered and perfected by the American people, is the ultimate form of living together. All men are created free and equal, and the United States has made this fact a living reality.

*But:* You would never get anywhere if you constantly left things to popular vote. No business could be run that way and, of course, no businessman would tolerate it.

Everyone should try to be successful.

*But:* The kind of person you are is more important than how successful you are.

Life would not be tolerable if we did not believe in progress and know that things are getting better. We should, therefore, welcome new things.

*But:* The old, tried fundamentals are best and it is a mistake for busybodies to try to change things too fast or try to upset the fundamentals.

Education is a fine thing.

*But:* It is the practical man who gets things done.

Science is a fine thing in its place and our future depends upon it.

*But:* Science has no right to interfere with such things as our fundamental institutions. The thing to do is to use science but not let it upset things.

No man deserves to have what he hasn't worked for and it demoralizes him if he gets it.

*But:* You can't let people starve.

Honesty is the best policy.

*But:* Business is business and a businessman would be a fool if he did no. cover his hand.[4]

Another aspect which produces some difficulty is that adults seem to have an implicit understanding that certain areas of our culture are not to be taught to adolescents. Such areas as sex, the power structure, and the contradictory nature of many of our norms are taboo in most high school classrooms.

## PREPARING FOR MARRIAGE AND FAMILY LIFE

Mental and emotional readiness for marriage and family life involves other developmental tasks. The boy must seek to gain economic independence and competence. The girl must obtain the skills and knowledge necessary for homemaking. Both boys and girls enter marriage with a concept of love based on the romantic theme. The romantic theme involves the notions of the perfection of the partner, exclusive rights to the partner's attention and affection, and the idea that the two persons were meant for each other. The romantic theme also involves physical desire and delayed consummation.

It has been suggested that romantic love motivates the individual to conform to the proper marital role in our society. It is also thought that romantic love is made possible through a combination of the isolation of the nuclear family from the extended family and the ability of the youth culture to free the individual from his nuclear family.[5]

The high divorce rate in the United States would lead us to ponder the question of the influence of the romantic theme on preparation for marriage and family living. William S. Kolb has pointed to the fact that the romantic theme is basic in our culture and that marriage counselors who attack it are, in effect, also attacking individualism and freedom.[6] Hugo Beigel has argued the romantic theme is not a cause of instability in marriage but rather has saved monogamous

[4] For a more complete listing of these dualisms, see Robert S. Lynd, *Middletown in Transition* (New York: Harcourt, Brace, & Co., 1937).

[5] Talcott Parsons, *Essays in Sociological Theory* (New York: The Free Press of Glencoe, 1949), pp. 187–89.

[6] William S. Kolb, "Sociologically Established Norms and Democratic Values," *Social Forces*, Vol. 26, 1948, pp. 451–56.

marriage from complete collapse.[7] On the other hand, many experts on the family have contended romantic love is immature and a poor preparation for marriage.[8]

## SUMMARY

Many of the problems of young adults result from adolescent development inappropriate to the demands of adulthood. This relationship between adolescent development and the ability to accept adult roles has been analyzed in terms of developmental tasks, based on a modification of a list of developmental tasks suggested by Robert J. Havighurst.[9] The tasks presented were:

1. Accepting one's physique.
2. Accepting a masculine or feminine role and proper relations with both sexes.
3. Emotional independence of parents and other adults.
4. Achieving assurance of economic independence in selecting and preparing for an occupation.
5. Developing intellectual skills and concepts necessary for civic competence.
6. Preparing for marriage and family life.

---

[7] Hugo G. Beigel, "Romantic Love," *American Sociological Review,* Vol. 16 (1951), pp. 326–34.

[8] See, for example, Ernest W. Burgess and Harvey J. Locke, *The Family* (New York: American Book Company, 1953), pp. 436–37; and Ernest R. Groves and Gladys Hoagland Groves, *The Contemporary American Family* (New York: Lippincott, 1947), pp. 321–24.

[9] Havighurst, *op. cit.*

# Chapter VII

# AGE AND SEX ROLES

Adolescence has many meanings which differ from one culture to another, from one subculture to another, and from one family to another. Whatever else adolescence means, it always involves an age status as well as certain rights and obligations associated with that status.

The rights and obligations of infants differ from those of the preadolescent child and these are different from those of adolescence, young adulthood, the aged, and so on. The interaction patterns between any two age statuses differ greatly. For example, we react differently with adolescents than we do with adults, but how we interact with adolescents also depends upon our own age. We accord respect to older persons, but this is less so as we grow older.

The rights, obligations, and expectations associated with any status comprise the roles assigned to that status. We may infer roles in many ways. Statements, oral or written, concerning what is expected of persons in a given status is one source. Statements of persons playing those roles as to what they think others expect of them is another. Or we may infer roles from the types of behavior which result in rewards and punishments. We would often draw different conclusions from each of these sources of information, for people often say (and believe) one thing but do (and believe) another.[1] Further, one segment of society will expect different things from a position than another segment will,[2] even when general agreement may exist on many of the basic aspects.

The importance of age roles in the study of adolescence cannot be overstated. Not only do the ambiguities, disagreements, and incom-

---

[1] For a list of "cultural dualisms" see Robert S. Lynd, *Middletown in Transition* (New York: Harcourt, Brace, & Co., 1937). For a discussion of explicit and implicit values see Lowry Nelson, Charles E. Ramsey, and Coolie Verner, *Community Structure and Change* (New York, Macmillian Co., 1960), pp. 95–97.

[2] For a discussion of the theory of roles, see Neal Gress, Ward S. Mason, and Alexander W. McEachern, *Explorations in Role Analysis* (New York: John Wiley, 1958), chap. 1, 2, 3, esp. pp. 21–47.

patible demands made upon statuses generally apply to the status of the adolescent, but, additionally, in American society we have not agreed upon even basic roles of the adolescent status. We only agree that the adolescent must have more obligations than a child and fewer rights than an adult. Adolescents must find their roles by trial and error, and the error is often expensive; the adolescent may pay for it throughout the remainder of his life.

Another important status is sex. The entire division of labor in adult society is influenced by sex. In American society, women usually are homemakers and men breadwinners. When women do work, they receive less pay for the same job, or they enter "female" occupations. Few men are nurses or secretaries, and women seldom enter a multitude of occupations. The well-known double standard in sexual relations is but another example of a societywide double standard.

The double standards in the work world and in sexual morality are only examples, but they are important to this study. Preparation for job and for marriage are two of the most important developmental tasks assigned to adolescents. Therefore, both age and sex statuses are necessary to understand adolescence.

Ralph Linton has pointed out that in every society persons are classified in several different ways simultaneously.[3] He has further commented that the age-sex categories are prerequisite to occupying practically any position within the social system. However, the exact age-sex category appropriate for any particular position varies from one culture to another and, as Linton has said, one must qualify even such an obvious generalization as the necessity of belonging to the adult male category before assuming the status of the father. The rights and obligations assigned to the social status of a father in American society, for example, are assumed by adult women in some African groups.[4]

Clearly, people in one age-sex category react differently to members of their own class than they do to members of other age-sex categories. Furthermore, as Linton remarks, there seems to be a universal tendency for members of all age-sex categories (other than infants) to develop some sense of solidarity. This solidarity, which may be due in part to common knowledge and interests, is an important factor in the ability of members of any one age-sex category to act as a unit when they feel threatened by another age-sex grouping.[5]

---

[3] Ralph Linton, "Age and Sex Categories," *American Sociological Review*, Vol. 7 (1942), pp. 589–603.

[4] M. J. Herskovits, *Dahomey*, Vol. 1, pp. 319–22.

[5] Linton, *op. cit.*, p. 590.

Although the age-sex categories are partially based upon physiological traits, the actions of members of an age-sex category as well as the actions of other groups toward them are clearly not based upon inherent physiological traits *in toto*. Societies vary greatly in the treatment of any comparable age-sex category, and it must be concluded that societies have a wide range of alternatives with respect to the social definitions placed upon any given age-sex category. Some societies have rituals at puberty through which the individual may clearly establish his identity as an adult. In such societies adolescence could hardly be said to exist [6] in the same sense it exists in American society. In other societies, as Linton shows in the case of Polynesians, adolescence is a clear-cut and distinguishable social classification. Adolescents are sharply differentiated from both children and adults. They are relieved of social responsibilities, and the rights and obligations attached to the adolescent status involve only amusement, personal adjustment, and courting.

The adolescent in American society finds himself in between these two extremes; the status is not absent from our social relationships but neither are the rights and obligations well defined. Adolescence is a distinct category in the sense the individual is not recognized as an adult until long after he is past puberty. Adolescents are also distinguished from the prepuberty child. However, the adolescent status is not as sharply differentiated as in Polynesia, partly because we feel ambivalence about the obligations of adolescents toward preparation of adulthood. Adolescents must attend school; they must achieve certain tasks; but the exact knowledge of the tasks and of the sources to achieve them is withheld.

Another important aspect of age categories is the abruptness of the transition from one category to another. In our society, the prepuberty child is treated as a child, and while he may be corrected for wrongdoing he is nevertheless immediately forgiven after such punishment occurs. The adolescent, on the other hand, is treated now like a child and now like an adult. "You cannot stay up and watch television because you are too young for that." And again in a few minutes, "Don't pick on your younger brother, you are too old for that." At the end as well as the beginning of the adolescent period, certain abrupt transitions occur for which the individual may be ill prepared. He can participate in the political structure at the age of twenty-one, although he may never have been treated as a decision maker and may have little experience in such a group process. Of course, he has

---

[6] *Ibid.*, pp. 595–603.

a superficial knowledge of political process from books, class discussion, and teachers. However, this is not the same as serious discussion and voting, which has consequences to his own welfare and to others'. This is only one example of the many abrupt changes required in transition from adolescence to adulthood.

We often protect our adolescents from knowledge of the less idealistic side of adult society, but at the same time we make them vulnerable to the consequences of their ignorance. Linton, in 1942, felt that it remained to be seen whether abrupt or slow transition of change from one age category to another has lasting effects on the personality of the individual.[7] However, it is fairly clear from anthropological data that differences of this sort are associated with other differences in the social structure.

Leonard S. Cottrell, Jr., has indicated adequate evidence exists to suggest that adjustment of persons to their age-sex roles is greater when these roles are more clearly defined.[8] Subsequent evidence in various studies of adults would seem to support this proposition, as in the studies of rural ministers,[9] county agricultural extension agents,[10] the public school superintendent,[11] and others.

Cottrell also lists three conditions which reduce the clarity of the definition of roles. The first condition is a difference between what is said and what is done behaviorally. Many of the ethical systems adolescents are told to learn are daily violated in one way or another by adults with whom they come into contact.

Role clarity is also reduced by disagreements among various people as to appropriate roles for the adolescent. For example, teachers, psychiatrists, and parents have different expectations of the adolescent in such areas as achievement, moral behavior, and healthy personalities. The most important differences in role definitions in the immediate experience of the adolescent are found between peers and adults. The adolescent is controlled either formally or informally by both adults and other adolescents. Ridicule and even ostracism from peer groups is not by any means unknown in our society for the adolescent who conforms to the demands of adults too much or too often. Likewise, the consequences of conforming too much to the "wrong" peer group may bring serious punishment from the adult community.

---

[7] *Ibid.*, p. 602.

[8] Leonard S. Cottrell, Jr., "The Adjustment of the Individual to his Age and Sex Roles," *American Sociological Review*, Vol. 7 (1942), pp. 617–20.

[9] Samuel W. Blizzard, "The Roles of the Rural Parish Minister," *Religious Education*, 1955, pp. 1–10.

[10] E. A. Wilkening, *Roles of County Extension Agents*, Preliminary Report No. 2, (Madison: University of Wisconsin).

[11] Gross, *et. al., loc. cit.*

The third condition which reduces clarity of roles is inconsistency in reactions of the same people to members of an age-sex category. The inability of the adult community to decide exactly upon the nature of the tasks necessary for adolescents to achieve demonstrates the presence of ambivalence and ambiguity in roles for the adolescent category. The notion of adolescence as preparation for adulthood versus adolescence as an advanced version of childhood play is only one inconsistency in the adolescent's relations with significant adults in his social world.

All three conditions are present in the adolescent world, and, therefore, we would expect difficulties of adjustment if we accept Cottrell's conclusion that lack of clarity in role definitions produces such difficulties.

Talcott Parsons has pointed out that a cross-cultural comparison of sex differentiation indicates the United States has fairly equal treatment of the sexes.[12] To illustrate this point he uses the practice of chaperonage. Although girls in the United States are somewhat more limited than boys at the adolescent age, the difference is not nearly so great as in Latin American and other countries where the girl is always chaperoned by an adult during courting. One long-standing difference of the sexes is the "curfew" for girls in college, but even this is disappearing due to a greater faith in the girls' self-control and individual responsibility. Some colleges have even eliminated "hours" for girls altogether.

Parsons also feels that one of the best single points of reference for describing youth culture in the United States at the start of the 1940's and earlier was the more irresponsible and less serious nature of the primary activities of youth as compared with the adult role. As evidence, he lists the emphasis on athletics.[13] This emphasis on less serious and "youthful" behavior was found by James S. Coleman in a comprehensive study of adolescents during 1957 and 1958 in ten communities in the north central part of the United States.[14] Recently (1962) Parsons indicated he believed youth have begun to accept more "progressive" and adult-oriented standards for achievement, although he still saw many strains of "regressive" activities, such as athletics and physical prowess generally.[15]

---

[12] Talcott Parsons, "Age and Sex in the Social Structure of the United States," *American Sociological Review,* Vol. 7 (1942), pp. 602–16.

[13] *Ibid.,* pp. 606–7.

[14] James S. Coleman, *The Adolescent Society* (New York: The Free Press of Glencoe), 1962.

[15] Talcott Parsons, "Youth in the Context of American Society," *Daedalus,* Winter, 1962, esp. pp. 113–20.

## SEX ROLES

The behavior appropriate to males and females is clearly distinguished in most situations in American society. Adolescents generally recognize this sex distinction, both when they rate occupations as male- or female-oriented and when they choose occupations. Outside the occupational field, however, the distinction between sex roles is often less clear. A higher value still, however, is placed on the male rather than the female roles. In one study, 100 single men and 100 single women at the University of California were given an adjective checklist to describe sex roles.[16] In general, the findings show that the roles of women and men are changing and are somewhat confused. Investigation of the content and implications of the stereotype of males and females revealed that women were more inclined to sex-type what they felt to be their "real self" and were more unfavorable toward this idea than were men. On the other hand, the women's "ideal self" was less sex-typed than the men's. Women, in describing their "ideal man," selected favorable female characteristics as often as they selected favorable male ones. Men, however, include favorable male characteristics less often in describing their "ideal woman."

A very early study indicated a considerable difference between boys and girls with regard to their orientation toward the major society. In this study, 784 boys and 857 girls in high schools in Tulsa, Oklahoma, and the Grover Cleveland High School in New York were given questionnaires.[17] The conclusion was that boys indicate a greater interest in safety, health, money, civic affairs, recreation and study, while girls are more concerned with personal attractiveness, etiquette, and getting along with other people. In an even earlier study, questionnaires were administered to 8,812 white students in grades two through twelve in the public school systems of Birmingham, Montgomery, and Mobile, Alabama.[18] In this study the largest number of cultural heroes or personal ideals were historical and public characters. This type of selection was found to increase with age. The second largest number of ideal persons was selected from the immediate environment—father, mother, teacher. However, at every age more boys selected ideal persons from the remote environment while the girls chose them from the immediate environment. In an-

---

[16] John P. McKee and Alex C. Sheriffs, "Men's and Women's Beliefs, Ideas, and Self Concepts," *American Journal of Sociology*, Vol. XLIV (1959), pp. 356–63.

[17] Percivale M. Symonds, "Sex Differences in the Life Problems and Interests of Adolescents," *School and Society*, Vol. XLIII (1936), pp. 751–52.

[18] David S. Hill, "Personification of Ideals by Urban Children," *Journal of Social Psychology*, Vol. I (1930), pp. 379–93.

other study, Ross L. Mooney submitted a problem checklist to 603 students in Stevens Lee High School in Asheville, North Carolina.[19] He concluded that the girls at all grade levels led the boys in the mention of problems in the areas of home, family, and social-psychological relations, while boys led the girls in the areas of adjustment to schoolwork and in future vocational and educational plans. From these studies we may conclude that girls as late as World War II were quite "feminine" in the American scheme of things. From their first doll, girls are treated as girls even though they are allowed some tomboy activities up to puberty. The change from the strictly feminine role doubtlessly produces part of the confusion; ambiguities always result from changes in established relationships.

The earlier studies reflect more conformity on the part of women. Robert A. Harper did a study, using questionnaires and interviews, with male students living in the dorms in a large state university, females in a small state school, males in a Catholic university, conscientious objectors in a civilian public service camp, and a group of incoming inmates of a Federal reform school for young men.[20] He found women tended to be conformists more than men; and that members of both sexes tended to conform with increasing age. Persons from small towns and from farm families tend to be conformists more than persons from larger cities and from nonfarm occupations. Panos Bardis did a study of 113 high school students aged from sixteen to twenty-one years.[21] The findings indicated that at all ages females were more conservative than males.

Many authors claim it is more difficult for girls to assume the feminine role than for boys to assume the masculine one. Myrra Komarovsky studied seventy-three senior members in a course on the family and eighty senior female members of a social psychology class, using interviews and autobiographical essays.[22] She found that female college students appeared to be confronted with mutually exclusive adult sex-role expectations: homemaker on the one hand and career girl on the other. She also found that some girls felt they must vacillate with the pressures of the moment and that all girls suffer from uncertainty and insecurity as a result of these role expectations. In a

---

[19] Ross L. Mooney, "Surveying High School Student's Problems by Means of a Problem Check List," *Educational Research Bulletin*, Vol. XXI (1942), pp. 57–69.

[20] Robert A. Harper, "Is Conformity a General or Specific Behavior Trait?" *American Sociological Review*, Vol. XII (1947), pp. 81–86.

[21] Panos Bardis, "Attitudes Toward Dating Among Students of a Michigan High School," *Sociology and Social Research*, Vol. XLII (1958), pp. 274–77.

[22] Myrra Komarovsky, "Cultural Contradictions and Sex Roles," *American Journal of Sociology*, Vol. LII (1946), pp. 184–89.

later study, using the same method upon middle-class, urban, married women, she concluded that the very strong ties the woman has with her parental family in earlier years makes it difficult for her to shift her devotion to her family of procreation.[23] She felt that men are given more freedom and privacy, and earlier in childhood. This enables them to prepare themselves psychologically for the future shift marriage demands.

Miss Komarovsky's earlier study was repeated by Paul Wallin, using a random sample of 163 female undergraduates in a university.[24] His findings were essentially in agreement with her report. Wallin felt, however, that the great majority of college women who faced an incompatibility in their sex roles either do not take the situation seriously or are readily able to solve the problem. Harold E. Jones did a study, using case history and systematic observation with peer-rating scales employed at certain stages in the development of each person.[25] These studies make it seem that girls face more serious difficulties in adjusting to changing social expectations than boys do. The findings indicate contrary expectations in the development for girls, including being quiet, unassuming, talkative, and showing aggressive good fellowship. Boys, on the other hand, appear to have a more uniform set of standards to meet in the process of developing their sex roles during a similar period of growth.

Wallin's conclusion seems worthy of a closer view. When we look not at the difficulties themselves but at their assumed consequences in role definition, we return a different verdict. It has been pointed out in many studies that boys are much more often referred to guidance centers than are girls.[26] It has also been pointed out by several authors that delinquency rates, however measured, are considerably higher for young males than for young females,[27] and that underachievement in school occurs twice as frequently among boys as

---

[23] Myrra Komarovsky, "Functional Analysis of Sex Roles," *American Sociological Review*, Vol. XV (1951), pp. 508–16.

[24] Paul Wallin, "Cultural Contradictions and Sex Roles, A Repeat Study," *American Sociological Review*, Vol. XV (1950), pp. 288–93.

[25] Harold E. Jones, "Adolescents in our Society," in Jerome M. Seidman, *The Adolescent—A Book of Readings* (New York: Holt, Rinehart and Winston, 1949), pp. 50–60.

[26] Department of Mental Hygiene, State of California: *Statistical Report, June 30, 1955.* (Sacramento: 1955). Department of Mental Hygiene, State of New York: *1956 Annual Report,* (Albany: 1957). G. M. Gilbert, "A Survey of 'Referral Problems' in Metropolitan Child Guidance Centers," *Journal of Clinical Psychology* Vol. 13 (1957), pp. 37–40. C. A. Ullman, *Identification of Maladjusted School Children,* Public Health Monograph No. 7 (Washington D.C.: United States Government Printing Office, 1957).

[27] E. F. Schwartz, "Statistics of Juvenile Delinquency in the United States," *Annals of the American Academy of Political and Social Science,* January, 1949.

among girls.[28] These facts suggest that the pressures on sex role adjustment are greater in the case of the male than the female, and more stress is implied. Several studies suggest that the pressures exerted upon boys at very early ages are greater than those exerted upon girls in terms of demands made upon them to accept the appropriate sex role.[29] These studies show that boys are aware of the demands for suitable masculine roles as early as kindergarten while girls may go on for as many as five more years before they are forced to take definite feminine roles.[30] One author suggests the anxiety resulting from these demands is increased by the fact that such advice as is given is primarily negative.[31] In other words, the boy is told what not to do rather than what he should do and anxiety is produced because he therefore knows he must assume the masculine role but has not been told how to do it or even what it is. Furthermore, as mentioned elsewhere, the absence of fathers from the home makes emulation for the boy more difficult than in the case of girls. Boys observed to have difficulty in assuming the appropriate sex role frequently report their fathers to be agents of punishment and their mothers to be protectors. Generally, in fact, fathers are perceived as agents of punishment.[32] It is further suggested that the male role is viewed by boys much in terms of decision making, independence, and physical strength. The actual practice of such role behaviors as are indicated in boys' views of the man's roles is hardly available to persons who in early childhood are protected, bossed, and outshown in feats of strength by a woman. On the other hand, the view of the female role has many common attributes with the actual interaction between mother and daughter.[33]

Let us turn now to some of the empirically determined similarities

[28] J. C. Gowan, "The Underachieving Gifted Child, A Problem for Everyone," *Exceptional Child*, Vol. 21 (1955), pp. 247–49, 270–71.

[29] D. G. Brown, "Inversion and Homosexuality," *American Journal of Orthopsychiatry*, Vol. 28 (1958), pp. 424–29. E. L. Cava and H. L. Rausch, "Identification and the Adolescent Boy's Perception of his Father," *Journal of Abnormal and Social Psychology*, Vol. 47 (1952), pp. 855–56. S. W. Gray, "Masculinity-Femininity in Relation to Anxiety and Social Acceptance," *Child Development*, Vol. 28 (1957), pp. 204–14. H. M. Hacker, "The New Burdens of Masculinity," *Marriage and Family Living*, Vol. 19 (1957), pp. 227–33.

[30] D. G. Brown, "Sex-role Preference in Young Children," *Psychological Monographs*, Vol. 70 No. 14 (1956). D. G. Brown, "Sex-Role Development in a Changing Culture," *Psychological Bulletin*, Vol. 54 (1958), pp. 432–42.

[31] Ruth E. Hartley, "Sex-Role Pressures and the Socialization of the Male Child," *Psychological Reports*, Vol. 5 (1959), pp. 457–68.

[32] W. Emmerich, "Parental Identification in Young Children," *Genetic Psychological Monographs, in press* (cited in Hartley, (*loc. cit.*)

[33] Ruth E. Hartley, "Children's Concepts of Male and Female Roles," *Merrill-Palmer Quarterly of Behavior and Development*, Vol. 6 (1959–60), pp. 83–91.

and differences between adolescent boys and girls which give insight into the sex roles within adolescent society itself. A general theme throughout Coleman's research is that both boys and girls strive for rewards given by peers.[34] However, the avenues open to each sex differ. Males can achieve the greatest rewards through athletics while females receive theirs through beauty, participation, and peer organizations. Athlete-scholars seem to receive a considerable amount of prestige from their fellows. However, the "scholar" is one who can get high grades with a minimum of study. Second to athletic star in the desire of boys to be remembered in certain ways was as a brilliant student; third was to be remembered as most popular.[35] Clearly, however, sports was preferred to studies as a path to success. Adolescent status within the peer group is therefore not exclusively an achieved status. In the case of girls, again, some of the characteristics required for high status among the peer group were beyond the person's complete control. Beauty, for example, was much more a criterion of high status than was scholarship, on the basis of persons who were members of the leading crowd in the school and in terms of the number of friends.[36]

The relations between boys and girls are also of interest in this analysis. Coleman points out that it would be plausible to expect that boys would be more inclined toward studies if the girls in the school valued good grades. However, he concludes from his data that a boy's popularity with girls is based less upon grades and studies than upon having a car.[37] Among girls, scholastic success is more important in popularity with other girls than in popularity with boys.

In the schools studied by Coleman, considerably more emphasis was put on being popular with the opposite sex than being popular with one's own sex. This status criterion among adolescents affected the girls' self-concept. For example, the girls named more often as best dressed said less often they would prefer to be someone different than themselves than did those girls less often named as best dressed.[38]

## AGE ROLES

Not much research has been done on the age differences within the broader age status we call adolescence. Any parent or teacher knows such differences exist and doubtlessly has hypotheses as to the nature

---

[34] Coleman, *op. cit.*
[35] *Ibid.*, p. 134.
[36] *Ibid.*, p. 165.
[37] *Ibid.*, p. 50.
[38] *Ibid.*, p. 54.

of the differences. Some evidence can be garnered from the comparison of studies by different behavioral scientists. Unfortunately, findings are influenced by methods.

We find in the few studies available that sometimes differences do exist and sometimes they do not. Even in an area so remote from the weekday concerns of adolescents as theology we find significant differences. In one study of 547 adolescents in the sixth, ninth, and twelfth grades, several statements concerning belief in religion and in God were administered by means of a questionnaire.[39] In general, the findings showed a rather consistent decrease in faith in fundamentalist religious beliefs from the sixth grade through the twelfth grade. This trend was especially noticeable in the following statements:

1. God is someone who watches you to see that you behave yourself and who punishes you if you are not good.
2. I know there is a God.
3. Hell is a place where you are punished for your sins on earth.
4. People who go to church are better than people who do not go to church.
5. Good people say prayers regularly.
6. Every word in the Bible is true.
7. It is sinful to doubt the Bible.

## Age Grading

Adolescents themselves often make finer distinctions with respect to age groupings with their peers than adults make with adolescents. The twelve-year-old may accept a fifteen-year-old as a leader and person to respect but may argue violently and consistently with persons closer to his own age. Age is reinforced by the system of classes in school. The bully of the eighth grade usually loses his self-confidence when a ninth grader "picks on him." If forced to fight, the eighth grader may win. Even if he is larger than the ninth grader, the thing for which he receives high esteem among his peers is that "he whipped a ninth grader."

There is considerable loyalty among persons of any one age grade, as suggested by Linton and described earlier in the chapter concerning more heterogeneous age groupings. An adolescent stood rather bored watching a parade until a group of persons his own age came along on horses: "Hey! a lot of those kids are in my class. (Pause) Pretty cool." Perhaps from an adult's point of view the preceding floats were more interesting.

There has been little research on the different forces which affect persons of particular age grades. However, some insight can be

---

[39] Raymond G. Juhlen and Martha Arnold, "Age Differences in Religious Beliefs and Problems During Adolescence," *Journal of Genetic Psychology*, Vol. 65 (1944), pp. 291–300.

gained through looking at the same thing from the other point of view: how differently persons behave in their social relations from one year to another within the adolescent period. A famous series of studies was completed by Arnold Gesell, Frances Ilg, and Louise B. Ames on this problem. The conclusions are presented in terms of typical behavior rather than precise measures of the variation that actually occurs at each age. However, the summary of their conclusion gives us insight into the varied ways behavior, overt and covert, changes from one year to the next. The reservation should be stated explicitly: the following conclusions do not represent uniformities to the extent that all persons of a certain age act alike or that all adolescents go through all of these "stages."

### Year Twelve [40]

At the twelfth year of life the youth begins to take on some of the characteristics of maturity. It is not that the "twelve-year-old is an adult in miniature" but rather that noticeable trends are beginning in maturation which indicate the directions the acceptance of adulthood will take. Compared to the eleven-year-old, the relations between the twelve-year-old and other persons are much more reasonable and companionable. He attempts to be an excellent conversationalist, even with adults. He develops a sense of humor, is less self-centered, and tries to negotiate sociability. There is definitely an attempt on his part to broaden his horizons beyond his own self-interest. His interest in self-chosen tasks is intense, and teachers report a great deal of enthusiasm in subjects frequently thought of as boring, such as arithmetic. There is an expression of interest in the opposite sex, although well-planned parties frequently do not turn out as well as the plan would indicate. Boys, especially, are likely to congregate and "show off" by annoying the girls. The reactions to schoolteachers are much in terms of the teacher's ability to be well-informed and to present her material in a lively fashion. Group loyalties are extremely strong, especially with the same sex, but do not necessarily result in antagonism to the teacher. Enthusiasm and spirit are characteristic of the friendship groups, as shown by language extremes such as "*loving* tomato juice and *hating* stewed tomatoes." Their conversation is interspersed with many superlatives. There is a strain toward conformity through the expression of great interest in how age mates think and feel about various problems. The researchers reported a large number of the twelve-year-olds were very curious about how

---

[40] Arnold Gesell, Frances L. Ilg, and Louise B. Ames, *Youth: The Years from Ten to Sixteen* (New York: Harper & Bros., 1956), pp. 104–38.

other youth their age had answered certain questions. Twelve-year-olds like to talk very much.

Their attitude toward work is much different than that found at earlier ages; they are beginning to recognize that work must be done and the sooner over the better. Children at this age like very much to try their hand at adult activity. Girls enjoy taking care of the house and cooking while the mother is gone. More boys are taking on paper routes and babysitting away from home in the evening. While the eleven-year-old has a great deal of difficulty with parents because of childish activities and the parents' combined annoyance, the twelve-year-old greatly reduces the annoying habits. His enthusiasm may produce some behavior which causes difficulty with parents, but life in general is smoother. The twelve-year-old begins to take some initiative in daily routines and in the kinds of activities that cause parents to think he is careless, lazy, and rude. However, he appears to accept parental criticism at face value, often politely or in a manner of pleasant humor.

Girls, much more than boys, are interested in the relations between the sexes. Part of this may be due to the shock of menstruation. Boys are still somewhat embarrassed to admit real romantic interest in the other sex.

The twelve-year-old is oriented toward older brothers or sisters of the same sex, especially those three or four years older. Some emulation occurs and the channelization of interests is definitely influenced by older siblings. The notion of a single best friend is very evident at the age of twelve, and these beginning adolescents delight at staying at each other's house and going together all the time. Within each group, there is common knowledge of which boy likes which girl and vice versa.

The interests of twelve-year-old boys appear to take two forms: either seasonal athletics or building things indoors. Hobbies are more socially oriented with many hours spent discussing collections previously private affairs. Radio and television do not have the grip they have on earlier ages. The middle-class twelve-year-old is greatly interested in having his own radio so he may keep it on long after he has gone to bed. There is much more inclination toward finding out about movies before attending them, whereas in an earlier age just the idea of a movie met with complete acceptance. The idolization of teachers which occurs at earlier ages is not found in the twelve-year-old. This does not mean there is not a real affection for the teacher; rather, the twelve-year-old allows her into any group if she wishes to be included.

### Year Thirteen [41]

All the maturation that occurred during the twelfth year receives an increment during the thirteenth, but it is rather complex because adolescence is now well underway. Compared to the twelve-year-old, the thirteen-year-old is much more likely to lapse into spells of silence. This may be mere daydreaming or reverie, but in any event he is much less open and communicative than was the twelve-year-old. The thirteen-year-old has a sense of duty, and despite his moodiness will prove to be adaptable and dependable. The strong worries about self and acceptance on the part of others begin about the thirteenth year. Long periods of silence and sudden disassociation from the family group indicate the beginning of probes into his self-concept and other problems which plague the adolescent in later years. The boisterousness and enthusiasm of the twelve-year-old gives way to perfectionist ways. The thirteen-year-old is very critical of his own performance as well as the performance of others in any task in which he is interested. The superlatives found in the twelve-year-old's language disappear. While the twelve-year-old accepts criticism at face value, the thirteen-year-old is very sensitive to criticism of his behavior. However, he is also perceptive of the emotional states of other persons. The broad and effervescent interest of the twelve-year-old gives way to a more discriminating taste in trends in interests and activities. The first beginnings of the extreme care with clothes and hair found among boys in later adolescence begins at thirteen, although it does not become fullfledged until later.

The thirteen-year-old is not uncooperative but is much less outgoing. His words reflect his discrimination, his attempt to find self, and his less complete orientation toward others: "to put it bluntly." His growing maturity is also reflected in such words as: "seldom," "harmonious," and "in my judgment." [42]

Younger siblings are sources of trouble but older siblings are sources of aid by way of confiding and self-supporting relations. Parents are frequently a source of difficulty in the sense they try to "improve everything about me." The thirteen-year-old is likely to withdraw from confidential relationships with parents and to find outward manifestations of affection embarrassing.

The looking glass becomes a help in learning to accept oneself. Boys as well as girls spend much time in front of the mirror, primping, carefully inspecting physical features, and making faces. As the

---

[41] *Ibid.*, pp. 139–74.
[42] *Ibid.*, p. 141.

chapter on developmental tasks indicated, learning to accept one's physical features is probably the most consciously difficult task for adolescents to achieve.

The researchers report the thirteen-year-old himself recognizes he is "not too good natured." However, he does not explode in anger as much as he did in younger years. He is often depressed, and usually calm. His attitude toward work has improved in large part. The girl will clean rooms other than her own in the house, and the boy enjoys "tinkering" jobs. His patience with things and people has increased greatly. The researchers feel he has mobilized his resources to understand himself and to learn to live with others, even with the opposite sex. However, many thirteen-year-old boys have not yet caught up with girls in size, and, to make matters worse for them, the girls are sufficiently mature to be attractive to and attracted by older boys.

In school, the orientation toward the "good" teacher continues and mischievousness may be the result when the teacher is not so defined. Considerable interest still exists in school subjects and voluntary contributions, such as newspaper clippings, are common. There is some tendency to separate the teacher from the subject she teaches at this time. The thirteen-year-old enjoys hearing stories others of his age have written about themselves but, consistent with his feelings of privacy in the home, he wants his own stories kept from his classmates.

The researchers recognize considerable variation in ethical sense among thirteen-year-olds. Some, mainly girls, are puritanical and do not tolerate violations of norms by others or themselves. Others, mainly boys, find their consciences only lightly stricken by such violations. More interesting, however, is the fact that in the thirteenth year many youth are beginning to be able to make ethical decisions and to do so with certain aspects of relative truth. They may tell "white lies," as often as not to protect the feelings of a friend.

### Year Fourteen [43]

In some aspects the fourteen-year-old returns to some of the ways of the twelve-year-old. He becomes less moody, more cheerful, and less withdrawn. The crystalization of the self during the periods of lonely contemplation in the previous year seem to bring about a more fully integrated structure of personality and an enjoyment of life.

In spite of considerable embarrassment at individual family members, the fourteen-year-old begins to accept responsibility toward other family members. Problems which occur, and they occur often, are handled in a less tight and insistent manner. He also begins to

⁴³ *Ibid.*, pp. 175–213.

learn how to get along with younger brothers and sisters. He is more interested in people as individuals and is aware of individual differences.

About a third of the fourteen-year-old boys date, but seldom do they go steady. The other boys do not like girls yet. About half of the girls date, but they do not go steady either. Generally, as in the earlier two years, girls like boys more than boys like girls. Nevertheless, girls are more interested in persons of their own age-sex status than in boys.

Girls are especially tireless in communicating with other girls. Such communication occurs at every possible time and every possible place, including an endless series of telephone calls, perhaps in anticipation of adult roles.

The fourteen-year-old's vocabulary is much larger and suggests nearly adult thought. He is now able to view two sides of issues and continues to see relativity in much of truth, as does his year-younger counterpart. He is much more able to think abstractly and propositionally.

The fourteen-year-old is easy and relaxed in the interviews reported by the researchers. He is also more cautious, reflecting his ability to view an issue from more than one frame of reference, and he is inclined to try to include too much into an answer, just as he tries to include too many things in his social life.

The attitude toward work progresses from the advances made by the thirteen-year-old. The girls begin to be a real help to the mother, if the mother develops this carefully. They scrub rooms in the house regularly and may do their own ironing. Boys can do man-size jobs, and often do, again if the development of work orientation is deliberately fostered.

The fourteen-year-old's attitude toward adults is positive in nature, and anger is more frequently controlled. His attitude toward age-grade mates still is one of solidarity and will remain so throughout adolescence. However, he recognizes greater difference among persons of his own age and between age mates and himself. Conformity in sex roles is evident: girls who would rather not remain like little girls may feel the necessity of wearing lipstick and of being boy-crazy. The fourteen-year-old is more likely to "kid" and "razz" than to make the antagonistic responses his parents expect on the basis of the previous year.

The study shows that girls are more sensitive to the feelings of others than are boys, especially with contemporaries. The friendship groups of girls are also inclined to be more differentiated on the basis of "best friends" than are the friendship groups of boys. Boys, on the other hand, are more likely to gang up with larger groups.

The fourteen-year-old is beginning to get his own set of morals and ethical system. His thinking concerning ethics extends beyond his own concerns to the family, teachers, and expecially others of his age. Again the researchers recognize variation: some fourteen-year-olds make decisions concerning ethical problems rather quickly from a "sense of right," others make theirs from the multiple influences of family and friends, and still others from a more deliberate and calculated decision process. In any event, their decisions are more inclined to be "other-oriented" than in the thirteenth year.

### Year Fifteen [44]

Rather than continuing in the ways of the fourteen-year-old, who seems to have found himself and is cheerful about the results, the fifteen-year-old may be confused about himself and confusing to others. He may react in an indifferent manner to almost all stimuli. His apparent apathy may be misleading according to the researchers, because he has returned to a moodiness and inward search for self. Compared to his earlier year, the adolescent becomes thoughtful, quiet, and serious. He is also oriented more toward secrecy and may often be seen as cold and hostile to some degree. Some fifteen-year-olds are more cautious in their speech and attempt to find just the right word to express themselves. This is consistent with a generally noticeable concern with detail.

The fifteen-year-old has become capable of holding grudges and seeking revenge. Delinquency and various other social disorders are often the outgrowth. The spirit of independence is evident and what the authors describe as a "cold war" may be carried on with parents. The daydream often expressed by fifteen-year-olds is going to school in a distant town. The fifteen-year-old is earnestly trying to become independent and not to be thought of as a child by parents and others.

On the other hand, the fifteen-year-old is still under considerable group pressures. He must find a way to be with his group and still assert his independence. He seems to be aware of the difficulty. He has the same situation with his family: he does not want to do anything suggesting dependence upon the family but neither is he rejecting the family. He gets on well with siblings, even younger ones, and he is concerned when parents do not get along with each other.

---

[44] *Ibid.,* pp. 214–49.

Boys are still less interested in the opposite sex than are girls, but a large percentage of both engage in kissing and in mixed parties. Girls prefer older boys, as is the case throughout early adolescence. Boys, for their part, begin the bragging stage and play the field with girls although in earlier ages interest in girls was a source of embarrassment.

As always, boys remain interested in sports but now an interest in cars becomes more important. Girls' activities are quite different from boys'. Compared to boys, girls are more inclined toward individual than group sports, and they like to walk and talk to friends at great lengths. Girls also become excellent correspondents more often than boys.

### Year Sixteen [45]

The near-adult status of the sixteen-year-old is recognized through various laws and customs. In most states, he can get a driver's license and quit school. Many sixteen-year-olds can interact with adults in various instances as a near equal, and they display greater self-assurance and self-reliance than before.

The sixteen-year-old is more tolerant of the world in general. He has greater facility with persons of all ages and may be quite cordial and "preadultish" in his handling of co-host duties in the home when an adult guest arrives. The time spent in the home decreases greatly, of course, but his sense of ties to the home has not diminished. Rather, he has assumed the broadening horizons characteristic of adulthood and is setting about developing the necessary relations as quickly as possible.

The sixteen-year-old has his emotions pretty much under control. He is not aggressive and he covers hurt feelings well; he is not moody and he often develops mechanisms for working off anger.

In this year his career plans begin to materialize. His high school curriculum forces him into an early general choice of college or non-college routes, but it also has helped him during the last year to crystalize his plans.

The sixteen-year-old has a more flexible ethical sense than in his earlier years. He is often somewhat surprised to find similarities in his ethical system with that of his parents.

It is unfortunate for our purposes that the study did not continue through the remaining years of adolescence. However, the years from twelve through sixteen give us some interesting detail into age and, to some extent, sex differences in role playing.

---

[45] *Ibid.*

## SUMMARY

Age and sex differences are of utmost importance in explaining differences between people and in their relations with each other. A degree of loyalty and exclusiveness is found among members of the same age and sex category. This solidarity is now well-documented for adolescent society.

The obligations and rights are ambiguous for both the adolescent and the adult. Whether this ambiguity is worse for the boy or girl is inconclusive. We have evidence in both directions.

Significant differences with respect to age-sex roles within the adolescent period are often overlooked in generalizations applying to the adolescent period per se. The development of the individual through various stages of maturation as represented by age differences in uneven and often reversals of traits are found from one year to the succeeding one.

# Chapter VIII

# OCCUPATIONAL CHOICE

Occupational choice may be studied within several frames of reference. Only three will be considered here.

The first is the point of view of our society. The general nature of the social structure strongly influences occupational choice in many ways. The amount of mobility and the degree of specialization are two important factors in occupational choice. What rewards are attached to various occupations and which occupations are most highly rewarded? How do status rewards and values affect choice?

The second frame of reference we will consider is social change. Trends in occupational structure are very important to the individual, for he is attempting to project these trends for a career of some forty-five or fifty years. It should be pointed out, however, that trends are less important than structural features of the society in terms of total understanding. The degree of mobility and specialization may greatly increase or decrease, but in either case mobility and specialization in the United States will be much greater than that faced by adolescents in many other countries.

The third frame of reference is the choice process itself, taken within the context of the structure and trends in the labor force. To the extent the adolescent considers thoroughly the factors that will later affect his job satisfaction he must assess the values attached to occupations and match them with his own values and attitudes; he must know enough about alternatives to accomplish this and he must anticipate his goals and interests in adulthood. Such a rational process seldom occurs. More often the adolescent makes a multitude of minor decisions which add up to commitment to a particular occupational line.

## SOCIAL STRUCTURE AND CHOICE

In a society in which there is little social mobility, that is, in which children assume the occupational roles of their parents, occupational choice is not a problem. The only occupationally related developmental task important in such societies is learning the skills, attitudes, and knowledge necessary to perform the role handed down from the father. In our society, as in most Western societies, occupational choice involves not only learning skills but choosing the occupational role the young person will assume upon entering the labor force. Therefore, the problem is greatly intensified for youth who live in societies with a considerable amount of social mobility.

The problem is further intensified because of the high specialization in many countries in which there is high mobility. Of course, a high degree of specialization itself is not sufficient to intensify the problem for youth. For example, India is very highly specialized but occupations are still primarily handed down from father to son within the caste system. However, once granted a high degree of social mobility, specialization has some consequences which make it difficult for youth to choose an occupation. First, the adolescent is given a very large number of choices. For example, in the various listings of occupations in the United States the number of occupations ranges from about 34,000 to 54,000.[1] The difference in these numbers depends upon how finely one wishes to define job roles as different occupations. Is an associate professor different from a full professor? In terms of the usefulness in the study of youth, such distinctions are probably not necessary. "Full professor" grows out of "associate professor" positions, and the role activities are essentially the same. Likewise, the difference between lawyer and judge is not a useful distinction in considering the occupational choice of adolescents. Many occupations are not open to youth first entering the labor force. It takes some time for a lawyer to reach the point where he may be appointed or elected a judge. Many other distinctions, however, are of utmost importance. For example, lawyers are either criminal or civil, and professors are always divided in terms of disciplines. The career pattern is different for each of these fields from the very beginning of college.

Let us assume that even the more conservative estimate of the number of occupations in the United States is double that which would be useful in the study of youth. This would leave more than 15,000 occupations for youth to consider. Obviously, then, a consequence of the high degree of specialization in our country for the problem of occupational choice is ignorance. Even professionals who specialize in the area of occupational structure can name only an extremely small percentage of the occupations open to youth. Choices will be made of occupations which youth know about and, therefore, a very

---

[1] For example see: Federal Security Agency, *Dictionary of Occupational Titles* (Washington, D.C.: U.S. Government Printing Office, 1949).

large number of occupations are not chosen until later in life. The mobilization of resources, efforts, and training begins very late for many of these occupations, which is well demonstrated by a study made of the occupations chosen by over 1,000 boys and girls in a rural county in New York state and by about 250 boys and girls from a school in Brooklyn.[2] Only 150 occupations were chosen by the boys in the study, and even fewer by girls. The occupations chosen may be characterized in two ways. Most are the familiar ones of the traditional rural community. These occupations have existed in our culture for a long time, and contact between members of these occupations and the families of the youth choosing them is frequent. The second type of occupation is the more glamorous position. Engineering is now a well-known occupation although the individual may not come into contact with it during his adolescence. For example, magazine advertisements mention engineering often and in the stories youth read an engineer is frequently the hero.

Parents are in the same position as youth; they do not know the occupations available to youth. Furthermore, youth is searching for independence from family and teachers and any help parents might be able to provide is often defined by the adolescent as the parents' effort to maintain control.

Further complicating the situation is the fact that our value system has traditionally held the individual is free to choose his own occupation. This is perhaps the freedom least infringed upon by those oriented toward control. This freedom is not complete, however. It has been pointed out that large groups of occupations are eliminated for certain children even before they enter adolescence. Those occupations which require a college degree are not generally available to youth who do not take the college curriculum in high school. The curriculum taken is largely determined by adults at the beginning of the high school period.[3] Nevertheless, in spite of the function of the school as a selecting agency the freedom to chose one's occupation is still not categorically limited. Many boys and girls placed in a non-college curriculum in high school may still enter college, although with greater difficulty.

Another, more general impact of the society upon the occupational choice of the individual is cultural influence—the value placed upon an occupation as desirable, both to the society and for the individual.

---

[2] Unpublished data from Charles E. Ramsey, "A Study of Decision-Making of Adolescents."

[3] For a discussion of this see Talcott Parsons, "The School Class as a Social System: Some of Its Functions in American Society," *Harvard Educational Review,* Vol. 29 (1959), pp. 297–318.

One theory holds this is the major influence in producing an inevitable stratification.

Kingsley Davis and Wilbert E. Moore published a theory in 1945 which is of considerable importance in developing any cross-cultural theory of occupational choice.[4] Their work gives us some insight into the possibilities of uniform or generalized influences upon the occupational choice within our own society. The theory begins with the assumption that positions within a society, including occupations, vary in four ways:

1. Some positions are defined in the culture as more important than others.
2. Some positions are inherently less pleasant than others.
3. Some positions require considerably more training than others.
4. Some positions have associated duties which must be performed more diligently than in others.

Therefore, it is up to the social system to provide some means of motivating persons with appropriate types and levels of talents to seek positions which are less pleasant, more functionally important, and require more training. A way must also be found to motivate the individual to perform those duties diligently.

The means found in all societies to accomplish these tasks is rewards: income, prestige, power, and the like. In terms of Davis and Moore's problem this produces stratification since this difference in rewards is exactly what we mean by stratification. For our purposes, however, this theory implies that the four factors listed above are social factors motivating the individual toward certain occupational choices and away from others.

The system outlined by Davis and Moore is a supply-and-demand theory to the extent that the scarcity of talent is a major factor in occupational choice. The theory is also a cultural one, since functional necessity is the other major factor.

The system, as outlined by Davis and Moore, does not work perfectly since occupational groups set up monopolies and through the exercise of power are able to produce scarcity of talent. Through public relations these groupings are also able to initiate a necessity which may not be functional.[5] Nevertheless, some cross-cultural evidence supporting the Davis-Moore approach can be seen.

Some evidence that subcultures influence occupational choice is found in a previous chapter. In the present chapter we will note some of the different ways this influence operates.

---

[4] Kingsley Davis and Wilbert E. Moore, "Some Principles of Stratification," *American Sociological Review*, Vol. 10 (1945), pp. 242–49.

[5] E. T. Hiller, *Social Relations and Structures* (New York: Harper & Bros., 1947).

The most important influence is apparently the occupation of the father. In our society, the occupational succession found in some other societies does not operate in a majority of cases. Nevertheless, many boys follow the father's occupation and an even larger proportion follows an occupation which is in the same status category as that of the father. For example, if the father is a physician the boy will choose either physician or some other profession. If the father is a skilled worker the boy will choose either the same or another skilled occupation.

The boy may also seek an occupation in the occupational category immediately above that of the father. If the father is in clerical work the boy may seek a position in the next higher category, managerial work. If the father is a businessman the boy may seek a job in the professions. If the father is in semiskilled work the boy will choose an occupation in skilled work. It has been estimated that about 67 percent of all boys choose an occupation in either their fathers' status category or the next higher one.

The tendency to reach the father's status varies according to that status. For example, more sons of higher status fathers aspire to the same status category than sons of lower status fathers. In the case of unskilled and service workers, few sons aspire to the same status.

The most frequent deviation from the tendency to choose the father's or the next-higher status is made up of an attempt to circumvent the entire status structure. The sons (and daughters) of low-status parents who wish to occupy relatively high positions within the community find education the only channel readily open to them. Therefore, of the one third who follows none of the patterns mentioned earlier, many go into the professions through education. In this way they move from the blue-collar positions of their fathers to the professions, whereas they could not reasonably expect to enter directly many occupations deemed lower in status than the professions.

It has been pointed out in the chapter on subcultures that only farmers' sons enter farming. One study showed that as high as 95 percent of the boys who chose farming as a career were the sons of farmers. The cost of entering farming, the decreasing number of farms, and the somewhat higher number of children in farm families doubtlessly reinforce this tendency. Business ownership is similarly transmitted from father to son, although the tendency toward exclusiveness may not be as great.

Boys choose much different occupations than girls, and they choose a wider range. Girls limit their choices for the most part to typical female occupations: nursing, teaching, and clerical work. In spite of the rapidly increasing trend for females to work full-time throughout much of their life, only a small percentage of adolescent girls choose occupations which indicate a major interest in a career. In any sample of high school adolescents practically all of the girls will state an occupational plan other than housewife. However, most girls view their occupational choice in two ways: a stopgap between graduation and marriage and an "insurance" against economic adversity during marriage.

The job ceiling, traditionally applied to members of certain minority groups, was described in the chapter on subcultures. Although the job ceiling has tended to rise, most minority group members have not prepared themselves to accept the higher level positions in the labor force.

Leila Sussman and Gars Norman Levine, studying the occupational-choice background of an entering class of freshmen engineers at the Massachusetts Institute of Technology, found parents the most important influence on occupational choice of business and professional sons. Sons of manual workers are most influenced by teachers in the later grades of grammar school and in high school. The study also showed that the parent's influence decreases as the adolescent grows older while the influence of friends becomes more important.[6]

In a study dealing with occupational choice and personal values among college students, Morris Rosenberg presents some interesting materials on differences in career choice and expressed values.[7] First, he finds (as might have been anticipated) careers play a more important part in the life plans of men than of women. When students were asked, "What three things in your life do you expect will give you the most satisfaction?" three times as many men selected career or occupation as did women. In addition to variations in the emphasis placed on career, male and female students were found to differ on the values they hoped to satisfy in their work. For the most part, women were found to be "people oriented" while men were "extrinsic-reward oriented."[8] When males and females are compared on the values they hope to satisfy in their work, interesting differences occur. Women who place career above family (and they are a minority) are more likely to have values similar to males than are women who choose family as their primary concern. In other words, women who depart from societal expectations are much like males in their

---

[6] Leila Sussman and Gars Norman Levine, *The Entering Freshmen at M.I.T.: Class of 61* (mimeo). No publication date given.

[7] Morris Rosenberg, with the assistance of Edward Suchman and Rose K. Goldsen, *Occupations and Values* (New York: The Free Press of Glencoe, 1957).

[8] *Ibid.*, p. 49.

value outlook. These findings suggest a relationship between the values one holds and the career he chooses. The more important question is which comes first: does holding a certain set of values lead one to a matching occupation, or does entrance and training in a specific occupation lead to a matching set of values? Since Rosenberg's research design was longitudinal, he was able to control for changes in both occupational choice and values over a two-year period. His conclusions show that a conflict between the values of a chosen occupation and the value orientations of the chooser tends to be resolved by a change of occupations so as to more nearly live up to the value orientations:

> It may be noted that 57 percent of the students selecting people-oriented values on both waves changed to people-oriented occupations, compared with 31 percent of those who did not select these values, a difference of 26 percent. On the other hand, 58 percent of those who chose people-oriented occupations switched to people-oriented values, compared with 47 percent of those who did not choose one of these occupations, a difference of only 11 percent. *This would suggest that values have a greater effect on changes of occupational choice than the other way around.* The overall effect of this mutual interaction is to reduce conflict between values and occupational choice."[9]

Rosenberg and his associates see in the deviant pattern a change of value orientations in the direction of the values emphasized in the prospective occupation, an element of anticipatory socialization.

> One potential problem involved in moving from the status of student to that of occupational incumbent is that there will be a certain amount of awkwardness and inefficiency in switching statuses. It might take some time for the individual to internalize the new status as an element of his self-picture and to learn the appropriate role-behavior. Even as a student, however, the individual is learning to think of himself as a doctor or lawyer or teacher, and is rehearsing, either in his mind or overtly, the behavior appropriate to that status. The data . . . suggested, for example, that the student may change his current values to accord with those which he believes will be appropriate for his chosen occupation. If the individual correctly learns the values, attitudes, and behavior appropriate for the occupational status he expects to occupy, and if he begins to internalize them, then he becomes "partly" a doctor or engineer while still in college. The transition to the actual occupational status then, can be accomplished relatively smoothly."[11]

The value orientations of the occupational chooser are, then, apparently a matter of who constitutes the reference group for the chooser. Presumably, value orientations on the threshold of the college career are a result of his interaction with family, teachers, and/or peers. A change of value orientation to reduce conflict with a chosen

---

[9] *Ibid.*, p. 19.
[11] *Ibid.*, pp. 125–26.

occupation is tentative evidence of the effect of an occupational culture on the student.

Next, we learn from the Rosenberg data that significant differences exist in values held and occupational preference. For example, Rosenberg asks each of his respondents to indicate his degree of "faith in people." From responses to five items, a scale of faith in people was constructed. In the table which follows the reader can see how several occupations ranked.

OCCUPATIONAL CHOICE AND FAITH IN PEOPLE

| Occupation | Per Cent with High Faith in People |
|---|---|
| Social work | 62 |
| Personnel | 59 |
| Teaching | 56 |
| Science | 51 |
| Government | 50 |
| Farming | 45 |
| Art | 43 |
| Hotel | 41 |
| Medicine | 40 |
| Journalism-drama | 39 |
| Architecture | 39 |
| Law | 39 |
| Engineering | 36 |
| Advertising | 36 |
| Business-Finance | 34 |
| Sales promotion | 22 |

Differences are also found when occupational preference is correlated with what Rosenberg refers to as the "Extrinsic Reward-Oriented Value Complex." This scale measured the individual's desire for an occupation which would give the extrinsic rewards of money and status. The lower the weighted average of the scale the lower the student's ranking of the importance of extrinsic rewards. The occupational group showing the highest desire for extrinsic rewards was real estate–finance; lowest were teaching and social work.

To summarize the Rosenberg findings: first, we see a relationship between value orientation and occupational choice. Second, values tend to remain constant with occupations replaced until there is a match between career choice and initial values. Three, women are most likely to hold the altruistic view and this view correlates most highly with the occupations women traditionally enter. The finding showing that the occupational values of the career women (as opposed to the family-oriented women) are almost identical with those of the career-oriented men would certainly suggest sex alone does not account for the altruistic value orientation of those who select the teaching career alternative.

From the occupational-choice studies discussed here, as well as from the materials presented elsewhere, we learn that the choice of occupations is a developmental process that starts in the prepubertal years. During the preadolescent and adolescent years the family is an important reference group to the individual as he moves toward a more narrow set of occupational alternatives. Contacts with members of a given profession, particularly if they are relatives, are also important. In the late years of adolescence and the early years of college, when the individual may be away from home for the first time, the friendship group helps him formulate his occupational ambitions. We also find that personal values play a significant role.

It is clear, then, that the choice of an occupation is a complex act which occurs in a complex situation. Generally it is not a decision made suddenly but rather a series of decisions that are part of a dynamic and on-going process.

Archibald O. Haller and his associates see the occupational act as part of a larger system of influences.[12] For them the system includes:

1. Occupational decisions.
2. The changing occupations of a changing society.
3. The immediate situation of the youth.
4. The youth's life decisions in areas other than occupations.
5. The youth's personality.

Of particular importance to our discussion of occupations and the transition from youth to adult roles is what Haller refers to as the *immediate situation*. Here he deals with the total environmental setting in which the young person finds himself. He points out, for example, that available school facilities may well play a vital part in the occupational selection process. If a young person is interested in chemistry and has the potential for such work but is unable to find competent adults to train him, his interest and skill are of little value. The importance of school facilities and staff can be seen in yet another way. From investigations conducted by a number of researchers we know that:

1. The larger the high school, the greater the probability of success in college.
2. The larger the high school, the more elaborate and impressive the teaching equipment, libraries and laboratories.
3. The larger the high school, the higher the probability of professionally trained and competent teachers.

---

[12] Archibald O. Haller, *et al.*, "The Occupational Choice Process: A Sociological View," in David Gottleib and Jon Reeves, *Adolescent Behavior in Urban Areas: A Bibliographic Review and Discussion of the Literature*, (Michigan State University, 1962).

Moving to less obvious factors in the immediate situation we can see the impact of such variables as parental influence, experience in the school situation, home environment, socioeconomic background, and peer-group involvement.

Parental insight and influence in relation to occupational choice can be noted in a number of ways, one of which is the ability of many parents to predict accurately the occupational interest patterns expressed by their children. Using the Kuder Preference Test, George E. and Richard M. Hole found that 80 per cent of the forty parents tested were able to match two or three of their child's top three vocational interests.[13] The authors point out that mothers were able to do somewhat better in prediction than were fathers. This difference could perhaps be explained by the fact that the mother's role, as noted earlier, requires greater contact and involvement with the child and hence offers a more accurate insight as to occupational preferences.

Parental influence is revealed also in how adolescents evaluate different kinds of occupations as well as their attitudes toward labor and collectivism. In these areas the adolescents' attitudes tend to conform to observed adult patterns. The extent of consensus, over time, between the occupational evaluations of youth and those of adults can be found in research conducted by Donald M. Valdez and Dwight Dean.[14] In their investigation they compare the prestige rankings obtained in the North-Hatt occupational stratification study of 1946 with rankings they received from college students some fifteen years later. With the exception of physicists—an occupational role which has gained somewhat in prestige during the intervening years—there are no significant differences between the evaluations of the college group and the adults who participated in the original North-Hatt study.[15] Valdez and Dean point out, in addition, that agreement among students as to occupational rankings remains high when comparisons are made between religious and public colleges; small and large colleges; and campus and community colleges.

Perhaps the greatest concentration of research pertaining to parental influences on occupational aspirations and expectations is in

---

[13] George E. Hole and Richard M. Hole, "Comparison of the Vocational Interests of Tenth Grade Students with Their Parents' Judgments of These Interests," *Educational and Psychological Measurement,* XVIII (Spring, 1958), pp. 173–78.

[14] Donald M. Valdez and Dwight Dean, "Teaching the Concept of Social Stratification." Paper presented at the Ohio Valley Sociological Meetings, Michigan State University, May 5, 1962.

[15] For a more detailed discussion of the North-Hatt research see "Goals and Occupation: A Popular Evaluation," in Reinhard Bendix and Seymour Morten Lipset (eds.), *Class, Status and Power: A Reader in Social Stratification* (New York: The Free Press of Glencoe, 1953), pp. 411–26.

studies dealing with child socialization. Although in recent years increasing attention has been paid in the literature of occupations and professions to the phenomenon of adult socialization, the great bulk of studies has emphasized child socialization and the term "socialization" has come to mean the process by which the individual is originally inducted into the social organization. "Socialization refers to the problem which is old and pervasive in human life—the problem of how to rear children so that they will become adequate adult members of the society to which they belong."[16] Under the influence of this orientation investigators of socialization have concentrated their attention on such phenomena as child-rearing practices,[17] family structure,[18] parental values,[19] and the effect of the peer-group culture as contrasted with the home culture.[20]

Perhaps under the influence of the Freudian conception of the relative completeness of the personality structure at the conclusion of puberty,[21] the study of socialization has until recently been more or less banished to the domain of child psychology. Given this orientation as to the saliency of the "early years" it is not surprising so many sociologists have concentrated on the content of the child-adult socialization process as observed in different cultural and socioeconomic settings.

Of particular importance to this discussion are the many studies dealing with social class and the occupational expectations and aspirations of American youth. With few exceptions, these studies begin with the assumption that differences in social class will lead to varia-

---

[16] Irvin L. Child, "Socialization," in Gardner Lindsey (ed.), *Handbook of Social Psychology* (Cambridge: Addison-Wesley Publishing Co., Inc., 1954), p. 655.

[17] Cf. Allison Davis and Robert J. Havighurst, "Social Class and Color Differences in Child Rearing," *American Sociological Review*, XI (1946), pp. 698–710; John W. M. Whiting, *Becoming a Kowma* (New Haven: Yale University Press, 1953); John W. M. Whiting and Irvin L. Child, *Child Training and Personality* (New Haven: Yale University Press, 1954); Robert R. Sears, Eleanor E. Maccoby, and Harry Levin, *Patterns of Child Rearing* (Evanston, Ill.: Row, Peterson & Co., 1957); D. R. Miller and G. E. Swanson, *The Changing American Parent* (New York: John Wiley & Sons, Inc., 1959).

[18] Cf. Talcott Parsons, Robert F. Bales, *et al., Family, Socialization and Interaction Process* (New York: The Free Press of Glencoe, 1955).

[19] Cf. David F. Aberle and Kasper D. Naegels, "Middle-Class Fathers' Occupational Role and Attitudes Towards Children," *American Journal of* Orthopsychiatry, XXII (1952), pp. 366–78; Melvin F. Kohn, "Social Class and Parental Values," *American Journal of Sociology*, LXV (1959), pp. 337–51.

[20] Cf. Meyer Rabban, "Sex-Role Identification in Young Children in Two Diverse Social Groups," *Genetic Psychology Monographs*, XLII (1950), pp. 81–158.

[21] Cf. Sigmund Freud, "Three Contributions to the Theory of Sex," *The Basic Writings of Sigmund Freud* (translated and edited, with an introduction by A. A. Brill) (New York: Random House, Inc., 1938), especially pp. 620 ff.; for negative evidence cf. Wm. H. Sewell, "Infant Training and the Personality of the Child," *American Journal of Sociology*, XVIII (1952), pp. 150–59.

tions in the kinds of values and attitudes transmitted from parent to child. The operational procedures employed in these studies are quite similar and tend to take the following form:

1. The investigator selects a stratified sample of young people and classifies them by social class. The social class position of the young person is usually determined by his father's class position. (Often, occupational status is used to determine this position.)
2. The respondents are presented with a series of questions either in the form of a paper and pencil questionnaire or through face-to-face interviews.
3. Responses obtained from these interviews are coded and comparisons are made between people from the different social strata.
4. End results are presented with the investigator commenting on the significance of association between social class and the dependent variable under investigation.

Dealing with a sample of 1,270 seniors from Michigan high schools, E. Grand Youmens notes the following social factors related to work attitudes and interests.[22] First, social class is significantly related to differences in youth socialization within the home, in the school, and in the total community. Second, social strata are more directly related to work attitudes than are school experiences or actual work experiences in the community. Three, actual work experience does tend to alter general attitudes toward work and occupational preferences are re-evaluated.

The problem of social status and aspirations has been approached in a number of other studies. Notable among these is the work conducted by W. H. Sewell, A. O. Haller, and M. A. Strauss.[23] Establishing a general hypothesis that, with the factor of intelligence controlled, the levels of aspiration of adolescents of both sexes are associated with the social status of their families, the authors surveyed a one-sixth sample of all nonfarm seniors in public and private schools in Wisconsin. The authors report that values associated with varying status positions are an important influence on the development of educational and occupational aspirations.

In yet another study, Bernard C. Rosen hypothesizes that achievement motivation (psychological) and value orientation (cultural) vary between the social classes.[24] This hypothesis is based on the notion that social mobility can be explained by the fact that members

---

[22] Youmens, E. Grand, "Social Factors in the Work Attitudes and Interests of 12th Grade Michigan Boys," *Journal of Educational Sociology*, XXVIII (September, 1954), pp. 35–48.

[23] W. H. Sewell, A. O. Haller, and M. A. Strauss, "Social Status and Educational and Occupational Aspirations," *American Sociological Review*, XXII (February, 1957), pp. 67–73.

[24] Bernard C. Rosen, "The Achievement Syndrome: A Psychocultural Dimension of Social Stratification," *American Sociological Review*, XXI (April, 1956), pp. 203–11.

of different social class groups vary in their values and motives. Rosen tested 120 male adolescents and reports that achievement motivation, but not value orientations, were related to high grades and that value orientations, but not achievement motivation, were related to educational aspirations. Taking the position that the various social classes will differ in values and motives, Rosen proposes middle-class children are more likely to be taught both the motives and values which lead to achievement.

Richard M. Stephenson examines three variables: mobility orientation, mobility resources, and mobility skill in determining social mobility within the class structure.[25] His sample consisted of 1,000 ninth-grade students in four semi-industrial medium-sized communities in New Jersey. His findings reveal that students do make a distinction between aspirations and occupations. The students seemed to show a fairly high degree of consensus in respect to aspirations but their expectations were very much influenced by position on the social class ladder. In this case, Stephenson found that the lower the socioeconomic status, the lower the level of expectations. He concluded that the common outlook on aspirations results from a common cultural orientation which cuts across social class groups while expectations are more of a realistic view determined in large part by the respondent's life experiences.

In most cases, investigations of social class and levels of aspirations are confined to differences between the classes with little attention to differences within the classes. LeMar Empey investigates both the inter- and intraclass differences among a one-tenth sample of all the male high school seniors in Washington state.[26]

Empey's findings would indicate that the absolute occupational aspirations of male high school seniors from the middle and upper classes are significantly higher than those of seniors from the lower social class groups. In addition, the relative occupational status aspirations of lower-class seniors would suggest they prefer and anticipate significantly higher occupational statuses than their fathers. Finally, high school male seniors of all social class groups show little difference in the degree to which they will reduce their occupational aspirations when faced with the necessity of choosing between their preferred and anticipated occupations.

In an investigation of twenty-four upper lower-class boys, including

[25] Richard M. Stephenson, "Mobility Orientation and Stratification of 1,000 Ninth Graders," *American Sociological Review*, XXII (April, 1957), pp. 204–12.

[26] LeMar T. Empey, "Social Class and Occupational Aspiration: A Comparison of Absolute and Relative Measurement," *American Sociological Review*, XXI (December, 1956), pp. 703–9.

twelve who were and twelve who were not planning to attend college, Joseph Kahl concludes that those aspiring to high educational and occupational status came from families which were unsatisfied with their positions and therefore encouraged their sons to seek higher occupational opportunities.[27] Holding to the notion that "college going" is a middle-class value, Kahl states that parents who encourage their children to attend college have taken on, at least in some part, the value system of the middle class.

From the studies discussed in this chapter it should be apparent that the social class variable is used quite frequently in sociological research. While there may be little consensus in the use of the term "class" in sociological research and theory, and even less consensus on how class is best measured, there is general agreement that it is a powerful variable and one which often accounts for much of the observed variation in human behavior.[28]

## SOCIAL TRENDS AND OCCUPATIONAL CHOICE

The trends in the labor force are occurring so rapidly we may lose sight of the fact they are merely trends in long-established patterns in the United States and not qualitative changes in the patterns themselves. Nevertheless, an occupational choice made in ignorance of these trends is likely to result in a boy put out of a job due to technological unemployment or in a boy who thought he would be receiving a high reward for his work but who actually lives at a marginal level of income and security.

A general summary of the trends related to occupational choice was completed by a North Central Regional Committee on the family and youth. This report points to three very important changes in our society which are of significance to occupational choice:[29]

1. The number of opportunities to enter farming declined during the last decade. Mechanization and increasing farm size reduced the number of operators required. Meanwhile, birth rates remained relatively constant. As a result, fewer farm youth can expect to enter farming—for example, only about one-third of the farm boys in the North Central Region (Kanel, 1960). Shoemaker (1958) estimated that only 10 to 15 percent of farm boys between 10 and 19 years of age could expect to earn reasonably satisfactory incomes in farming from 1955

---

[27] Joseph A. Kahl, "Educational and Occupational Aspirations of 'Common Man' Boys," *Harvard Educational Review*, XXIII (Summer, 1953), pp. 186–203.

[28] John F. Cuber and William Kenkel, *Social Stratification in the United States* (New York: Appleton-Century-Crofts, Inc., 1954); Milton M. Gordon, *Social Class* (Durham, N.C., Duke University Press, 1958); Joseph A. Kahl, *The American Class Structure* (New York: Rinehart Co., 1957).

[29] Lee G. Burchinal with Archibald O. Haller and Marvin J. Taves, *Career Choices of Rural Youth in a Changing Society*, North Central Regional Publication Number 142, (Minneapolis: University of Minnesota, 1962), pp. 4–6.

to 1962. The United States Department of Labor predicts a 17% net decline in farmers and farm workers in the present decade.[30]

Entrance requirements in farming are also changing. Capital investments necessary for successful farm operations are increasing. Furthermore, reduced availability of sufficient farm units limits entry. Successful farming today requires greater production, marketing, and business management skills than ever needed previously.

When thinking about nonfarm occupational opportunities, farm youth may want to consider the vast expansion in farm-related industries. Persons with a farm background and equal levels of training with nonfarm competitors may have an advantage in entering the farm supply, sales, and service fields of agribusiness. Otherwise, the degree that farm-related businesses and other nonfarm occupational fields will absorb farm and rural youth will depend largely on their ability to meet changing job requirements.

2. Another change, affecting rural and urban youth alike, is the composition change of the labor force. Between 1960 and 1970, while employment in farming will decline about 17 percent, the percentage of the labor force composed of unskilled workers will decrease. But, large increases will occur among occupations requiring the greatest education and training—up to 40 percent for professional and technical people. Growth will also continue among proprietors; managers; clerical; sales, skilled and semiskilled workers.

3. The last change involves youth themselves. About 50 percent more young persons, 2.6 and 3.8 million, will reach 18 years of age in the United States by 1965 than did so in 1960. Competition for education and jobs will be keener than for previous generations. But today's youth cannot merely prepare for today's occupational opportunities. Their preparation must also be for the labor market of the future decades.

These continuing changes require that rural youth assess accurately their interests and abilities and match these closely with developing occupational opportunities. Unless information on careers and vocational guidance programs effectively help this process, problems in occupational choices will increase. At least three kinds of losses are likely to occur:

*a*) Loss in productivity of the economy due to poorly trained persons.
*b*) Unemployment among the unskilled.
*c*) Losses in satisfaction that come from not matching persons with the jobs.

Any attempt to develop a comprehensive theory of occupational choice must be tentative. Nevertheless, such an attempt organizes our present knowledge. This report attempts to aid by presenting one generalized and tentative description of the occupational choice process.

Free choice of occupation assumes that: (1) there are alternative courses of action, and (2) one is free to choose among available alternatives. The American labor force includes an almost unbelievably large assortment of occupations. Each has its distinguishing pattern of required abilities, interests, values, and work roles. Yet, each occupation can be filled by individuals varying greatly in abilities, interests, etc.

There are certain sociological limitations, such as the generally accepted division of labor. Certain occupations are open to men; others to women. Age and race limitations are found in many fields. Policies of business organizations encourage or discourage employment in various ways. Moreover, present methods of disseminating occupational information limit the number of occupations about which the individual is informed.

Some conditions related to freedom of occupational choice are inherent in the

---

[30] U.S. Department of Labor, *Manpower Challenge of the 1960's,* October 1960. p. 11.

occupational structure itself. Distribution of occupations at any given time limits how many persons can enter various fields. The rate of turnover in occupations and the growth of the economy also determine the number of job opportunities. If the economy is expanding, there are more jobs of various kinds than if the business cycle is stationary or declining.

The changes referred to in point two of the discussion above might well be expanded somewhat. In this study, as in many others, occupations are classified according to Alba M. Edwards' scale of three criteria: the amount of education required, the amount of income received, and the amount of skill required in the job. Numerous studies have shown that Edwards' original assumption is correct, that these are more than status groupings, they are subcultures. The differences between the occupational groupings are significant for almost every human behavior including delinquency rates, divorce, I.Q., occupational choice, religious denomination, organizational participation, and a long list of other variables. The occupational groupings are:

1. Professional.
2. Proprietary, managerial, official.
3. Clerical.
4. Skilled work.
5. Semiskilled work.
6. Unskilled work.

Many add "service workers" as a seventh category and some add "semiprofessional" after the top category. Farmers are difficult to place. Probably for the nation as a whole farm owners would be near the second category, farm tenants near the third or fourth, and farm laborers with unskilled workers.

The changes in these categories are projected from 1960 to 1970. Lee Burchinal stated that unskilled workers would remain the same, farmers would decrease greatly, and professionals would increase over 40 percent. All other occupations will increase from about 15 to 30 percent, with clerical work increasing the most. These changes reflect the general trend in our society of letting machines do our hand labor while we plan for them, control them, and keep a record of their production.

## OCCUPATIONAL CHOICE FROM THE POINT OF VIEW OF YOUTH

When occupation is viewed from the point of view of the individual adolescent, the requirements for any generalizations and principles concern occupational choice as a process. Perhaps the classic study in this area is the one by Eli Ginzberg and his associates.[31] Ginzberg comments that while many people explain their occupational choice as accidents such choices are not accidents in the real sense of the word but rather were affected by something beyond the control of the individual—"An unplanned exposure to powerful stimulus."[32] Ginzberg also cites what might be described as "impulse" theories. These ideas rest primarily upon psychoanalytic theory and indicate that occupational choice may be explained in terms of early interests of a subconscious nature. He points to one study in which the conclusion is drawn that a child who has been able to repress sadistic tendencies may become a successful butcher or a great surgeon. Such a theory would fall down as a total explanation because the jobs to which anyone's subconscious tendency may lead vary greatly with the jobs available at the time and place. Therefore, one would necessarily need to consider factors in the society in which the person lived. Such a theory, again as a total explanation, would fall down also in that choices are changed as situations surrounding the person change. Nevertheless, as a single set of factors which may influence choice, the subconscious cannot be ignored. There are other theories which might be of importance to guidance counselors, parents, and teachers. However, our purpose here is to understand the occupational-choice process itself.

Ginzberg begins his theory by stating the assumption that decisions with regard to phenomona such as occupational choice are not made at a single point in time but over a longer period. Such decisions involve a series of "subdecisions," all of which, taken together, lead up to what may be viewed by the observer as the decision of occupational choice.[33] Many decisions made as part of the total occupational-choice process limit the individual for later freedom of choice. For example, a commitment of time, effort, and money into certain college careers makes it extremely expensive to change to another career pattern late in college, even though the individual might find the other field more interesting. Furthermore, decisions as to minor issues within the choice process may affect the ability of the individual to achieve the original goals. Decisions with respect to doing homework, for example, may greatly limit the ability of the student to enter college even though he has definitely decided upon a career involving

---

[31] Eli Ginzberg, Sol W. Ginsburg, Sidney Axelrad, and John L. Herms, *Occupational Choice: An Approach to a General Theory* (New York: Columbia University Press, 1961). Many of the interpretations are the responsibility of the present authors.
[32] *Ibid.*, p. 19.
[33] *Ibid.*, p. 27.

college. Each of these decisions is strongly affected by the amount of knowledge and exposure to alternatives at any given point of time. Ginzberg's theory of the process of occupational choice takes these factors into account.

Maturation involves learning to understand both oneself and one's environment. Therefore, as the adolescent matures he is able to consider more intelligently the matching of his individual characteristics with the available occupations in the society. He also learns to exercise increasing control over the environment and over himself.[34]

Ginzberg finds that the first consideration of occupational choice is *fantasy choices.* Although in many cases the fantasy choice comes over into later ages, generally we may identify this early fantasy choice with the latency period and, to a smaller degree, with the preadolescent period.

Even during the fantasy-choice stage some degree of differences may be found. Very early in the latency period the child may respond in true fantasy, hour by hour, on occupational choice. Later, the fantasy is narrowed to more reasonable types of choice, but they may change frequently. During this period the child may "spring" a new occupational choice on the parent for reality testing. These choices may be responses to immediate stimuli in the environment, such as contacts with a man whom the child respects.

During the period of the fantasy choice the child is under no urgency to make a realistic occupational plan and need not assess his ability to play the role associated with these occupations.[35] Furthermore, he is under no obligation to plan in any detail the manner in which he will implement such an occupational plan. Nevertheless, it is during these years that the child is able to narrow the occupational choices to a fairly small range. This does not mean the narrower range of choices involves occupations which either match his talents or interests or are similar in nature; a child during the period of the fantasy choice may be considering college professor, airplane pilot, and lumberjack. The narrowing in range is a strictly quantitative matter in the sense that only the number is reduced.

Children find themselves in a "suspended state" at the end of the latency period.[36] The child is dissatisfied with previous fantasy choices, a situation partly produced by pressures from parents in terms of taking the occupational choice outside the realm of "play." On the other hand, he is ill-equipped to make a more realistic plan. He has

---

[34] *Ibid.,* p. 29.
[35] *Ibid.,* p. 60.
[36] *Ibid.,* p. 65.

had little help, he knows little about the social structure, and his self-assessment is only beginning.

Following the fantasy choice is the stage Ginzberg calls *the tentative choice*. This is characteristic of the preadolescent and the young adolescent up through high school. Many of the more dramatic choices made during the fantasy period are now eliminated. For example, it was found in earlier studies that adolescents frequently chose baseball star, movie actor, and airplane pilot. Obviously, the future of some children might be in these areas, but far fewer than make such choices. Ginzberg feels that for many the tentative choice often stretches throughout high school, ending for noncollege careers around eighteen. However, it can still be tentative in the sense that choices are frequently changed in college throughout the twenty-first or twenty-second year.

It is important in understanding the process to recognize that occupational choice is not the only important decision for the adolescent during these years. He is attempting to gain emotional independence from his parents and to learn more of himself. These actions all influence each other greatly, especially in the identification of self on the one hand and finding self-interests and career patterns on the other. Another factor strongly influential at the tentative choice stage is the future educational plan. For example, the high school senior who does not plan to go to college knows he must move out of the tentative choice at high school graduation. Even earlier, the high school student beginning the sophomore year (in the six-three-three system), knows he will need to take certain courses if he is to go on to college. This may not necessitate specifying the occupational choice clearly but it usually involves limiting the choice to a group of occupations requiring college training.

During this period occupational choices change from time to time, but the more important feature is the assembling of evidence both on the self and on society for reality testing of the tentative choice. Ginzberg points to the principle that throughout the tentative choice the adolescent attempts to integrate his current role and his future role.[37] That is to say, the adolescent's present activities are more oriented toward his future role than they were previously.

Ginzberg further divides the period of the tentative choice into four substages. The first of these, when the youth first enters adolescence, Ginzberg calls the interest stage. At this point, the adolescent makes his choice primarily in the light of his likes and interests. This is a

---

[37] *Ibid.*, p. 74.

transitional stage between the fantasy choice and the tenative choice.

The second substage, which usually occurs around the ages of thirteen or fourteen, Ginzberg calls the capacity stage. During this period the adolescent becomes aware of role requirements, of differing rewards associated with different occupations, and of the necessity of different preparation to enter such roles. Primarily, however, he is thinking of his own abilities with regard to these requirements.

The third substage, which Ginzberg calls the value stage, is around the ages of fifteen and sixteen and is characterized mainly by associating occupational roles with interests and values dear to the adolescent at that period. Consistent with the findings of Gesell on the adolescent's general approach to life, the youth at this point attempts to synthesize interests, values, capacities, job requirements, and the like. He is able to consider a larger number of factors during this period and is not obsessed with one or two conditions of himself or of the occupation of interest.

The fourth and last substage posited by Ginzberg is the transition period, usually around the age of seventeen. It is the transition from the tentative to a realistic choice. The school and the peer group are beginning to exert strong pressures on the youth, and a very strong pressure is exerted by the fact that he knows he must make a definite decision at the end of high school. He will or will not go to college; if he does not go to college, he must chose a job. He begins to shift from such factors as interest capacities and values to the reality conditions of the society about him. He no longer has the protection of parent and school to avoid facing the fact that society imposes upon him very limiting conditions for entering the labor force. Colleges have requirements, his application for any job at the end of high school must be accepted by someone beyond his control, and he cannot for long refuse to recognize such facts of social life. Further, the school itself may provide a guidance course or more time with guidance counselors. Thus the adults, who know much more about the limitations of the social structure, force him to recognize these limitations through either the requirements of classes or the informal rapport between the guidance counselor and the person.

The third general stage, after the fantasy and tentative choices, is *the realistic choice*. This stage, in turn, can be divided into three substages. The first is exploration. It involves a more intensive search of knowledge, often through first-hand experience. During this period the adolescent may himself wish to take courses in occupational guidance or to try various majors in college.

The next substage is crystallization. At this point all the factors the adolescent has learned during the transition stage may be integrated into a single set of choices very narrowly defined. He is finally able to commit himself.

Then he is able to move into the last stage of realistic choice, which Ginzberg terms specification. He narrows a general choice such as physicist into a certain area of physics. This stage may be determined by available opportunities. Once he has narrowed the alternatives to an area he will make contact with persons who have positions which may be open to him.

In general, the three stages of choice—fantasy, tentative, and realistic—as well as their substages represent a rational model of occupational choice. Of course, this theory, like any theory, does not describe all the individuals who go through such a process. Many nonrational factors, many apparent accidents of opportunity, and many oversights on the part of the individual would cause variation from this general process. Ginzberg recognizes this fact. His intent was to develop a theory which would then be tested in the description of the occupational-choice process. He did not intend it to be all-inclusive. Nevertheless, we feel this is an important step forward in understanding occupational choice as it may occur through time for a large segment of the adolescent population.

Some important variations may enter into the application of Ginzberg's theory to certain groups of adolescents. In the first place, as Ginzberg notes, the theory was based primarily on interviews with upper income families. The alternatives open to such adolescents would doubtlessly allow more ability to make rational choices in a broader scope. The alternatives of certain occupations for lower income adolescents are much narrower. There is no reason why recognizing limitations would not be simply another factor in the rationality of the choice of an adolescent from a lower income family. Nevertheless, when one's alternatives are limited to a small number of occupations, the detail of the stages may be greatly reduced. We have attempted to apply Ginzberg's theory in general to all high school people, but the exact modifications of the theory for lower income groupings is not known. Another factor which may enter into this is the resignation found among many lower income children. Their families do not encourage them to aspire high, and resignation itself is a characteristic of many of the parents. Doubtless, this is often contagious.

Several case studies indicated the lower income group had much earlier crystallization of the occupational choice. Part of this may be due to their greater work experience. Another factor which may enter into the deviation from the model by the lower income groups is their inability to resolve the problem of choice within the limitations set by their parental income. On the whole, however, the choices of lower income groups seem to parallel those of the theoretical model presented here.[38]

A second question of deviation from the theoretical model arises in the case of girls. The authors tentatively concluded that girls parallel two stages of the process, namely the fantasy and tentative stages. However, the difference between boys and girls, especially college girls, is in the focus on goals and values. Girls are more inclined to look at college in terms of self-development and social experience rather than in terms of vocational aims. Primarily, girls are marriage oriented. Nevertheless, because of the interim between graduation and marriage, girls do give some consideration to working. One can generally say, then, that it is probable the theory applies to girls up to the point of graduation from high school. At that point the problems girls will face are different and, therefore, the choice process itself is different.[39]

## SUMMARY

Occupational choice may be viewed from many frames of reference, only three of which are considered here. The first is from the point of view of the social system. American society is characterized as having a high rate of mobility from the father's occupation and a high degree of specialization. The combination of these two characteristics presents difficulties to the adolescent in that he must, within our value on free choice, choose among a vast number of alternatives. He knows little of these occupational alternatives. Many positions are filled by persons who neither planned for nor even knew about the occupation during the time they were preparing for economic independence.

The second frame of reference is the trend of the structure of the labor force. Generally, occupations which require higher degrees of education are increasing greatly while those which may be entered with less education are either decreasing or remaining the same.

The third frame of reference is from the point of view of the adolescent himself. A rational model of the occupational-choice process is described in terms of three stages: the fantasy stage, the tentative stage, and the realistic stage. The model needs further testing in terms of (1) nonrational factors which enter into the process and (2) its application to types of students who were not included in large numbers in the study.

---

[38] *Ibid.*, chap. 11.
[39] *Ibid.*, chap. 12.

# Chapter IX

## COURTSHIP AND THE ROMANTIC THEME

Courting, romance, and love are an integral part of American life. As we view the right of every man to find his place in the economic and social order inalienable, so we insist each person find romance and a lifelong companion. The image of dating, courtship, marriage, children, and the family is very much a part of the socialization process. Through the words of parents, teachers, peers, clergy, and the mass media the child is taught from an early age that marriage is the great divider between the time of youth and the age of adulthood. In many respects we encourage this notion by forgiving errors of judgment in matters of romance as long as they occur prior to the wedding ceremony. Young people are told to "be sure this is the right person." It is often assumed that, given sufficient opportunity to meet members of the other sex and to date, the adolescent will work through the various crushes and stages of "puppy love" and be prepared for the "real thing." This notion of the validity or desirability of a variety of premarital experiences may help explain why so many adults are opposed to early marriages, early engagements, and the whole business of adolescents going steady. But at the same time adults are insisting young people not make any rash judgments or take any hasty actions, society is providing numerous situations which encourage and actually demand early mate selection.

In this chapter we will examine the factors in our social system which lead to the romance and courtship theme while noting some of the processes by which adolescents enter into heterosexual associations and the nature of these relationships.

### INDIVIDUAL CHOICE

Unlike some other societies we place great stress on the freedom of choice in mate selection. While the notion is that marriages will have a higher probability of success if entered into by people of similar racial, religious, and class backgrounds, nonetheless parents rarely control fully the choice of marriage partners. On the contrary, practical concerns are often kept in the background while true love is pictured as the force which can overcome most obstacles. The idea that marriages will be arranged by parents without the opinions and sentiments of their children taken into consideration is not part of the American approach to marriage. At the same time, it would not be accurate to leave the impression that parents and others are uninvolved in steering youth toward specific types of marriage partners. Homogeneity in class, racial, and religious background is most frequently emphasized. If placed on a continuum of importance no doubt race would be considered most salient, followed by religion and, finally, social class position. Although in a few instances people of different racial backgrounds do marry, these are exceptional cases rarely accepted by most members of the society.

In terms of interreligious marriage the evidence available would indicate that while this phenomenon is far from growing, the frequency of "out-marriages" has increased over the past twenty years. From a number of scattered empirical studies we know most young people prefer to marry someone from their own religious group, although how strongly these sentiments are felt does vary. A survey conducted by *Fortune Magazine* in 1942 indicates that seven out of ten Jewish adolescents in an Eastern industrial city said they would not want to marry someone outside their religion.[1] It is important to note, however, that the same survey points out many Jewish youngsters were "uncertain" as to how they would feel about marrying a non-Jew. A national survey of high school students also reported in the same issue of *Fortune* shows that 52 per cent of the Protestants and 59 per cent of the Catholics would not consider marrying a Jew. In respect to marriage there definitely are degrees of acceptability between the various religious groups. In all probability Jews and Catholics would place the strongest sanctions against marriage between Jews and Catholics while both groups would be more amenable to marriage with Protestants. Despite these variations it would appear that the socialization of the child includes pressures opposing interreligious marriage.

The extent of marriage between people from different socioeconomic groupings rarely has been studied by American sociologists. The few investigations available are the work of Europeans who attempt to compare their countries and the United States. One such study was conducted by J. R. Hall. He reports that England, Wales,

---

[1] "The Fortune Survey," *Fortune Magazine,* November, 1942, p. 10.

and the United States provide relatively frequent opportunities for marriage between the classes.[2] The findings of Hall along with the work of Gottlieb and Spaeth suggest that marriage between individuals from different social class groupings is no longer rare in this country. Gottlieb and Spaeth examined the marriage patterns of a national sample of American graduate students. They found that over 30 per cent of the male graduate students had married women either above or below their own socioeconomic grouping.[3] No doubt the rate of marriage across class lines is correlated with level of formal education. We would propose that by the time students complete four years of college, differences in outlook as determined by family socioeconomic background will be at a minimum. The college, in fact, acts as a social class equalizer, bringing together people from a variety of statuses and teaching them a common set of attitudes, values, and behavior patterns. In addition, the formal democratic climate of many colleges and universities tends to limit many forms of social class segregation. The exception would, of course, be colleges that cater only to an economic elite and certain fraternities and sororities which limit membership to the more affluent students.

Despite these informal restrictions which may act to control the kinds of mates people will select, the prevailing sentiment in our society is with the individual. In the final analysis he is expected to initiate and negotiate the courtship and marriage process. The fact that the individual must both find and convince a potential mate, with a minimum of interference from outsiders, leads to an early concern with courtship and marriage.

## INSTITUTIONAL SETTINGS ENCOURAGING EARLY HETEROSEXUAL RELATIONSHIPS

Many popular critics of the American scene have commented on the overorganization of our leisure-time activities. From the writings of these critics it would appear that many Americans, and this includes the young, do little as individuals but in fact spend most of their time with others within some organized activity. There can be little doubt that many American schools—ranging from the elementary schools to institutions of higher education—do provide numerous programs of an extracurricular nature. It is not uncommon for ele-

/cont

---

[2] J. R. Hall, "A Comparison of the Degree of Social Endogamy in England, Wales and the U.S.A.," David Glass, (ed.), *Social Mobility in Britain* (London: Routledge and Kegan Paul, 1954).

[3] David Gottlieb and Joe L. Spaeth, "The Carrot and the Stick: Some Financial Patterns of American Graduate Students," paper read at the 1959 meetings of The Society for Social Research.

mentary schools to conduct classes in popular dancing and to foster any one of a number of clubs not officially affiliated with the formal school program. As we go up the academic ladder the number of such activities increases, with the American high school and college attaining the maximum in outside activities and programs. The following announcement from the first page of a high school newspaper is indicative of the importance and visibility of these activities:

> It is important, of course, to know your school work and get those lessons done but don't overdo it. Most people feel that too much study causes you to neglect some of the other important parts of growing up. Now is your chance to go further and develop a well rounded personality. Don't be a creep—learn to dance and see how much fun school can be. Today at 4:00 there will be free lessons in the gym class on the Frug, Bossa Nova and Fox Trot. You don't have to be the one that never gets a date. Learn the steps and practice with a guy or gal from our school. Remember 4:00 for those of you who want to do more.

While some schools would be less emphatic in their approach, the motivations for such activities are similar in many places. The idea seems to be that the "well-rounded person" must have more in his day-to-day activities than just serious academic content. Although the school is not the only adult-directed agency which provides for the leisure-time pursuits of the young, it is probably the most important. Acting as a source for the organization of these activities, the school does encourage early heterosexual interaction. Being without a date for the Friday evening football game, the class dance, the school play, homecoming events, the Coronation Ball, and so forth lessens the prestige of the student and gives him a feeling of isolation from the mainstream of school activities. Since many of these activities actually demand couples it is not strange that at a fairly early age students begin to groom themselves for entrance into the events. Since these extracurricular programs rarely call for intellectual skills it is not surprising that the criteria for popularity are rarely related to academic achievement. On the contrary, as James S. Coleman and others have noted, popularity within the school setting increases with the possession of attributes such as fashionable clothing, proper grooming, athletic skill, possession of a car, personal looks, and financial status. Coleman points out that for the boys in his sample high schools being an athlete was more likely to be correlated with popularity among girls than being a scholar. As for the girls, he finds that an important path to fame and popularity in the high school is dating popular boys and that girls successful with boys received greater recognition from other girls than did girls classified as brains.[4]

---

[4] James S. Coleman, *The Adolescent Society* (New York: The Free Press of Glencoe, 1962), pp. 143, 165.

Popularity among college students follows a similar pattern. Studies of university students at the University of Chicago[5] and Purdue University[6] suggest that for boys the major concern is with the girls' romantic sex appeal, a well-proportioned body, and affectionate responses. The girls stressed social sophistication, moderation in behavior, and financial status.

The extent these criteria are accepted by all youth or even a majority will be discussed in a later section of this chapter. For the moment, however, it is sufficient to point out that the school does provide a multitude of nonacademic programs for the young and that these programs frequently call for the participation of male and female partners. In addition, the criteria for mate selection do not necessarily reflect the formal declarations of the academic system.

Aside from the school, other social institutions and agencies supply leisure-time pursuits for the young. Again, as in the case of the school, a number of these activities either encourage or stimulate dating. Youth programs of various church groups frequently include dances, picnics, hayrides and parties. In each case these hetrosexual social events act to encourage an interest in members of the opposite sex.

We may well ask the question: what kinds of young people are *not included* among those who participate in the heterosexual activities based on dating? Two students at a large Midwestern state university attempted to get some answers by observing students in the university library on Friday and Saturday evenings during the course of a five-week period. Their observations and impressions are reported below:

> With the exception of the period prior to mid-term examinations we found the following: (1) Few of the students in the library were members of a Greek organization (fraternity and sorority); (2) most of the girls were not of the type that would be considered cool on this campus. They tend to be heavy, not well dressed and not very attractive. The boys were very much the same with few wearing the kinds of clothes considered acceptable in current college fashions. A lot of the boys wore glasses; some had beards. The boys were either very fat or very thin; (3) Most of these kids were studying by themselves. Kids who were on study dates seemed to look different, dress different and act different.

While these comments are not based on a tight systematic analysis, we, from our own different kinds of academic experiences, would concur in general with the reported observations. This does not mean that youth who are not part of the popular culture will not become involved in heterosexual activities. On the contrary, although the

[5] Eleanor and J. H. Greenberg, "Courtship Values of a Youth Sample," *American Sociological Review*, VIII (December, 1953), p. 635–40.

[6] Harold T. Christensen, *Marriage Analysis* (New York: The Ronald Press Co., 1950).

empirical evidence available is limited it would seem safe to say that many young people do find some peer group which will provide potential dating partners. The nature of these associations and the makeup of the different youth subcultures will be discussed in our chapter on adolescent relationships with peers and adults.

Strange as it might seem, the socialization agency which provides the fewest organized activities for youth is the family. This is not to say parents are uninvolved in furthering the emphasis on early heterosexual activities; rather, the family per se does little, with the exception of birthday parties and graduation celebrations, to organize leisure-time events for adolescents. Parents are, however, very much concerned with the social status and activities of their children and frequently attempt to provide the kinds of materials and encouragements which will lead to popularity. This phenomenon of parental encouragement and pressures is most likely to manifest itself during the time the child is in high school or college.

Most parents are not oblivious to the many social events that are part of adolescence and will show concern when their youngsters are not included in these activities. The degree of parental sophistication and involvement is no doubt related to socioeconomic status. Because of their greater involvement within the school and community middle-class parents will have a greater awareness of these social activities and play a more active role in moving their children into these events. Middle-class parents, as compared to those from the lower economic groups, are more likely to enroll their youngsters in dance classes, provide financial assistance, and teach the importance of social graces. In addition, many middle-class adults have been to college and therefore recognize the importance of nonacademic programs in the everyday life of the college student. Involvement of parents is also related to the sex of the child. We would speculate that many parents of older female adolescents begin to experience some anxiety as they recognize their daughters are not part of adolescent social life.

The extent to which young people find "good times" outside of the home can be noted from the research of George Lundberg and his associates.[7] The authors find that the great majority of young people studied (796 cases) state that some other place than home was the scene for "the most enjoyable activity" of the year. Five per cent of the boys and less than 20 per cent of the girls selected home. In most cases, for both boys and girls the setting for the most enjoyable ex-

---

[7] George A. Lundberg, Mirra Komarovsky, and Mary Alice McInerny, *Leisure: A Suburban Study* (New York: Columbia University Press, 1934).

perience was some informal gathering with a group of peers. Boys placed heavy importance on such activities as sports and outings while girls chose these along with parties and dances.

The social programs of the various institutions discussed create a situation where young people must, if they are to remain part of the adolescent society, enter into heterosexual relationships. From an early age the young person comes to recognize that acceptance by peers and by many adults will be influenced by involvement in these social events. By the time youths enter junior high school many activities are of a type which demand a companion of the opposite sex. Failure to attend these events is frequently taken as an indication the individual is unable to find a willing partner. The nature of these activities and the frequency with which they occur stimulates an early concern with dating popularity and heterosexual behavior.

## THE MASS MEDIA AND ROMANTIC LOVE

The romantic love theme seems to be characteristic of Western society and is perhaps most elaborate in the United States. To some degree at least, the romantic climate may be attributed to the various outlets of the American mass media. As was noted in chapter two, much of the formal communication directed at young people in our society stresses the importance and goodness of being part of a romantic relationship. The many teen magazines supply cues as to the attributes needed to attract a member of the opposite sex as well as the names of potential romance partners. The popular music directed at adolescents usually describes love among young people. Many of these songs emphasize the enduring fidelity of young people who hold onto their chosen mate despite adult interferences. The song "Patches" is but one example that can be cited. This is the story of a young girl who comes from "the other side of the tracks" and is loved by a middle-class boy. The boy's parents are opposed to the relationship and prevent the young man from seeing his girl. So great is the sorrow of the girl that she commits suicide and is found "floating face down in the river." Contrary to the notion that young men are frivolous and insincere, our young man does not forget his love. His reaction to the news of the girl's death leads him instead to say, "no matter where you are I will join you tonight my Patches." The popularity of this song is not unique and, in fact, it would appear that many of the songs most endorsed by youth are ones that follow a similar theme. Love that is misunderstood or destroyed by an unsympathetic adult world is an intrinsic part of songs which have been most popular with adolescents. In addition, we find that those songs declaring that being in love is part of growing up or is part of the youthful years are the ones that become "teen hits." We would question the notion that it takes only a loud voice or a fast melody to make a musical hit with youth. The words of the song are important and in many cases young people will dedicate songs to peers which they feel express their most sincere sentiments.

Aside from popular music and the teen magazines there is the romance-encouraging phenomen of television and the movies. In this case the media may work in two ways: first, they give young people popular heros they can identify with and include in imaginary romance relationships; second, they may reinforce the already prevailing climate which stresses the saliency of romance. We are not suggesting there is always, or even usually, a direct one-to-one relationship between the stimuli of the media and the behavior of the adolescent. Rather, we would take the position that the mass media provide ideas and cues which the adolescent may incorporate into his thinking about dating, romance, and perhaps marriage. Regardless of the direct impact of the mass media on youth behavior—and there is little consensus among adults on this issue—it seems fair to say these media do little to thwart the young person's concern with matters of love and romance.

Up to this point we have discussed the factors within the structure of our society which contribute to the importance of the romantic theme among adolescents. In the remaining portions of this chapter we will deal with the factors which adolescents appear to take into consideration when selecting a date partner, and the sexual behavior of young people.

## SELECTION OF PARTNERS AND THE DATING PROCESS

In many parts of the United States dating as a relationship involving two members of the opposite sex occurs when the child is about twelve years old. At this stage the date is usually centered about some activity such as a party, picnic, dance, or hayride. Rarely are young people of this age category involved in a date independent of the peer group. Usually date partners will be youngsters from the same school class or children familiar to the parents of those involved in the date. Chaperones are not uncommon and frequently adults will plan and supervise the activities of the young couples. These group dating activities will, in most instances, involve youth of similar socioeconomic and experience backgrounds. Concern is not so much with the individual characteristics of the date partner but rather with previous acquaintanceship. No doubt the fact that these activities are sponsored by adults will act to limit the scope of possible dates. In addition, since this is a new experience both partners are less anxious when there has been some previous social interaction. For this age group the first date is often a cooperative event involving members of two cliques from the opposite sex. The following illustration written by a high school girl describes the process:

> I had my first date when I was in the eighth grade. This was a hayride followed by a party at the house of one of the girls. All of the kids knew each other since these were the same boys that we had known in school and in the neighborhood. All of the girls were so excited about the whole thing. We were calling each other on the phone a week before the party and a week after the party. After this party there were many more. Usually one of the girls' mothers would arrange the whole thing. There were a couple of parties at the homes of the boys. They were usually to celebrate a birthday. There were no regular dates; usually you would go with a different boy to each party. Most of the times a girl would ask the boy and you did not want the boy to know you liked him so you asked a different one each time. I guess you could not really call these dates. We really started to date during the ninth grade.

A more definitive dating process becomes clear during the fourteenth year. This stage of development sees a growing concern with the more personal attributes of the dating partner, a greater range of mate selection, and a shift away from group-centered dating activities. In August Hollingshead's study of *Elmtown's Youth*, 20 per cent of the girls and 15 per cent of the boys reported they had their first dates when they were thirteen years of age. By the fifteenth year Hollingshead notes that over 90 per cent of the boys and girls are dating.[8]

The rapid increase in dating from the ages of twelve to fifteen can be explained in several ways. First, overt parental opposition to dating decreases. Second, the number of activities open to adolescents which call for dating partners increases. Third, the scope of potential dating partners increases because the high school, which enrolls students of various backgrounds, places adolescents in a position where they are likely to come in contact with other young people different from themselves in respect to social class, religion, values, and interests. As a result, the possibility of youth-adult conflicts increases, too. At the earlier stages of development, parents play an important role in the selection of the dating partner and the nature of the date. But by the time the adolescent is involved in the high school social system, dating activities have moved from the control of parents to agencies outside of the home. This shift from the home keeps parental involvement in the content of the dating activity at a minimum.

---

[8] August B. Hollingshead, *Elmtown's Youth* (New York: John Wiley & Sons, 1949), p. 225.

In addition, contact with a more diverse population of adolescents may create situations where parents and adolescents disagree as to the acceptability of a particular dating partner. This is not to suggest that parents are no longer in a position to block the dating process, but rather that the probability of youth-parent disagreements will increase since there is now a greater chance the youngsters will associate with individuals who do not fit the ideal held by parents. The comments of one high school girl provide some insight as to how these conflicts might arise:

When I was in the tenth grade I met a boy whom I liked very much. We never really dated but just talked together in the hall and once in a while we had a Coke. After a few weeks he called me at home and asked if I would go to a movie with him. I said yes. I told my mother about the date and she wanted to know all about the boy. I knew that once she found out he was Catholic it would cause trouble so I never told her about that. That Saturday night he came over to the house to pick me up. I introduced him to my parents and he was very nice and so were they. Later that evening when I came home my mother asked me more questions. Finally she came right out and asked about the boy's religion. I said he was Catholic and she was quite upset. She said that she did not think it was a good idea for me to date a Catholic boy and that it would only cause trouble later on. I said that he was a nice boy and that his religion was not that important to me. She then started to talk about marriage and how if I started to date a Catholic boy I might want to marry one when I got older. I told my mother that was a silly idea and just because you date a boy does not mean you will marry him. It went on like that for quite a while and my mother finally insisted that I could no longer date this boy. After that I would meet him at school and see him around but he never took me out or came to my home.

Aside from the greater range of dating activities and the availability of more dating partners, the change in dating patterns from the younger ages is very much influenced by the ownership or use of an automobile. The car gives the adolescent "wheels" and permits a greater range of mobility as well as greater freedom from adult supervision. Each of these factors—expectations that high school students will date; increase in dating activities available to the adolescent; broader range of dating partners; and the automobile—contribute to a growing interest in dating and a higher frequency of dating among young people.

From the observations and research of those concerned with adolescent dating behavior it would appear that during the high school period change also occurs in the criteria employed by adolescents in their preferences for dating partners.

As has been pointed out, the first dating pattern is based on clique activities involving youth who have known each other from early childhood. The emphasis is not so much on the personal attributes of the individual as on previous social interaction and activity interests.

Once group-centered dating activities have changed to those involving two members of the opposite sex as a social unit, concern with the personal characteristics and attributes of the potential dating partner becomes greater.

In discussing what it takes to be popular with peers in the American high school, Coleman finds that both boys and girls place greater importance on "nonacademic" qualities than on attributes directly related to the formal educational process. As noted in a previous chapter, when boys are asked what impresses the girls they rank "being an athlete" first, followed by "being in the leading crowd" and "having a nice car." The girls in the Coleman study perceive that popularity with boys will be determined by "being in the leading crowd," "a leader in activities," and "having nice clothes." For the most part both boys and girls endorse the same items with the girls substituting "nice clothes" for a "nice car." It is interesting to note that for both sexes little importance is attributed to "coming from the right family" as a source for popularity. This is further indication that adolescents appear to be more concerned with achieved status than with ascriptive factors.[9]

Other investigators who have examined the dating behavior of high school and college students conclude that dating prestige is related to the possession of specific symbols. Willard Waller, in his study of college students, finds successful men belonged to a better fraternity, danced well, and were socially active. He adds that this elite group dressed well and had a car as well as a good line. They preferred girls who were attractive, danced well, dressed well, and were popular.[10]

In a test of the saliency of these symbols, Robert O. Blood, Jr., studied a sample of students at the University of Michigan. He found that while "personality factors" were ranked above other items, male students felt their dating currency was enhanced by possession of looks, cars, clothes, and membership in an elite fraternity.[11]

Whether the concern is with high school youth or college students, most investigators agree dating popularity is very much related to the physical presentation of self. In the competition for dates girls face the more severe obstacles since they are required to meet the expectations of the male pursuer. In many cases the girl who best fits the male ideal has the higher dating potential. On the other hand, the girl who is less able to conform to the ideal type may resort

---

[9] Coleman, *op. cit.* pp. 45–50.

[10] Willard Waller, "The Rating and Dating Complex," *American Sociological Review*, Vol. II (October, 1937), pp. 727–34.

[11] Robert O. Blood, Jr., "A Retest of Waller's Rating Complex," *Marriage and Family Living*, Vol. XVIII (February, 1955), pp. 41–47.

to socially unacceptable behavior in order to inflate her dating status.

An additional factor which will play some part in the dating process is the age of the individual. Among adolescents of the same sex, we find that younger students may be left out of certain activities while older students frequently take over leadership positions on both the formal and informal level. Since in dating as well as in marriage males are expected to be older than females, the younger boy within a particular high school or college may find himself with limited dating potential. On the other hand, older girls might find themselves unable to obtain dates since they are too old for males of their own age grade as well as for males who are younger. In some American colleges this period of date scarcity is referred to as "senior slump" by older female students.

In discussing research dealing with dating criteria it is important that the reader recognize the shortcomings of some of these investigations. The term "date" does not have universal consensus and may take on different meanings for different youth in different settings. A "coffee" or "Coke" date is not the same as a "study" date and all three differ from a date involving a formal dance followed by a late supper. The selection of a partner for a dorm picnic or a "grasser" (an informal off-campus affair usually held in some secluded field where beer drinking seems to be an essential element) may involve different criteria. By allowing the adolescent to define the term "date" as he wishes, the investigators may be dealing with a multitude of activities as opposed to some single variable.

A second methodological shortcoming of these studies is that attempts to validate the young persons' responses are rare. The lack of confirmation of actual dating behavior means there is little control over individuals who have a need to overestimate their dating record; nor is there any way to evaluate the reliability of reports of dating patterns which occurred in years gone by.

Finally, most of these dating studies have dealt with youth in high school or with a select group of college students. We know little about the dating history of nonschool adolescents or the criteria they employ in selecting dating partners. Nor, by concentrating on fraternity and sorority members at specific types of colleges, can we learn much about the total dating picture among many college students. Members of fraternities and sororities doubtlessly will differ in some respects from other college students in their choice of dates and in the nature of their dating activities. Studies dealing with college students from many schools would certainly indicate that not only are there great variations in the social climates of the schools themselves but that college students are not a homogeneous population in respect to values, attitudes, aspirations, and behavior. David Gottlieb and Benjamin Hodgkins in their study of college students identify four student sub-cultures classified as "vocational," "deviant," "academic," and "collegiate." The authors show that each of these groups differs significantly in grade point average, concern with religion and politics, involvement in extracurricular activities, and postcollege plans.[12] Clearly there would be every reason to believe that students from these various subcultures will differ to some extent in what they see as the ideal dating partner. In addition, we would expect that attitudes toward the "ideal date" will change once the young person reaches the stage where he begins to give serious consideration to selecting a spouse. The more visible attributes as well as the possession of certain status symbols will no doubt be challenged by the desire for a serious, dependable, and capable partner.

## THE SEXUAL BEHAVIOR OF ADOLESCENTS

The shortcomings of research in the area of dating and dating partners are only slight when compared with available studies dealing with the sexual behavior of youth. Each of the methodological factors noted earlier is greatly exaggerated in these reported accounts of adolescent sexual activities. To the best of our knowledge, no behavioral scientist has ever attempted to measure the intensity of sexual relations among any segment of the population by actual observation. In every case the approach is to ask the respondent what he did, when he did it, and how he did it. This is one area of human behavior virtually impossible to study by actual observation. The investigator must, by necessity, base his findings on what he is told. The unfortunate problem is that many behavioral scientists dealing with this area make the assumption that what the respondent says is "the gospel." In writing up their research findings there is a tendency to pass over the factual situation—that these are the expressions of respondents—and treat the data as if they were based on empirical observation. Our emphasis on the limitations of these investigations is not meant as an attack on our colleagues but rather as a warning to the reader. Given these problems in the study of adolescent behavior, we turn now to a review of the materials which have been published in this area.

Most investigators suggest that heterosexual behavior falls into spe-

---

[12] David Gottlieb and Benjamin Hodgkins, "College Students' Subcultures: Their Structure and Characteristics in Relation to Student Attitude Change," *The School Review*, Autumn, 1964.

cific categories of developmental intensity. The stages appear to range all the way from no physical contact at one end of the continuum, through the holding of hands, a single kiss, kissing, body embrace, and the fondling of the body, to sexual intercourse at the other. Generally, this developmental process is seen to be related to age and personal experiences. The young person is likely to go through each of the stages noted above, with perhaps some modifications. Personal attitudes and situational opportunities will, of course, play some part in how rapidly the adolescent moves through the various stages and there can be no guarantee each stage will be covered prior to marriage. From a developmental point of view, the "hand holding" phase would occur in early adolescence while premarital sexual intercourse would most probably be between the eighteenth and twentieth year. Obviously, the probability of intimate sexual relations will be associated with the situation in which the individual finds himself with respect to the availability of partners and the prevailing value system. Winston Ehrman, for example, in his study of premarital dating behavior points out that veterans are more likely to have experienced sexual intercourse than nonveterans.[13] This finding would be anticipated since veterans in college are usually older than nonveteran peers and have usually had a greater exposure to potential sexual partners.

As the adolescent grows older the opportunities for heterosexual association increase and the prevailing social climate becomes less and less restrictive. Necking and petting are not uncommon in many American high schools and in some schools the girl who refuses to enter into these activities finds herself without a date. On the other hand, the girl who "goes too far" may lose both her reputation and respect from both male and female peers. It would seem that some unwritten or unstated norm exists as to acceptable sexual behavior and the adolescent who does not abide by the norm will be penalized. The system, as noted earlier, will place some adolescents in a difficult situation since heterosexual popularity is related to variables such as good looks, nice clothing, money, and proper group membership. The young person who does not possess these attributes is less able to compete in the dating market and may resort to unacceptable sexual behavior in order to enhance dating potential.

On the college level there is some modification in the value system and generally a lowering of personal restrictions on what is and what is not acceptable sexual behavior. This does not mean a formal decla-

_/ cont._

---

[13] Winston Ehrman, *Premarital Dating Behavior* (New York: Henry Holt & Co., 1959).

ration that sexual intercourse is now acceptable but rather that under certain conditions sexual intimacy may be forgiven, or at least understood. One primary condition which makes sexual intercourse more understandable among college-age students is sincere love and some formal marriage commitment on the part of the couple. Where such a commitment is apparent fewer sanctions seem to be imposed by peers. Again, however, it should be noted that the reaction of peers will be related to the particular value system of the peer group. Among some college youth rejection of premarital sexual relations is viewed as part of "middle-class morality" and therefore a value to be flouted. For many other college students the expressed feeling on premarital sex relations is one of personal rejection along with the idea that "what others do is their own business."

Regardless of peer-group sentiments it is apparent a double standard does exist among adolescents on the question of proper sexual behavior. With few exceptions most investigators report agreement among males and females that males have had more extensive sexual experience; that they should have more experience; and that while a male nonvirgin is acceptable as a marriage partner, a female nonvirgin may not be considered suitable. The impact of this double standard can be seen all through the various periods of child development and adulthood. The male who engages in early sexual activity will be considered somewhat of a popular hero by his male peers while the promiscuous female will frequently meet with scorn and contempt. Beyond the age of adolescence a similar double standard can be found. Few adults would endorse adultery but they are less likely to become indignant when the act is committed by a husband than by a wife.

Studies of the incidence of sexual intercourse among adolescents would certainly indicate the male has the greater premarital sexual contact. In reviewing some eighteen studies concerned with the sexual behavior of young people, we find great variation in the proportion of males who say they have engaged in premarital sexual intercourse. The average incidence is about 50 per cent. In other words, if we look at the findings of numerous researchers who have studied this phenomenon we see that about one out of every two males interviewed reports premarital sexual relations. For the females the range averages to about 25 per cent, or one out of every four females interviewed.[14] As was noted earlier, the significance of these findings must be evaluated within the framework of our cultural norms—norms

---

[14] For a more detailed discussion of the studies referred to here, the reader should see Ehrmann, *op. cit.*, pp. 33–37.

which would no doubt cause an inflation of the reported incidence among males and a deflation among females.

A further indication of the operation of a double standard is found in the work of Gilbert. His research conducted with adolescents in 1951 shows that 72 per cent of the females, but only 27 per cent of the males, were willing to marry a nonvirgin.[15] From the material presented by Gilbert as well as the data collected by others it appears that females are more liberal in their consideration of marital partners. This attitude on the part of the female is certainly influenced by our value system which tends to encourage male promiscuity while placing strict prohibitions on the actions of females. In addition, the sentiments of the females reflect a greater concern with the love theme—a theme built around the notion that sexual intercourse is not merely a means to biological gratification but an expression of a constant and sincere attachment to another person.

Differences in how males and females view premarital sexual intercourse can be seen in how both groups respond to questions dealing with reasons for "not going farther in heterosexual behavior." In ranking reasons, Ehrmann reports that "morals," "fear," and "no desire" were most frequently mentioned by the females in his sample. Males, on the other hand, mentioned "dates would not," "respect for date," and "morals" as their primary reasons. As Ehrmann points out, "Female sexual expression is primarily and profoundly related to being in love and to going steady. Male sexuality is more indirectly and less exclusively associated with romanticism and intimacy relationships."[16]

Males are not unaware of the females' concern with love and greater hesitancy in becoming involved in intimate sexual relations. Keeping this in mind, the male will frequently attempt to convince the female of his love and devotion. Ernest Smith refers to this phenomenon as "the ritual of the line," a process in which the boy seeks to convince the girl that "he has fallen in love with her and is thereby inviting her to reciprocate and permit intimacies."[17]

Although a double standard does exist we should not assume the female is entirely passive in matters of heterosexual behavior. Generally there appears to be a system of mutual exploitation with males seeking the sexual exploitation of females and females seeking the

---

[15] Gilbert Youth Research, "How Wild Are College Students?" *Pageant*, 1951, 7: pp. 10–21.

[16] Ehrmann, *op. cit.*, p. 269.

[17] Ernest A. Smith, *American Youth Culture* (New York: The Free Press of Glencoe, 1962), p. 165.

social-economic exploitation of males. Ehrmann, after studying the premarital sexual behavior of college students, concludes:

Yet in more ways than one it is a sorry picture, where both boys and girls are offered exploitative roles, the boys playing on each girl's hope of permanence and early marriage to get cheap and immediate and unsatisfactory sexual compliance, the girl playing on the vulnerability of the boy who begins to court her by entangling him in sexual intimacy which will propel him toward marriage.[18]

## SUMMARY

In dealing with adolescent courtship and the romantic theme we have attempted to pinpoint the factors in our society which contribute to an early concern with heterosexual behavior. We have shown how our system of individual choice, the structure of our social institutions, and the mass media combine to enhance the probability that young people will move toward both a concern for and involvement with members of the opposite sex. In later portions of this chapter we dealt more specifically with the dating process and sexual behavior of young people, indicating that research pertaining to these phenomena must be subject to careful re-evaluation since reported findings are based on expressions of behavior as opposed to actual empirical observation.

We attempted to show there are probably differences among young people in how they view dating, their criteria for date selection, and their feelings toward intimate sexual behavior. While one single theme may dominate in date selection and sexual behavior among young people, the situation is such that we are not able to generalize to all adolescents in all settings.

Finally, we have emphasized the notion of the double standard in adolescent heterosexual behavior in order to show how members of both sexes view the total rating, dating, and courtship complex. Generally, it would appear the female does take on the role of the pursued while the male plays the part of the pursuer. Yet the double standard is not completely unjust since the female can, if she so desires, control the level of sexual intimacy and exploit, to some extent, her male partner.

---

[18] Ehrmann, *op. cit.*, p. xvii.

# Chapter X

## SOCIAL CONTROL: RELATIONSHIPS
## WITH PEERS AND ADULTS

A central theme in this book is that youth shifts, over time, from social control by adults to a growing influence by peers, and then, once again, to a concern with the attitudes, values and expectations of the adult world. This process can be seen in the diagram below.

FIGURE 10–1    AGE STATUS AND PRESTIGE-GIVING FACTORS

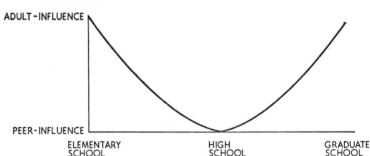

Several points must be clarified in regard to this diagram. First, we are dealing here with youth within the formal educational system and not young people outside the social structure of the school. Second, this is a general model and does not take into account the obvious deviations which will be found among certain students in certain kinds of schools. The model itself is based on the observations of numerous investigators who have dealt with the general problem of youth societies and youth behavior. Three, an inherent assumption in the proposed model is that young people as well as adults will be guided in their interpersonal relations by the degree to which these interpersonal relations provide some goal fulfillment. In other words, people will differ in their preference for certain kinds of personal recognition and rewards and will move toward those reference groups perceived to be most able to fulfill the end goals. We are pro-

184

posing that students, as they progress through their academic training, will change in the kinds of recognition they desire. We have dichotomized these recognitions along an academic-nonacademic continuum. The nonacademic is identified as "social-personal" as contrasted with the normative recognition for scholarly and intellectual recognition. Finally, we are suggesting that adults within the formal school setting are identified with the academic goals while peers are seen as best fulfilling the desire for social recognition. Generally, then, the model presented in Figure 10–1 suggests it is at the very beginning and very end of one's educational involvement that we find the greatest concern with academic recognition, and this type of recognition is seen as coming from adult members of the school system. By the time the individual is well into his high school studies the desire for academic recognition has shifted dramatically to a preference for social status within the school community. It is in the high school, as we and others have noted, that the adolescent society comes into full bloom. The student moving out of high school and into college is still concerned about peer-oriented rewards, but this tends to decline as he moves through college and all but disappears by the time he begins his professional graduate training.[1]

The incoming school child sees the school as a setting where learning in the formal sense is to take place. Parents, in anticipation of the first day of school, encourage their children to be good and "listen to the teacher." As the child moves from one grade to the next the student culture takes hold and personal and social factors tend to become more salient. Apparently, personal and social factors attain their maximum influence at the high school level; at this point of development the adolescent is between age-grade stages and is most dependent on his peers. This appears to be a most crucial point in the young person's life with respect to identification with specific roles. It is at this stage that young people in our society exhibit the greatest conflict as to where they belong vis-à-vis the adult world. The formal educational process is directed at teaching them that they have a responsibility to their family and to the community while in reality the society is structured in such a manner that involvement in "grown-up" activities is kept at a minimum. For many young people the only alternative available seems to be a greater involvement with the peer group. Certainly the dimensions of the youth society are clear and apparent to the adolescent. He knows what it takes to attain

---

[1] This model and much of the discussion which follows appeared in W. B. Brookover and David Gottlieb, *Sociology of Education* (rev. ed.; New York: American Book Company, 1963).

‐status and acceptance with his peers while he is uncertain just what adults prefer.

The disparity between what the adolescent feels and what he thinks adults feel can be seen from the research of Robert D. Hess and Irene Goldblatt. The investigators asked a sample of adolescents to make ratings on: (1) the average teenager, (2) the average adult, (3) teenagers from the viewpoint of an adult, and (4) adults from the viewpoint of an adult. Similarily, parents of the young people included in this study were asked to rate (1) the average teenager, (2) the average adult, (3) teenagers from the viewpoint of a teenager and (4) adults from the viewpoint of a teenager. In this way the authors were able to note areas of agreement and disagreement in how adolescents and parents view one another. The authors found:

1. Adolescents and parents agree in expressing mildly favorable opinions of teenagers.

2. Adolescents tend to idealize adults—that is, they have much higher opinions of adults than the parents have.

3. Adolescents see a relatively greater status difference between teenagers and adults than the parents see.

4. Adolescents believe the average adult has a generalized tendency to depreciate teenagers. They feel teenagers have a uniformly low reputation among adults.

5. Parents anticipate teenagers will have a selective tendency to undervalue adults. They predict adults will get lower ratings than they merit on items which refer to interpersonal relationships, but that they will be accurately evaluated on noninterpersonal-maturity items.

6. Adolescents believe the adults will evaluate themselves relatively accurately.

7. Parents believe teenagers have unrealistically high opinions of themselves.

8. Both adolescents and parents believe the status difference between teenagers and adults will be distorted to approximately the same extent by the other group.[2]

These findings would certainly indicate a lack of consensus between adolescents and adults as to just where each stands within the social order. Again, we suggest that the lack of clarity as to what adults expect and desire is one factor contributing to the adolescents' tendency to move toward peer-group involvements.

As the transition from high school to college takes place, the importance of the social-personal factors gradually declines until at the graduate school or adult level, the academic aspects of the social system become most important again. Part of the decline in personal-social factors may be attributed to student selectivity. In other words, the more education a person undertakes beyond high school the more serious he will be about his academic activities and training. Al-

---

[2] Robert D. Hess and Irene Goldblatt, "The Status of Adolescents in American Society: A Problem in Social Identity," *Child Development*, Vol. 28 (1957), pp. 459–68.

though we have not tested this theoretical curve empirically, we feel there are data to support its validity. Talcott Parsons, in a discussion of the classroom as a social system, notes that the elementary school phase is concerned with the child's internalization of motivation to achieve and that the focus is on the level of capacity. The secondary school, because of its abundance of activities and variety of curricular matter, subjects the student to a wider range of statuses, peers, and adults, and forces him to choose among alternatives within the framework of the system.[3]

Several researchers have emphasized the importance of personal and social factors as status determinants at the high school level. Gordon notes the importance of semiformal organizations (extracurricular activities) and of the informal organization of students as agencies where students gain or lose personal prestige. Although it is difficult from his analysis to determine the total impact of each of his organizational components, it is clear that knowledge and concern with intellectual pursuits does little to enhance a high school student's standing with his peers.[4]

James Coleman points out some consequences of the student culture. His research indicates that a possible effect of the student value system on education is removal of the highly intelligent students from an academic achievement orientation to one that holds greater prestige among peers. Coleman contends that academic achievement as a status-giving item is of such little importance to students that some potentially excellent students move away from academic achievement to concentrate on participation in extracurricular activities because these are the things that give a student status with his peers.[5]

On the college level we see a similar picture. Philip E. Jacob concludes that institutions of higher education do little to alter the value systems of their students. He contends that changes in college student values are not so much a product of faculty and formal influences as they are of peer-group pressures. Again, the student shows a greater concern with what he sees as important to his peers than with what he sees as important to the faculty or in accord with the expressed values of the institution.[6]

---

[3] Talcott Parsons, "The School Class as a Social System: Some of its Functions in American Society," *Harvard Educational Review* (special issue on sociology and education), Vol. XXIX, No. 4, p. 299.

[4] Wayne C. Gordon, *The Social System of a High School* (New York: The Free Press of Glencoe, 1957).

[5] James S. Coleman, "Academic Achievement and the Structure of Competition," *Harvard Educational Review*, Vol. XXIX, (Fall, 1959), pp. 330–51.

[6] Philip E. Jacob, *Changing Values in College: An Exploratory Study of the Impact of College Teaching* (New York: Harper & Bros., 1957).

Moving to the graduate-school level, while the personal factor is still of importance there is a shift to identification with the more academic elements as a basis for attaining prestige with one's peers. William Erbe investigated how a national sample of some 3,000 students in American graduate schools responded to questions asking what attributes they saw as important in giving a student prestige with faculty and peers.[7] He found that students working at the masters' level were more likely to choose "a pleasing personality" as a factor giving prestige with peers or faculty than were students enrolled at the doctorate level. In addition, he notes that while a pleasing personality ranked first out of eight items listed as a factor giving prestige among students it ranked third when applied to the faculty. Generally, the Erbe study would indicate that social-personal factors are considered more important among peers than faculty and that as the graduate student comes closer to completing his doctorate he moves closer to a concern with academic characteristics as opposed to the social-personal ones.

From this brief overview of research dealing with student values, the model outlined in Figure 10–1 does seem to reflect, at least in part, the student culture as observed in various educational institutions.

To this point we have examined specific structural conditions in our society which move individuals toward and away from the controls of youth peers and adults. Basically, our position has been that the society provides numerous activities which act to stimulate adolescents to form their own relatively isolated age-grade social systems. Secondly, it was proposed that while the adolescent society makes its expectations and values clear to the adolescent the adult world tends to present demands which are both vague and conflicting to the eyes of the adolescent. Finally, we suggest that the adolescent will turn to his peers, as opposed to adults, in an attempt to attain youth-endorsed goals. Each of these factors is interrelated and, as a total complex, acts to move the adolescent from adult social controls into the realm of peer-group domination.

## SOME VARIATIONS IN THE BEHAVIOR AND VALUES OF YOUTH: COLLEGE STUDENT SUBCULTURES

The degree to which any young person will respond to the influences of his peers will, of course, be determined by a variety of factors. Some of these intervening variables have been discussed in Chapter

---

[7] William Erbe, "Informal Group Membership and its Consequences for American Graduate Students" (paper read at the Institute for Social Research, University of Chicago, May 21, 1960).

4. Certainly, differences in the socialization and experiences of the child will play some part in the direction the individual takes as he enters and goes through the age of adolescence. In some cases, for example, he will have a choice in the selection of end goals while in other instances the structure of the society is such that freedom to choose among alternatives will be limited. The sex of the individual will place limitations on the kinds of activities he will find available. Race and socioeconomic status also contribute to the direction taken by youth and the means by which the young person seeks to attain desired goals. Despite these intervening factors, we have taken the position that young people will move through a process of alienation from adult controls to a growing dependency on age peers. Again, however, it is important to point out that the degree to which the individual relates to his peers will vary, as will the nature of these relationships. Differences will be found among adolescents in the kinds of values they endorse and in the behavior they exhibit. In terms of broad comparison, we can see the apparent contrast in the behavior of delinquent gang members as opposed to members of 4H clubs. Both groups, however, will be concerned with the preferences of peers and will have some degree of affiliation with the peer group.

In order to give the reader some added insight as to variations in youth "types" within our society, we turn to a report of research dealing with college-age individuals. Our purpose here is to identify different kinds of youth subcultures and the general nature of their attitudes, values, behavior, and expectations.[8]

While each of us would agree the behavior of youth varies, there is a tendency in our society to make broad, sweeping generalizations about young people, particularly about college students. Too often college students are described as if they were cut out of a common cloth, united in a desire to maximize social prestige even at the expense of personal integrity and general academic standing. We see in Jacob's position a furthering of the notion proposed by others who have been concerned with American youth—namely, that young people are more likely to take on the values of peers than adults even though the peer values may conflict with the values expressed by the adult population.

Given that there is diversity in the sociocultural system of America and variations in the background experiences of young people, we

---

[8] This discussion of material dealing with college youth subcultures is based, in large part, on on-going research being conducted by David Gottlieb and Benjamin Hodgkins. An initial report of these materials is published in *School Review*, Autumn, 1963, pp. 26–49, under the title, "College Student Sub-Cultures: Structure and Characteristics."

would anticipate that attendance at high school or college would not have the same net effect on all individuals. It is important, then, to determine the possible consequences such student diversity will have on attempts by a given educational institution to influence students in a specific way.

Two points must be taken into consideration when studying the influence of the educational setting upon the student: the social origins of the student and the sociocultural system implicit in high school and college life. The dynamic interaction that results when young people from diverse social origins, holding variant value orientations, attend a high school or college with yet another value orientation is of central importance if we are to understand why students hold the values they do and the extent to which they turn to peer as opposed to adult influences. We suggest, then, that there are differences in the kinds of social and academic climates that exist between schools as well as differences in the value orientations of students. Where perceived consensus exists in the mind of the student between his values and the value climate of the school, we will get one type of student behavior. When, however, there is a lack of agreement between what the student sees as important and his perception of what the school represents, we will get another. Interaction between the student and the institution does not always result in the uniform embracing of formal school values, and all this implies, but may result rather in a subgrouping of the student body, based in large part upon the student's response to the academic and social milieu of the school. We have identified such subgroups as "subcultures." Because there are no phenotypic criteria for differentiating such groups, their subtle influence is often overlooked by others.

Descriptively, we would define such a subculture as *a segment of the student body at a given institution holding a value orientation which varies sufficiently from that held by other members of the educational community.*[9] Although the research reported here deals with college students we feel the theoretical orientation presented would be applicable to high school age youth as well.

A method of identifying these subcultures is both desirable and essential. We have adopted the classifactory system suggested by Martin Trow [10] which posits the existence of four subcultures. The reason

---

[9] Some sociologists would restrict "subcultural" to cases in which the individual can meet all of life's needs from birth to death within the sub-culture. See Milton M. Gordon, "The Concept of Sub-Culture and Its Implications," *Social Forces,* Vol. 26 (October, 1947), pp. 40–42.

[10] Martin Trow, "The Campus Viewed as a Culture," *Research on College Students* (Boulder, Colo.: The Western Interstate Commission for Higher Education, 1960).

why this particular classifactory system was adopted will not be discussed here. We would only note that the terms employed by Trow agreed essentially with our own observations of student differences. Within the scope of our preceding discussion, then, these subcultures are identified as:

*Vocational.* The students within this subculture accept the vocational goal, with its emphasis on class attendance, study, and good grades, and tend to withdraw from both intellectual pursuits and social activities offered by the institution. Being "job oriented," they find little appeal in the nonapplied aspects of academic life.

*Nonconformist.* The students of this subculture are, in a sense, unique, for while coming closest to the intellectual value orientation traditionally associated with academic life, and rejecting the vocational or social phases of it, they tend to reject also the prescribed means for attaining their intellectual goal. They are intellectually curious but are nondisciplined as far as conformity to the prescribed "balance" approach to college is concerned.

*Academic.* The students within this subculture hold a value orientation closely similar to that of the college sociocultural system. Thus, while primary interest is on a broad education, vocational proficiency and social adeptness are considered desirable and are actively sought.

*Collegiate.* The students within this subculture value highly the ability to get along with and manipulate other people. Their value orientation is such that, besides enjoying social activities, they perceive them as indispensible for their later success in life. Accordingly, the intellectual and vocational aspects of academic life are minimized.

Summarizing our model, then, we have posited a unique sociocultural system existing at most institutions of higher learning. As a result of socially heterogeneous student bodies attending these institutions, with value orientations different from those of the college sociocultural system, subcultures develop within the student body which are instrumental in determining the effect college ultimately has on the student. The manner in which these subcultures develop is explained in terms of the strain for self-consistency by the individual and subsequent alienation from that part of the sociocultural system which is incongruent with his cognitive set.

Since the cognitive set of the individual is an important key to adequate classification, an instrument is necessary whereby the individual could classify himself into one of the four categories. For this instrument we developed a descriptive paragraph, based upon available research on student attitudes and behavior, for each subculture. These statements were then read to an introductory sociology class of undergraduate students about equally divided among freshmen, sophomores, and juniors (with a few seniors added). They were asked to write down anonymously which description was most appropriate to each of them as individuals and why it was. From their answers new descriptive statements were developed which incorporated to the fullest extent possible the expressions used by the students themselves. These new statements were then pretested on a fraternity and a group of students judged *a priori* by the authors to fall into specific subcultures. Approximately 80 per cent of the responses on the pretest agreed with our *a priori* judgements. It was concluded, therefore, that for preliminary research the statements would be reasonably satisfactory. The statements were subsequently included in an "Experience Inventory" containing questions relative to the students' attitudes, beliefs, and behaviors. The research instrument was completed by 977 college seniors at a large Midwest public university. The descriptive statements used for each of the subcultures were:

*Type W (vocational).* This kind of person is interested in education, but *primarily* to the point of preparation for his occupational future. He is not particularly interested in the social or purely intellectual phases of campus life, although he might participate in these activities on some limited basis. This person does his homework so that grades can be maintained, but otherwise restricts his reading to the light, general entertainment variety. *For the most part, this person's primary reason for being in college is to obtain vocational or occupational training.*

*Type X (nonconformist).* This person is interested in learning about life in general, but in a manner of his own choosing. He is very interested in the world of ideas and books, and eagerly seeks out these things. Outside of the classroom, this person would attend such activities as the lecture-concert series, Provost lectures, foreign films, etc. This person wants to go beyond the mere course requirements and will frequently do extra readings in order to obtain a more complete understanding of the world in which he lives. From a social point of view, this person tends to reject fraternities, sororities, and the social events that are a part of campus life. When this person does join, it will usually be one of the political or more academic campus organizations. *For the most part, this person would consider himself to be someone who is primarily motivated by intellectual curiosity.*

*Type Y (academic).* This person is in many respects like Type X noted above. He is concerned with books and the pursuit of knowledge, *but* is also the kind of person who does not cut himself off from the more social phases of campus life. He is interested in getting good grades (and usually tries to maintain a fairly high grade point average). *He is the kind of person who will work with student government, the campus U.N. and activities of this type. He is the kind of person who feels that the social side of college life is not the most important but is certainly significant for his general development.*

*Type Z (collegiate).* This is the kind of person who is very much concerned with the social phases of college life. He identifies closely with the college and tries to attend as many of the campus social and athletic events as possible. This person *may* be interested in intellectual kinds of things but will, for the most part, find greater satisfaction in parties, dances, football games, etc. He is concerned about his education, but feels that the development of his social skills is certainly important. His college years are centered about fraternity and sorority activities even though he might not be a member. *This person attempts to "make grades" but will rarely go out of his way to do extra or nonassigned readings.*

The most tangible evidence of differences in the composition of these groups was anticipated from two sources of information, the social origin of the individuals and their academic performance, as measured by their grade-point average. The results of the analysis on social origins are seen in Tables 10–1, 10–2, and 10–3.

Inspection of the data presented therein shows significant differences between the proportion of students from each social class (as measured by fathers' occupation) who identify themselves as belonging to one of the four subcultures. As might be anticipated, students from the higher socioeconomic backgrounds show a greater tendency to identify with the academic subculture, while the lower-class students are more vocationally oriented.

TABLE 10–1

PROPORTION OF STUDENTS IN EACH SUBCULTURE BELONGING TO UPPER, MIDDLE, OR LOWER SOCIAL CLASS AS (MEASURED BY FATHER'S OCCUPATION)

| Nonconformist | Academic | Vocational | Collegiate | Total | N |
|---|---|---|---|---|---|
| Upper class ........14% | 49% | 24% | 13% | 100% | (244) |
| Middle class ........20 | 39 | 31 | 10 | 100 | (507) |
| Lower class ........19 | 32 | 37 | 12 | 100 | ( 78) |
| $X^2 = 13.6010 \, P < .05$ | | | | | Total $N = 829$ |

Table 10–2 indicates that differences in rural-urban origin are also significant in determining how a student will classify himself. Students from farms are predominantly vocational in orientation while the highly urban areas seem to produce more students identifying themselves as academics. It is of interest to note, however, that a proportionally greater number of farm students are self-identified as nonconformist than are the urban students, which may suggest a social "alienation" factor influencing farm students to a greater extent than urban subjects. This finding would suggest that even when individuals select the same subcultural grouping the motivating factors are not necessarily similar.

TABLE 10–2

PROPORTION OF STUDENTS IN EACH SUBCULTURE HAVING A FARM, VILLAGE OR SMALL TOWN, OR LARGE TOWN OR METROPOLITAN ORIGIN

| Nonconformist | Academic | Vocational | Collegiate | Total | N |
|---|---|---|---|---|---|
| Farm ............22% | 29% | 44% | 5% | 100% | (118) |
| Village or small town ......21 | 40 | 28 | 11 | 100 | (327) |
| Large town or metropolis .......14 | 46 | 27 | 13 | 100 | (384) |
| $X^2 = 27.541 \, P < .05$ | | | | | Total $N = 829$ |

Identification with the "deviant" group by rural youth is not so much, we would speculate, the result of an intellectual process as it is a reaction to an unfamiliar or threatening situation.

Table 10–3 indicates that significant differences are found between the students' religious affiliation and student subculture orientation. The Protestant group is divided between the more "standard" (noted as Protestant I) and the more fundamentalist (noted as Protestant II) faiths.

TABLE 10–3

PROPORTION OF STUDENTS IN EACH SUBCULTURE BELONGING TO SPECIFIC RELIGIOUS GROUPS

| Nonconformist | Academic | Vocational | Collegiate | Total | N |
|---|---|---|---|---|---|
| Jewish ...........21% | 45% | 10% | 24% | 100% | ( 29) |
| Protestant I ........18 | 45 | 23 | 14 | 100 | (230) |
| Catholic ..........16 | 43 | 30 | 11 | 100 | (146) |
| Protestant II .......18 | 38 | 34 | 10 | 100 | (392) |
| $X^2 = 20.499\ P < .05$ | | | | | Total $N = 797$ |

The data shown in Table 10–4 note cumulative grade-point averages for the students in each subculture group. As can be observed, members of the nonconformist group are the best performers and those in the collegiate group are the poorest. This finding may, of course, be influenced by variations in grading and by selectivity in course selection by students. Such differences are, however, significant and in the direction anticipated by the authors. The nonconformist's intellectual commitment, to the exclusion of social or vocational goals, allows a focus of his efforts in this direction. Thus, for example, while the academic student spreads himself out, in a sense, and dissipates his efforts, (the nonconformist concentrates in one area. So also, the collegiate group, in its desire for social success, must sacrifice academic performance to attain its goal. Finally, the vocational student, tending to view college much in the instrumental fashion of the collegiate student, does not have the self-commitment to intellectual achievement held by his nonconformist and academic counterparts. Therefore, while grades are important they are so only in the context of "getting a job" upon graduation.

TABLE 10–4

MEAN GRADE-POINT AVERAGE OF STUDENT SUBCULTURES

| | Nonconformist | Academic | Vocational | Collegiate | Total |
|---|---|---|---|---|---|
| N ...........193 | | 384 | 280 | 106 | 963 |
| X ..........2.72 | | 2.66 | 2.49 | 2.32 | |
| $F_0(3, \infty) = 26.10 > F_{.05}(3, \infty) = 2.60$ | | | | | |

Table 10–5 deals with responses to the question, ". . . Which of the types comes closest to describing the typical student at your university?" These responses give an indirect indication of how the student tends to view the general student body.

TABLE 10–5
PROPORTION OF STUDENTS IN EACH SUBCULTURE PERCEPTION OF THE "TYPICAL" STUDENT

| Subcultural Membership | Noncon- formist | Academic | Vocational | Collegiate | Total | N |
|---|---|---|---|---|---|---|
| Nonconformist . .5% | | 21% | 21% | 53% | 100% | (189) |
| Academic ......3 | | 29 | 13 | 55 | 100 | (373) |
| Vocational .....2 | | 20 | 27 | 50 | 100 | (277) |
| Collegiate ......4 | | 13 | 8 | 75 | 100 | (106) |
| | | | | | Total N = 945 | |

Approximately half or more of the students in each subculture view the typical student on this campus as "collegiate." Three quarters of the students in the collegiate subculture, however, perceive the student body to be similar to themselves. Such a finding strongly suggests that the need for group support and unity may be greatest among the individuals of this subculture since their activities and values are in the largest contrast to the expressed goals of the formal educational establishment.

In terms of changes in attitude, values, and behavior since first coming to college, Gottlieb and Hodgkins found that:

1. Collegiates were more likely than any other subculture to become more dependent on peers as they progressed through college.

2. Nonconformists were more likely than respondents in other subcultures to report a decline in their feelings of religious commitment and need for a religious faith.

3. Nonconformists were lowest and collegiates highest in indicating a shift in attitude toward the importance of rules and regulations. Nonconformists were most likely to say they saw rules and regulations as unimportant while collegiates took an opposite position.

4. Nonconformists were highest in expressing a negative attitude toward those in positions of authority compared to students from the other subcultures.

5. Nonconformists were highest in expressing an expectation to attend graduate school upon completion of undergraduate work, followed by the academics with the vocationals and collegiates lowest in this respect.

6. Nonconformists and academics were highest in expressing a preference for posteducational occupations in the areas of teaching and research while collegiates were highest in the area of administrative positions.

The research findings presented here give good reason to re-examine certain of the prevailing conceptions about student behavior and values. More specifically, we can see that broad sweeping generalizations in regard to all youth in all places leave much to be desired. It is apparent that the degree to which a young person will be influenced by various groups will depend on the situation in which he finds himself and his previous experiences and perceptions, as well as the values he holds paramount.

## SOCIAL CONTROL AND THE YOUNGER ADOLESCENT

Let us move now from research dealing with college-age youth, to look at the influence of peers and adults on the younger adolescent.

Discussions of the functions of the peer group in the life of the adolescent characteristically note the role of the peer group as an aid in the adolescent's emancipation from his family. The support he gains from the peer group encourages him in his struggle against parental authority and adult control. Harold Phelps and John E. Horrocks have shown in an intensive study of 200 adolescent boys and girls that the most important over-all reason for the formation of informal groups among adolescents is the desire to achieve freedom from adult supervision.[11]

Outside of its specific support in the struggle with adult authority the peer group is seen as an insulator against the frustrations and anxieties in the shift from adolescence to adulthood. It supports the adolescent by offering him a source of status and a training ground where he can experiment with interpersonal relations, gain heterosexual experience, and develop social contacts which will be of future use to him. Several authors note the influence of the peer group in the later formation of personality characteristics. A most interesting study conducted by Seidler and Ravitz reveals the impact of peer influences on the attitudes and adult-oriented goals of a group of Jewish adolescents. The authors show that the internalization of peer values was so great that the peer group took on the function of a primary socializing agency. In many respects the peer group seemed to assume responsibilities traditionally left to the family. The authors support their contention by noting the number of out-group marriages and nonconformist ideas, and the trend—as adults—away from business occupations to professional and service occupations.

While some investigators have taken the position that the youth peer group acts as a "buffer" against the adult world, others propose that, in fact, the peer groups serve the function of preparing adolescents for future adult roles. In the latter view the adolescent is seen as working out certain transitional problems inherent in the shift from

---

[11] Harold Phelps and John E. Horrocks, "Factors Influencing Informal Groups of Adolescents," *Child Development,* Vol. XXIX (March, 1958), pp. 69–86.

adolescent to adult status. The peer group offers an opportunity to test one's leadership qualities and general abilities. Within the peer group the young person is able to get some idea of how he is viewed by others so that he can make appropriate changes in respect to his own future. Those who contend the adolescent peer group is but a reflection of adult cliques tend to minimize the conflict between youth and adults. Caroline M. Tyron, for example, feels the adolescent sees his peer group as a reflection of the form and purpose of an adult counterpart. She sees a definite similarity of general characteristics between the adult peer group and the adolescent group.[12]

Whether one sees the age of adolescence as a period of conflict among youth and adolescents or merely a time of "learning adult roles," there is general agreement that the peer group does influence the behavior of the adolescent. We have already noted the impact of the peer group in matters dealing with the selection of dating partners and general prestige within the high school and college. Evidence is also available which would support the idea that peer-group involvements are very much tied in with the self concept of the adolescent. In 1959, Leanne G. Rivlin, investigating the self attitudes and sociability of adolescents, applied fourteen criteria of creativity to a group of 126 tenth and eleventh graders in New York City high schools. After establishing a creative and noncreative group, he compared the two groups on their self attitudes and sociability. This comparison revealed the creative group was more sociable and had more confidence in its interpersonal relations than the noncreative group. In this work we see the interrelationships between social interaction within the peer group, self concept, and creativity. Although it is difficult from the research of Rivlin to pinpoint the independent and dependent variables, it does appear that involvement with the peer group leads to self-confidence and a more favorable self concept.[13]

Finally, we are able to see the influence of the peer group on the adolescent's future educational and occupational aspirations. Alan B. Wilson, in his discussion of the residential segregation of social classes and the aspirations of adolescents, showed that the values of the membership group influenced the development of aspirations. He noted that the concentration of social classes in specific areas of a city means the values of the particular classes are also concentrated in

---

[12] Caroline M. Tyron, "The Adolescent Peer Culture," *43rd Yearbook of The National Society for Education,* Part I (February, 1944), pp. 217–39.

[13] Leanne G. Rivlin, "Creativity and the Self Attitudes of Sociability of High School Students," *Journal of Educational Psychology,* Vol. I (August, 1959), pp. 147–52.

that area. For Wilson, the values reflected by the peer group influence not only educational aspirations but also occupational aspirations, academic achievement, and political preferences.[14]

## SUMMARY

In attempting to understand processes of social control in the life of the adolescent we have introduced several central ideas. First, we took the general position that dependency on peers will shift markedly as the adolescent moves from the elementary-school level to high school and through college. Those who go beyond college will increasingly tend to move back again to adult controls.

Next, we have proposed that three structural factors in our society act to move the adolescent toward his peer group and away from adults. The increase in social activities and programs which demand peer group participation is the first. As was noted earlier, this concentration of activities reaches its maximum point during the high school and college period. The clarity of adolescent expectations as opposed to the vagueness of what adults want from adolescents is the second structural factor contributing to involvement with peers. Again, adolescents make clear that which is needed for status and prestige within the youth society while the adult society presents a variety of conflicting expectations. The third element leading to greater peer involvement stems from the fact that adolescents are rarely allowed to enter the adult world until they go through certain rites of passage. Even here, however, there is a lack of agreement among adults as to when a young person is officially ready to take on adult roles. Marriage is not always considered a sufficient indication, nor is membership in the armed forces, attainment of a certain age, or academic achievement. The fact that we have no precise time or act which signifies completion of the transition from youth to adulthood adds to the continuation of a youth society.

We have also indicated that it is not empirically accurate to talk in terms of a single "youth culture," rather we must be aware of the great variations which exist in the behavior, values, and attitudes of youth in different settings. As was noted in our discussion of college youth, it is possible to find differences among young people. Although our concern was with college-age individuals it seems fair to say that similar differences can be found among younger adolescents.

---

[14] Alan B. Wilson, "Residential Segregation of Social Classes and Aspirations of High School Boys," *American Sociological Review,* Vol. XXIV (December, 1959), pp. 836–45.

# Chapter XI

## JUVENILE DELINQUENCY

It is difficult to determine the most important area of conflict between the generations, and it is a moot point as to whether such a question is itself important. However, it is probable that adult action programs will more often be directed toward the areas of adolescent behavior which are defined in public discourse as the most important. Clearly, juvenile delinquency is considered by the adult community as the most important area for study and action if the public press is a valid indicator of the degree of concern.

In this chapter we will document the degree and nature of the concerns with that adolescent behavior considered a problem by the popular press. Then we will review the research on the nature of and trends in juvenile delinquency. Next, we will consider some of the theory on sociological factors in juvenile delinquency. Last, we will take up the treatment of delinquents in the community and in the courts. All these considerations have at least one important factor in common: it is most difficult to understand the entire area of delinquency in the United States today. It is difficult to diagnose delinquency; it is difficult to treat the delinquent. All these difficulties rest upon the fact that it is nearly impossible to arrive at generally accepted definitions and generalizations concerning delinquency.

### CONCERN IN THE POPULAR PRESS

Much of the information and ideas adults have about youth comes from the popular press. The discussion which follows is limited to popular-magazine articles. A content analysis in the comparison of magazines with the few radio and television programs presented by Denver stations between 1960–63 revealed no outstanding differences in either problems or approaches.

The following analysis is based on sixty-seven articles about adolescence found in popular magazines between 1960 and 1963. The method is a simple content analysis of each article to determine the types of adolescent problems with which adults seem most concerned and the approaches to these problems taken by adult authors. A more general analysis then determines the nature of the assumptions made concerning youth. The articles were all written by adults but were addressed variously to adults and adolescents.

## Problems

Adults appear always to have been concerned with the antisocial behavior of youth. Many of the authors state antisocial behavior, either generally or in some specific form, as the problem of their articles. Other authors take some assumed cause of antisocial behavior, such as the carnal nature of youth or the narrow-minded approach of parents as the problem. In the sixty-seven articles studied, four were concerned with the problem of sex or venereal disease, two with drinking, one with secret organizations, six with rebellious behavior, and nine with various other forms of delinquent behavior. In all, one third of the articles directly stated adolescent antisocial behavior as the problem of the article. Eight articles blamed parents for this, six attributed it to physical and emotional problems, and five more or less closely related it to school systems. In total, twenty-nine authors stated problems indirectly or causally related to antisocial behavior. Only seventeen articles could be said not to be directly or indirectly concerned with some form of socially disapproved behavior while fifty were so concerned.

Of the seventeen not concerned with antisocial behavior, four lamented the fact that youth are complacent and not rebellious; five described positive programs of action which seemed to help adolescents avoid trouble. Four articles stated no problem in the usual sense of the word but rather lauded youth for their idealism. Two articles considered movies a problem for youth, one encouraged self-understanding, and one safe driving.

## Some Assumptions in Popular Literature on Adolescence

It is clear from a content analysis of the literature on adolescence found in popular magazines that several assumptions are made by the authors. It is also clear that not all of these assumptions are compatible. However, the disagreements among authors are not unique to the field of popular literature, for similar disagreements are found among authors of scientific research articles and of theoretical articles on adolescence.

It would behoove us to look more closely at some of the assumptions in the popular literature, since these represent the popular image of adolescents among adults. Many of the assumptions are made or tested by authors of more scientific, if less readable, articles on the subject.

The first assumption that appears throughout most of the popular literature is that adolescence is a time of stress, confusion, and difficulty. Some of the articles consider such stress inherent in adolescence due to the physiological changes which occur, especially early in the period. Other articles, particularly those written to teenagers, accept the stress by making it a challenge. One contradictory set of assumptions concerns the solution of such storm and stress. One approach found in popular and scientific literature is that the adolescent needs something to rebel against and thus parents should not go far in smoothing out difficulties which seem to them usually ridiculous and always painful. Other articles implicitly assume (1) that either adolescents or parents or both may reduce, if not eliminate, the stress through certain courses of action and (2) that the reduction of stress is desirable, thus contradicting the notion that adolescents need something to rebel against. These two assumptions are inferred from the fact that advice is given to adolescents or to the parents on the manner in which tension can be reduced.

Still another assumption of great significance is that the role expectations of the adolescent are neither understood by him nor clearly defined by adults. Most authors of scientific and research articles, including the authors of the present volume, seem to concur on this assumption. However, some authors feel role definitions are more clearly defined and understood than formerly.

Most popular authors think there is a distinct and separable adolescent society. Some of the popular literature recognizes fully that adult society treats the aggregate of adolescents as if a teenage culture and society exist. Advertisements are directed at adolescents, magazines are written for them, and distinct characteristics are attributed to them.

Many authors feel adolescence on the whole is a period of idealism and, further, that the idealism, perspective, and serious thinking of youth are increasing and are greater today than formerly. Many other authors, however, cite the statistics which indicate increasing delinquency, venereal disease, and promiscuity among adolescents and hypothesize the degeneration of today's youth. Thus are found the contradictory trends of increasing idealism or conservatism on the one hand and increasing delinquency and antisocial behavior on the other.

Contradictions in assumptions may be found in the recommendations made by authors as well as in their notions as to the nature and causes of adolescent behavior. One most interesting contradiction in recommendations is between authors who challenge youth to learn more about the adult world and to gain depth in understanding of themselves and of others and authors who lament of "growing up too soon." The latter writers discourage adolescents from going steady, from marrying too young, and from taking life too seriously. These authors also admonish parents not to "push" their child too much in school or in accepting responsibility.

Still another contradiction in assumptions regarding recommendations is the "disciplinary" versus the "permissive" approach. Actually, the authors making either of these two approaches usually write in a much different vein. Those who believe more supervision and discipline are needed give recommendations primarily, although they may do some analysis by accounting for the antisocial behavior of today's youth in terms of lack of supervision. Those who appear to believe in a more permissive outlook more often approach the problem in terms of analysis—primarily from the point of view of factors leading to self-control.

The disagreements among the popular authors are also characteristic of the more scientific works on adolescent-adult conflict and juvenile delinquency. The primary difference in popular and scientific literature on these topics is in the degree of caution.

## NATURE OF DELINQUENCY AND TRENDS

"Juvenile delinquency" is a very abstract term in the sense that it classifies greatly different behaviors as identical on the basis of a single, narrow feature of those behaviors. In New York state, delinquency is defined as any act which, if committed by an adult, would be a crime. This is as close to an operational definition as we may find in the literature. Yet it is not adequate. Many instances of adolescent behavior treated as delinquency would not be considered a crime if committed by an adult—for example, truancy and ungovernability. Indeed, ungovernability is the most frequent offense for which girls are brought into court.

The definition of delinquency is greatly complicated by the fact that some "delinquent" behavior is consistently defined as violating our norms, while other "delinquent" behavior is defined by one person, but not all, as violation. For example, armed robbery is considered by all adults as morally and legally wrong. However, an all-night pajama party held by girls will be accepted by one parent and considered ungovernability by another. In other words, some delinquency rests entirely upon deviant and "old-fashioned" definitions placed on a behavior which is accepted as moral by most people. Rather than add another definition of delinquency to the already-long list, let us look at the types of charges, formal and informal, made by adults which result in adolescents being brought before the juvenile court. This procedure is possible because we know more about the nature of delinquency than our lack of a formal definition might imply.

### Nature of Delinquency

Table 11–1 is a list of those offenses which resulted in boys and girls being brought into court in Denver, Colorado, during all of 1962 and from January through May of 1963.[1]

TABLE 11–1

CHARGES AGAINST JUVENILE OFFENDERS, DENVER, 1962 AND JANUARY–MAY, 1963

| Offenses | 1962 | | 1963 | |
|---|---|---|---|---|
| | Boys | Girls | Boys | Girls |
| Robbery | 15 | 3 | 10 | 0 |
| Assault | 29 | 13 | 55 | 11 |
| Burglary | 259 | 21 | 134 | 19 |
| Larceny, under $50 | 130 | 39 | 83 | 45 |
| Larceny, over $50 | 15 | 3 | 14 | 1 |
| Auto theft | 290 | 14 | 187 | 11 |
| Unauthorized use of weapons | 4 | 0 | 0 | 0 |
| Sex misconduct | 18 | 11 | 3 | 6 |
| Drugs | 0 | 1 | 0 | 0 |
| Drunkenness (including glue sniffing) | 29 | 10 | 22 | 15 |
| Disorderly conduct | 8 | 12 | 8 | 14 |
| Vandalism | 46 | 10 | 53 | 4 |
| Arson | 2 | 0 | 0 | 0 |
| Forgery | 2 | 0 | 0 | 0 |
| Runaway | 3 | 49 | 3 | 45 |
| Truancy | 42 | 19 | 20 | 15 |
| Curfew violation | 0 | 4 | 1 | 0 |
| Ungovernability | 83 | 181 | 26 | 68 |
| Totals | 975 | 390 | 619 | 254 |

The relative rank of offenses is fairly consistent between the two periods. Without reviewing the findings in detail, we may draw several conclusions from this table which are consistent with similar tables from other cities and other years.

The types of offenses for which boys are brought before the juvenile court are quite different from those for which girls are brought in. Auto theft and burglary are the two most frequent offenses found

---

[1] *The Denver Post*, June 21, 1963, p. 29.

among male juvenile offenders, while ungovernability is most characteristic of female offenders.

Male offenses are most often against property while female offenses are most often rebellion against the family and, to a lesser degree, the school. Further, almost three times as many boys as girls are brought into juvenile courts. For the most part, the more frequent male offenses are specific while the more frequent female offenses are vague or general.

### Trends of Delinquency

During the twelve years from 1948 to 1960, the number of cases of juvenile delinquency taken to the courts increased more than 100 per cent. During the same period, the adolescent population increased slightly less than 30 per cent. There is little question that since 1950 the same trends have been observed in Austria, Australia, England, Greece, Finland, Japan, and the Philippines. Doubtless, at least part of this trend is due to the greater willingness of people to handle juvenile cases through the court system rather than to settle them informally between parent and victim. Further, many acts once defined as mischief are now defined as delinquency.

However, it is doubtful whether all of the apparent increase in delinquency could be explained by these changes in attitude. Certainly, an increasing number of delinquents is apprehended by the police and an increasing number of crimes appears to be committed by juveniles. This increase is great. However, the apprehension of adolescents by the police is most misleading. Police forces are more effective. Approximately two thirds of the adolescents actually apprehended are sent home with a warning to them and their parents and no official recording of the apprehension. Even the cases which go into court are largely released on probation and an even larger number of cases is merely held open without any specific action taken. It is true, however, that almost all the adolescents taken into court are judged delinquent.

Delinquency rates have always been higher in cities than in rural communities. However, the greater increase is currently being experienced in rural communities. Again, this is probably due to the decrease in the informal handling of cases between adults without resorting to police in court processes. The attitude toward official handling appears to be changing more rapidly in the rural areas than in the urban ones.

Statistics on trends cannot be completely trusted for several reasons. The increasing willingness to report such acts as vandalism to the police has already been mentioned. The way in which statistics are compiled presents another difficulty. National trends are compiled ultimately from reports from the local communities. The tendency for victims to report minor offenses varies greatly by community. Doubtless, the efficiency of police departments both in keeping records and in reporting offenses also varies from one community to another. The responsibility of local officers is to the local governing body, not to the state or nation. However, efficiency and completeness in reporting are increasing.

Moreover, local police operate under a system of laws concerning delinquency made at the state level for the most part, and at the local level for the remaining part. These laws vary by state and by community, and within the same jurisdiction from one time to another. Therefore, to some extent the compilation of statistics at the national level is like the summation of apples and oranges.

## FACTORS IN DELINQUENCY

There are many studies of factors in delinquency. Typically, these studies use one of two methods in measuring delinquency. The first method is to divide areas of a city into those with high and low delinquency rates and compare the areas with high delinquency rates to those with low delinquency rates in terms of social and economic characteristics. The social and economic differences are then considered factors in delinquency. In this method, however, one measure of delinquency rates is based on the number of crimes known to the police. This measure has two difficulties. In the first place, police may find a young person driving while under the influence of alcohol but only warn the person and send him home. Thus, some delinquency is not reported by the policeman. The tendency of police not to report delinquent acts differs by areas, depending upon the socioeconomic characteristics of the area. Second, there is some difficulty in determining whether a particular act has been committed by a juvenile, insofar as the offender was not apprehended. Vandalism is usually a juvenile offense but it is much more difficult to determine whether a burglary was done by an adult or a juvenile.

The second method used in studies of delinquency is comparing nondelinquents with delinquents. After studying the two groups' social, psychological, and economic characteristics, any significant differences are concluded to be factors in delinquency. This method is by far the most frequently employed, but it involves several difficulties.

It will be shown that all adolescents commit acts which under some circumstances are defined as delinquency. Only a few adolescents are sent to a reform school. Between the commission of a delinquent act and the reform school are several points at which delinquency may be measured. Paul Tappan[2] lists the following places in this process at which such measurement may occur:

1. All children's behavior.
2. Specific delinquent conduct.
3. Discovered delinquency.
4. Delinquency resulting in arrest or report.

*Court delinquency*

5. Delinquency alleged to court.
6. Delinquency resulting in court hearing.
7. Unofficial court delinquency.
8. Official adjudicated delinquency.
9. Delinquency commitments to institutions.

*Delinquency handled in social agencies, public and private*

10. Delinquency submitted to agency intake.
11. Cases of delinquency accepted for treatment.
12. Cases recorded by agencies as delinquent.

TABLE 11–2

DELINQUENCY BY SOCIOECONOMIC STATUS:
INSTITUTIONALIZATION AS THE CRITERION OF DELINQUENCY

| Socioeconomic Status | Training School Boys | | High School Boys | |
|---|---|---|---|---|
| | No. | Per Cent | No. | Per Cent |
| I (Lowest) ... | 73 | 50.0 | 112 | 13.3 |
| II .......... | 48 | 32.9 | 333 | 39.6 |
| III.......... | 19 | 13.0 | 282 | 33.5 |
| IV (Highest).. | 6 | 4.1 | 114 | 13.6 |
| Total ...... | 146 | 100.0 | 841 | 100.0 |

$X^2 = 117.0$
P is less than .001
$C = .45$

TABLE 11–3

DELINQUENCY BY SOCIOECONOMIC STATUS:
REPORTED BEHAVIOR AS THE CRITERION OF DELINQUENCY

| Socioeconomic Status | Most Delinquent (Scale types 8–15) | | Least Delinquent (Scale types 1–7) | |
|---|---|---|---|---|
| | No. | Per Cent | No. | Per Cent |
| I (Lowest)..... | 42 | 16.0 | 69 | 12.0 |
| II ............. | 101 | 38.4 | 233 | 40.4 |
| III ........... | 91 | 34.6 | 191 | 33.1 |
| IV (Highest) ... | 29 | 11.0 | 84 | 14.5 |
| Total ........ | 263 | 100.0 | 577 | 100.0 |

$X^2 = 4.2$
P is less than .30
$C = .10$

[2] Paul Tappan, *Juvenile Delinquency* (New York: McGraw-Hill, 1949), p. 32.

TABLE 11–4

DELINQUENCY BY FAMILY STATE:
INSTITUTIONALIZATION AS THE CRITERION OF DELINQUENCY

| State of Family | Training School Boys | | High School Boys | |
|---|---|---|---|---|
| | No. | Per Cent | No. | Per Cent |
| Unbroken ........ | 81 | 51.9 | 934 | 80.5 |
| Broken .......... | 75 | 48.1 | 226 | 19.5 |
| Total ......... | 156 | 100.0 | 1160 | 100.0 |

$X^2 = 63.7$
P is less than .001
$C = .34$

TABLE 11–5

DELINQUENCY BY FAMILY STATE:
REPORTED BEHAVIOR AS THE CRITERION OF DELINQUENCY

| State of Family | Most Delinquent (Scale types 8–15) | | Least Delinquent (Scale types 1–7) | |
|---|---|---|---|---|
| | No. | Per Cent | No. | Per Cent |
| Unbroken ........ | 281 | 76.4 | 653 | 82.4 |
| Broken .......... | 87 | 23.6 | 139 | 17.6 |
| Total ......... | 368 | 100.0 | 792 | 100.0 |

$X^2 = 5.9$
P is less than .02
$C = .11$

The findings from research will differ according to the particular type of delinquency which is being distinguished from "nondelinquency." It is generally known that delinquents are more often from poor economic circumstances and more often live in the slums. However, it is also known that law enforcement is uneven in that the cases of middle-class adolescents caught in delinquent acts are handled at a much earlier point in the process described above. The policeman may only warn the boy and, possibly, his parent. However, the books on delinquency report numerous cases of lower-class boys arrested and even incarcerated for offenses identical to those for which middle-class boys are only warned. There are even cases in which a middle-class boy and a lower-class boy commit an act together and the class bias in handling the case results in the middle-class boy being sent home and the lower class boy going to a reformatory. Therefore, the lower we get in Tappan's list of categories of delinquency the higher will be the relationship between delinquency and socioeconomic status.

James F. Short, Jr., and F. Ivan Nye clearly demonstrate the difference in relationships found with different means of measuring delinquency.[3] Delinquency was measured in two ways. First, training school boys were compared with high school boys. When this was done, the correlation between socioeconomic status was .45, a moderately high relationship for a single factor. (See Table 11–2.) However, delinquency was also measured in terms of boys who were "most delinquent" and "least delinquent" from the "noninstitutionalized" population. In this case, the correlation between socioeconomic status and delinquency was only .10, a very low correlation. (See Table 11–3.)

Short and Nye made similar findings with respect to the relationship between delinquency and the broken home. Boys in a training school were much more often from broken homes than were boys in the high schools. The correlation was .34. (See Table 11–4.) However, when "most delinquent" and "least delinquent" were compared there was little difference, with a correlation of only .11. (See Table 11–5.) This much-talked-about factor in delinquency was further questioned by Nye in a separate article.[4] He found that children from broken homes reported a lower incidence of delinquent behavior than did those children from unhappy homes which were not broken by divorce.

In a now-famous study by Austin L. Porterfield, over 300 people were asked to report the offenses they had committed as juveniles.[5] All the respondents were college and precollege men and women. Table 11–6 indicates their response.[6]

TABLE 11–6

PERCENTAGE OF STUDENTS REPORTING THE COMMISSION OF ONE OR MORE OF
THE FIFTY-FIVE OFFENSES CHARGED AGAINST CHILDREN IN THE COURT AND
AVERAGE NUMBER OF OFFENSES REPORTED BY EACH

| Offending Group | Number in Group | Percentage Reporting One or More of the Offenses | Average Number of Offenses Reported |
|---|---|---|---|
| Precollege men ............200 | | 100.0 | 17.6 |
| College men .............100 | | 100.0 | 11.2 |
| Precollege women .........137 | | 100.0 | 4.7 |

The second column is a most significant finding. Among precollege men, college men, and precollege women, 100 per cent of those

[3] James F. Short, Jr., and F. Ivan Nye, "Reported Behavior as a Criterion of Deviant Behavior," *Social Problems*, Vol. 5 (1957), pp. 207–13.

[4] F. Ivan Nye, "Child Adjustment in Broken Homes and in Unhappy Unbroken Homes," *Marriage and Family Living*, Vol. 19 (1957), pp. 356–61.

[5] Austin L. Porterfield, *Youth in Trouble* (Fort Worth: Leo Potishman Foundation, 1946).

[6] *Ibid.*, p. 38.

responding reported one or more offenses. One of the present writers, recognizing the extreme importance of this study in measuring delinquency but being skeptical of the findings, attempted to test the extent to which people would tell the truth under such circumstances. He asked a group of students in a delinquency class to indicate by "yes" or "no" whether or not they had committed an offense. He also asked them to indicate the nature of this offense. Then he asked them to throw away the answers and take out another piece of paper. The first question of this second set was whether or not they had admitted to an offense. The second question was whether or not they had told the truth. The papers were anonymous and printing with pencil was required. On both questions on the second page, there was a 100 per cent "yes" answer. This raises a significant question with relationship to the division of adolescents into the categories of delinquent and nondelinquent on the basis of official records or incarceration.

Let us return to the relationship previously discussed between delinquency and slum dwelling. It was pointed out that the relationship is moderately high when adolescents in institutions are compared with the high school population generally but that the relationship is greatly reduced when the "most delinquent" are compared with the "least delinquent." There are reasons for these findings in addition to those mentioned.

A concept useful in sociological analysis is the definition of the situation or the self-fulfilling prophecy. This concept involves the notion that if we think a thing to be true, it is true in its consequences. Applied to the relationship between slum dwelling and rates of delinquency as measured by the percentage of boys in reform school or in police records, we can find the self-fulfilling prophecy operating. The research findings support the stereotype of the lower-class slum teenager as a delinquent. This stereotype affects the organization of the police force as well as judges. Therefore, we concentrate our police force in those areas where we expect them to be most needed. The results are not surprising—there is a greater probability of apprehension in the slums.

The rates of Negro delinquency are higher than those for whites, when police records and incarceration are used as indices. All of the factors previously discussed in relation to the slums are relevant in helping to explain this higher rate for Negroes. Negroes are concentrated in the slum. However, there is an additional reason. Negroes, for the most part, are highly visible. When police are given a description of someone reported in misconduct, the additional information that the alleged offender was a Negro is helpful to them in apprehending him, because they may immediately eliminate all whites who otherwise fit the description. Since whites outnumber Negroes in most areas, this facilitates the work of the police.

In spite of all the difficulties in accepting the findings of studies based on the rates of areas and on the comparison of delinquents and nondelinquents, many findings are worthy of consideration. In a comparison of the institutionalized population of delinquents with a matched sample of "nondelinquents," Sheldon and Eleanor Glueck found a number of factors in the family background of delinquents which warrant further study.[7] One important factor which seems to be associated with delinquency is the lack of supervision of the boy by his mother. Also, when the boy experiences a lack of affection on the part of either the father or the mother, delinquency is more likely to appear. A lack of cohesiveness generally in the family also seems to be associated with delinquency as it is measured in this study.

### Delinquency as a Gang Behavior

It has been estimated that about 90 per cent of the boys brought into court for juvenile offenses had one or more accomplices. These gangs, usually thought of as most characteristic of the lower class, are apparently persistent through several generations. For example, the gangs found by Thrasher in 1924 in El Paso, Texas, were of a similar nature and were known by the same names by Harold J. Rahm and J. Robert Weber in 1958.[8]

Two interesting theories have been presented in recent years concerning why the gangs in the lower classes may exhibit such tendencies. The first, by Richard A. Cloward and Lloyd E. Ohlin,[9] assumes that middle-class goals have been accepted by most or all boys. These goals involve a regular job, spending money for recreation and nice clothes, and the like. Most middle-class boys and many lower-class boys are able to achieve these goals through legitimate means; however, some middle-class boys and a large number of lower-class boys are not. Various factors may influence their inability to achieve these goals legitimately; inadequate support from parents, poor study habits, lower intelligence, and discriminatory treatment in some schools appear to be among the more important ones. Since they cannot give

[7] Sheldon and Eleanor T. Glueck, *Unraveling Juvenile Delinquency* (New York: Commonwealth Fund, 1950), p. 353. See also same authors, "Early Detection of Juvenile Delinquents," *Channel of Criminal Law, Criminology, and Police Science,* Vol. 47 (1956), pp. 353–64.

[8] Harold J. Rahm and J. Robert Weber, *Office in the Alley* (Austin: University of Texas Printing Division for the Hogg Foundation, 1958), p. 357.

[9] Richard A. Cloward and Lloyd E. Ohlin, *Delinquency and Opportunity: A Theory of Delinquent Gangs* (New York: The Free Press of Glencoe, 1960), pp. 357–71.

up the middle-class goals, indeed they are sanctioned if they do, their only resort is to illegitimate means. They are further encouraged in delinquent ways by the frustration resulting from the fact that the adult community sets goals for them for which no means are provided. It is small wonder, then, that the lower-class boy becomes disgusted with the adult community and loses respect for police, law, and order.

Within this theory, then, the opportunities available to the boys determine the nature of their antisocial behavior. If the community is stabilized through either legitimate or illegitimate power structures, the boys are likely to become an adolescent prototype of adult crime. They enter the fringe of a syndicate and participate in burglary and theft. They have means of disposing of the stolen goods through the adult crime organization. If the community does not have sufficient stability in the legitimate or illegitimate power structure to provide boys with an outlet for stolen goods, their frustration is let out through gang warfare. Gang warfare does not give them money or property but it does provide them with a feeling of manliness and excitement. If neither theft nor gang warfare occurs, the boys turn to other forms of delinquency which are retreat from the more aggressive forms such as theft and gang warfare. In this case we find alcohol and drugs as the main outlets for their frustration. Since parties involving drunkenness and drug addiction are often gang functions, we may still refer to this as gang delinquency.

A contrary theory is offered by other experts on juvenile delinquency.[10] According to this theory, lower-class boys accept lower-class goals and means and reject the middle-class goals assumed by the theory given above. Therefore, the assumption of basic orientation is different from that of the previous theory. The characteristics associated with lower-class culture are those which tend to get the boy into trouble: being tough, outsmarting others, seeking excitement, individualism, and fatalism. The gang in this case merely reinforces the lower-class values which are found troublesome by the middle class. The exceptions to this theory, namely boys in the lower class who do not become delinquent, are explained in terms of their ability to cast aside lower-class values and attempt to achieve middle-class status. The values on hard work, education, property, cleanliness, and ambition are characteristic of the middle class. Within this theory it is thought that education, the church, and other features

---

[10] For example, see William D. Kvaraceus and William E. Ulrich, *Delinquent Behavior: Principles and Practices* (Washington, D.C.: National Education Association, 1959), pp. 365–66.

of the community are helpful in aiding the boy to accept and conform to approved behavior in a middle-class society. This might be regarded as a culture-conflict theory.

## The Theory of Differential Association

The famous theory of differential association, attributed to Edwin H. Sutherland, needs much more study but it appears to be one of the most profitable approaches to delinquency.[11]

This theory begins with the assumption that criminal behavior, delinquency included, is learned from others through interaction and the process of communication. As with all learning, most of this occurs within the primary group—those which are intimate and face to face. Basically, two things are learned in such groups: the techniques of living—in this situation, the techniques of anti-social behavior and crime; and the motives, drives, rationalizations, and attitudes associated with this behavior. These psychological states and processes may be referred to as definitions of situations. For example, in interacting with others the person may learn to define other persons as deserving consideration and respect. On the other hand, the adolescent may learn to define other persons as means to the adolescent's ends. There are, of course, many such definitions. Some regard persons; some regard property; some the desirability of obeying norms; and some the hierarchy of values on money, hard work, and the like.

A person becomes delinquent because of an excess of definitions favorable to vilification of norms as compared with definitions favorable to obeying norms. The superiority of either set of definitions depends upon the source from which these definitions have been learned in the first place—in other words, differential association. This theory denies the theories of values described earlier. Sutherland and Cressey say, "While criminal behavior is an expression of general needs and values, it is not explained by those general needs and values since non-criminal behavior is an expression of the same needs and values." [12]

This theory is, of course, consistent with the long-standing notion that many boys get into trouble because of running with a "bad crowd." While this is not a total explanation, there is clear evidence that many adolescents do get into trouble in exactly this manner.

We hypothesize that the theory of differential association might

---

[11] Edwin H. Sutherland and Donald R. Cressey, *Principles of Criminology* (New York: Lippincott, 1960), chap. 4.

[12] *Ibid.*, p. 79.

also explain how some adolescents may learn delinquent behavior from their families. For many youth, delinquency might truly be said to have been learned in the home. During the depression a not-unusual means of obtaining coal for heating the home was to pick it up from the railroad tracks. That such coal was both the property of and on the property of the railroad made little difference. The railroad did not pick up the coal after it had fallen off the cars. But there was a small difference between picking up the coal after it had fallen, or obtaining it while it was still on the coal car. The categorical property rights had already been violated. The coal may change to apples or bread, but the principle of learning is the same in many homes of extremely low income. Such learning may not be limited to lower-class homes. Indeed, who has not heard parents laugh with pride at the stealing of watermelons. And further, no small proportion of adolescents has heard the reminiscences of wild times when a friend from college days visits the father.

On the other side of approaches taken by parents is the strict family which tries so hard to rear a good boy that life becomes intolerable. True, this is indirect learning, but the sources of the resulting delinquent may well be the catharsis experienced after antisocial behavior.

Even in less strict homes there is always a potential conflict between the adolescent's parent and peer. Everyone needs friends and feels this need consciously. In order to assure friendship among peers many adolescents either find or feel they must lie to their parents. We may assume most adolescents would prefer not to lie and therefore come to reject their parents more completely as they define them as old-fashioned. At this point, parental advice is ignored and parental control is strongly weakened through patterned evasion on the part of the adolescent.

Still another interesting hypothesis as to learning delinquency within the family stems from the approximation of a corporate structure in many families. An allowance is set, and the offspring learns to manipulate the parent for extra money needed. Certainly a rigid allowance "teaches the child the value of money," but at what cost to other values? We are not recommending a complete abandonment of allowances, but we are suggesting such a policy in the family may lead to a definition of money as an end and other people merely as means. It is possible a more reasoned approach would recognize that the need for money varies greatly from week to week and that a discussion between parents and adolescents would better meet both the needs of the adolescent for money and the needs of the parent to become more familiar with the day-to-day life of the adolescent. More important, however, is the main point we wish to make: we need not look only to major crises in the adolescent's life to find the sources of learning delinquency; we may look to the seemingly minor, repetitive patterns of interaction between the adolescent and the others significant in his daily life.

## THE JUVENILE COURT

Only about one third of the adolescents apprehended by the police for offenses considered delinquent are taken to the police station or the juvenile court. However, those adolescents who do reach the courts find a much different court than do adult offenders. The juvenile court, as it is structured today, lags far behind the laws which were passed which might implement a more intelligent handling of juvenile cases. This has always been so.[13]

Juvenile court actions, as in criminal courts, are ordinarily initiated in one of two ways: police may initiate court action after a formal arrest of a juvenile, or a private party may sign a complaint. Sometimes the private party is a parent, especially in the case of ungovernability and incorrigibility. A large number of the cases are disposed of before they officially reach the judge's chambers. The "intake" agencies often handle juvenile cases through the approved processes appropriate to their profession. Many times special officers or social workers are appointed for this job. But we are concerned here with the official handling of cases through the court process.

After the case comes to the attention of the court, arraignment is similar to that found in criminal courts where minor violations are in question. The charge is read to the juvenile and the meaning of the charge and his rights are explained to him. Nevertheless, the inexperience of the juvenile usually means his fears and misunderstanding are more important than the explanation of the charges. Many of the newer and experimental courts deviate from the usual procedure in minor criminal cases. Here the court is adjourned immediately after the arraignment and a social investigation is conducted. The theorists who have promoted this policy in juvenile cases contend the misconduct is not at issue but rather the adjustment of the child to his society. It would follow, then, that the investigation should consider the social, economic, and psychological factors which lead to the child's being in court.

In criminal court, where minor violations are involved, the court is also adjourned immediately upon arraignment in many cases, in order

---

[13] Tappan, *op. cit.*, chap. 8.

to contact witnesses. This is sometimes done in the case of juvenile offenders, but more often few or no witnesses are involved. The adjournment after arraignment is for the purpose of social investigation. In the more traditional courts, the hearing is conducted immediately after arraignment. The court is then adjourned for some time and disposition is made of the case at a later date. Where social investigations are involved, the time between arraignment and the hearing ranges about from one week to one month. Frequently the case is dismissed after a very brief hearing, even for those juveniles who reach the court. Warnings to the adolescent or lectures on moral behavior constitute the only court action taken in many cases.

Two extremely important differences occur between the juvenile case and the adult criminal case. The first difference is that the hearings are private rather than public. Criminal courts have had the power of excluding the public for certain types of cases for a long time. However, it is seldom done by most judges except with juvenile offenders. The juvenile cases are almost always heard in the private chambers of the judge. The second difference is the absence of either a prosecutor or a defense attorney. It is the right of the offender or his parents to be represented by counsel, but such representation is seldom seen. Part of the lack of legal representation is due to the fact that the middle-class parent is more likely to hire a defense attorney but the middle-class offender is less likely to get to the courts.

The probation officer is present and often acts as a prosecutor. He describes the case and the situation which lead to the offense. The assumption is that the boy or girl was an offender, or the court would not have taken the time and money for a social investigation. This is evidenced by the fact previously mentioned that almost all cases which reach the court end with a decision that the juvenile is a delinquent.

Increasingly, juvenile judges are specialists in juvenile cases. This does not mean characteristically that they are trained in other than law schools. Nevertheless, the team work between probation officer, the social worker, and the judge usually means the case involves, in a significant way, psychology, sociology, and criminology, as well as the legal aspects of the judgment. Juveniles are asked questions and are expected to answer them—a process that clearly violates the legal precedence of not demanding a person testify against himself. The informality of the actual procedure leads to a conclusion that the juvenile who refuses to talk is sullen and uncooperative and, therefore, guilty.

Part of the reason for the privacy of the situation of the juvenile court is the social stigma attached to being brought into court. It is the feeling of the persons who work in juvenile courts that the community would place the child at a disadvantage for the rest of his life if his offense were publicly aired. In many states the newspapers do not even publish the names of juvenile offenders when they write up stories concerning a juvenile offense.

Following from the absence of prosecutors and defense attorneys, the use of evidence is much less rigorous than in the case of the public hearing where both the people and the alleged offender are represented by counsel. In general, then, there are many violations of due process of law in the case of the juvenile offender. Clearly these violations rest upon a sincerity of interest in protecting the offender against future stigma, but one side effect is the much higher proportion of decisions which, in effect, is a finding of "guilty."

Many persons feel the juvenile court and its team of specialists should orient themselves toward the prevention rather than the punishment of delinquents. This is an unreasonable expectation because of the way in which juvenile offenders reach the juvenile court. In the first place, the court "team" could under no circumstance have jurisdiction unless at least one delinquent act had been committed and the person had been apprehended. Only at this point could the court intervene legally. It should further be pointed out that unless the offense is a serious one juveniles do not ordinarily reach the juvenile court unless they are habitual delinquents and have been caught repeatedly. Therefore, the court could not handle the real preventive program for those delinquents who escape detection. Further, it would be difficult to work with those who are caught by the police and released with only a warning to them and their parents. Other delinquents are apprehended and brought into the official agencies but never reach juvenile court. Therefore, those brought into court are frequently already aggravated, possibly irremediable, and mature delinquents. Tappan says, "The record of failures in dealing with delinquents, even first offenders, is far too bleak to justify courts in experimenting with children who have committed no acts in violation of legislatively established policy." [14]

Many persons believe the court should not place delinquents in reform schools, especially those delinquents who have committed few delinquent acts and are not yet hardened to a criminal pattern of behavior. Juveniles presumably learn better techniques and more appropriate attitudes from the more hardened delinquents they meet in the reform school. Certainly the rates of recidivism are high. Fre-

---

[14] *Ibid.*, p. 201.

quently delinquents are merely warned by the judge with a brief lecture and permitted to return home. In a large number of cases those who have committed a delinquent act are able to give a convincing story to the judge and then hold the court and the law in contempt after they are permitted to leave without any punishment. It would appear, then, that at present we are caught between two extremes and either course of action would result in fostering rather than deterring further delinquent behavior.

## SUMMARY

The public and the popular press are more concerned with delinquency than with any other aspect of the study of youth. A study of sixty-seven articles in the popular magazines in 1962 and 1963 revealed that fifty were either directly or indirectly concerned with delinquency. Many contradictory assumptions are made concerning the nature of adolescence and the causes of delinquency.

Actually, delinquency is an abstract term which refers to a greatly diverse set of phenomena. Delinquency ranges from serious offenses against persons and property to behavior characteristic of most adolescents but which, for particular adolescents, becomes delinquent because of conservative attitudes on the part of parents and guardians.

Boys are brought into court for different offenses than are girls. Boys are also much more often involved with the police than are girls. The lower classes are much more often involved with the police than are middle-class adolescents. In a criticism of the research on slums and the broken home, we pointed out several significant principles in the sociology of delinquency:

1. Practically all adolescents commit acts which are usually considered delinquent.

2. Because we believe delinquency is more characteristic of the slums, we concentrate our police force there. Therefore, a delinquent living in the slums is more often apprehended. This also partly accounts for the higher delinquency rates among Negroes.

3. The stereotype of delinquency as a slum (and Negro) characteristic leads to the more permissive handling of middle-class offenders.

4. There is a slight tendency for boys from the lower class to commit delinquent acts. The probability of incarceration is much greater for delinquents from lower classes.

5. Adolescents from broken homes are less often delinquent than adolescents from homes which are unhappy but not broken.

6. Adolescents appear to be more often delinquent when the family fails to give them affection and consistency in supervision, and when the family has less solidarity.

7. One theory holds delinquency is a result of the discrepancy between middle-class goals, which practically all adolescents accept, and the means

available to achieve these goals, which get some adolescents into trouble with the middle-class controlling element in the community.

The juvenile court varies from the criminal court in actual practice. Most delinquents never reach the courts, but when they do they are almost always, informally, found guilty. The delinquent is usually not represented by counsel, nor is there a prosecutor. The person, in practice, must testify against himself or he is thought to be sullen and uncooperative. "Trials" are private, because a public trial would bring a social stigma to the person. Some have suggested that the juvenile court should be oriented toward prevention rather than cure, because incarceration merely brings the adolescent into contact with technically more proficient delinquents. However, the courts more often get the matured delinquent. Further, it is not the function of courts to work on prevention in our social structure. Still further, many feel the courts do not have a sufficiently favorable record to warrant their experimentation with prevention—recidivism rates are high.

## Chapter XII

# MINORITY GROUP STATUS
# AND ADOLESCENT CULTURE

### by Francis A. J. Ianni

It is generally believed that ethnicity, race, and religion continue to produce identifiable minority groups in the United States. Mexican-Americans, Italo-Americans, Negro-Americans, Japanese-Americans, and American Jews are still considered to inhabit subcultural worlds within the larger world of our national culture. Each of these cultures within a culture is also commonly believed to provide its own characteristic ways of thinking and acting—stored learned behaviors which mold the beliefs, attitudes, values, and actions of its members. If we accept the existence of these subcultural worlds (and by no means all social scientists do) then it is legitimate to ask if each also has its own characteristic ways of handling adolescence which results in a pattern of teen-age culture in each minority group that differs from other such groups as well as from the generalized teen-age culture.

There is no simple answer to this question. As indicated above, some social scientists now hold that minority subcultures no longer exist, and even the existence of a distinctive youth or adolescent culture as a dominant pattern among adolescents in American life has been questioned.[1] Other social scientists, however, not only accept the existence of youth subcultures but describe in some detail the pertinent and distinctive characteristics.[2]

Even an introspective appeal to my own adolescence does not seem to help resolve the question to my satisfaction. I spent the major portion of my own adolescence in an Italo-American community, a "Little Italy" which had its own distinctive normative system, values, and patterns of behavior. As I have listened to friends and colleagues whose adolescent years were spent in other cultural situations—Negro, Jewish, white Protestant middle class—I know that my own

---

[1] Frederick Elkin and William A. Westley, "The Myth of Adolescent Culture," *The American Sociological Review*, Vol. 20, No. 6 (December 1955), pp. 680–84.

[2] See, for example, Talcott Parsons, "Psychoanalysis and the Social Structure," *Psychoanalytic Quarterly*, Vol. 19 (1950), pp. 371–84; Arnold Green, *Sociology* (New York: McGraw-Hill, 1952), p. 95; and Ernest A. Smith, *American Youth Culture* (New York: The Free Press of Glencoe, 1962), pp. 4–18.

adolescent attitudes and behaviors were different. Yet, as I think of the differences, the religious ceremonies and "festas," the food habits, the feelings of love and warmth and belonging, I *know* that I shared these with my family, but I do not (or will not) remember ever sharing them with my peers. These were ideas about life I held because my parents said I should; they were values I accepted because they were part of family life. If I ever discussed them with my peers I am sure we talked about them as part of the family life which each of us shared with his family, but not with each other. What kept us together as teen-age friends were other values and behaviors which emerged from the conflict-laden situation of marginality in which we found ourselves and which we could never share with our immigrant parents. Now, conceivably we had evolved a distinctive pattern of adolescent culture which was neither Italian nor American but a hybrid pattern somewhere in between. But I do not think this was the case and if it were we, at least, were totally unaware of it. Certainly we had interests, games, tastes, and ideas which were different from any other subcultural group, but I do not think these were formalized enough to form a cultural milieu strong enough to mold our behavior. And more important, any subcultural elements we shared were not characterized by the permanency and intergenerational persistence usually associated with the concept of culture.

What was happening to us, and what I suggest happens to most minority teen-age groups, is that we were discovering (and in some cases inventing) behavior norms from the surrounding dominant culture and these norms conflicted with what our parents expected of us. We had not developed a new Italo-American teen-age culture—an all-inclusive system of behavior which provided guides for everyday life—we had simply found some ways by which to adjust conflicting parent-expectations with dominant culture expectations. What emerged for us was not a distinctly Italo-American pattern of behavior but rather what have come to be called "contracultural patterns of values and behaviors based on conflict."[3]

All of this is not to say that the cultural world of the adolescent minority group member is not different from teen-age life in general. Rather, it is intended as a caution to the assumption that teen-age culture in any minority group is simply the result of the admixture

---

[3] Yinger's definition of contraculture is: "I suggest the use of the term contraculture wherever the normative system of a group contains, as a primary element, a theme of conflict with the values of the total society, where personality variables are directly involved in the development and maintenance of the group's values, and wherever its norms can be understood only by reference to the relationships of the group to a surrounding dominant culture." J. Milton Yinger, "Contraculture and Subculture," *American Sociological Review*, Vol. 25, No. 5 (October 1960), p. 629.

of the minority group subculture and the dominant American culture, or that there is, within the minority group, an established, permanent, and persistent group attitude and normative pattern of behavior which tells adolescents what to believe and how to behave. The patterns of adolescent culture characteristic of a minority group simply evolve on an *ad hoc* basis as the youngsters adjust to life around them. Thus, minority group youths' behaviors are essentially the result of emergent norms rather than established cultural patterns.

Despite the lack of agreement as to the existence of distinctive minority group adolescent subcultures, differences in attitudes and behavior on the part of minority group teenagers as individuals are well accepted. Differences in parent-adolescent relationships, achievement motivation, delinquency rates, gang behavior, and many other areas of teen-age behavior have been well documented. Generally these studies have indicated that minority group teenagers differ from the nonminority group teenagers and that the various groups differ from each other as well.

Before taking up these differences, however, it would be well to consider the cultural history and present teen-age behavior patterns of some American minority groups. Such groups do differ from each other and the reasons for these differences are often visible in the social and cultural history of the group at the time of immigration and since. We will examine these groups; an ethnic group (the Italo-Americans), an ethnic religion (American Jews), and a racial group (the American Negro).

## THE ITALO-AMERICAN TEENAGER [4]

The Italo-American teenager of today is the third-generation grandchild of the Italians who swarmed to the United States in the great wave of Italian emigration at the turn of the century. During the decade 1900–1910, a total of 2,104,125 [5] Italians emigrated to the United States, mostly from Southern Italy and Sicily. [6] The vast ma-

---

[4] This section is adopted from Francis A. J. Ianni, "The Italo-American Teen-Ager," *The Annals*, Vol. 338 (Nov., 1961), pp. 70–78 and, by the same author, "Residential and Occupational Mobility as Indices of the Acculturation of the Italians in Norristown, 1900–1950," in Sidney Goldstein, *The Norristown Study* (Philadelphia: University of Pennsylvania Press, 1961), pp. 230–44.

[5] This figure is based upon the number of Italian immigrants who entered the United States regardless of the length of their stay. It is computed from tables in the U.S. Bureau of Immigration, *Report of the Commissioner-General of Immigration, 1930*, pp. 175–76.

[6] There are many definitions of Southern Italy. The one Italians commonly accepted, which includes the provinces of greatest emigration, encompasses the provinces of Apulia, Calabria, Campagnia, Lucania, and Abbruzzi and Molise, and the Island of Sicily. More generally, this may be described as all of Italy south of Rome.

jority came from agricultural villages where they had been peasant farmers (contadini), farm day laborers (*giornatori*), or, in a few cases, artisans.

In Southern Italy, the peasant family at the turn of the century was the basic social and economic unit of this traditional folk society. Patriarchal, well-integrated, and almost self-sufficient, this family unit engaged in an active family- and village-centered life. The typically large family was dominated by an authoritarian father whose control and right to punish his children, even into adulthood, was unquestioned. Sons and daughters were expected to contribute both financially and affectionally to the family. Even after marriage, the son's first responsibility and the new daughter-in-law's subservience were to the husband's family. All recreation was centered in the family and any extrafamilial contact was almost entirely restricted to the village.

Adolescence as a distinct age grade was almost nonexistent, for the boy assumed the responsbilities of adulthood very early; young boys from the age of ten usually tended the flocks. By the time the boy had reached fifteen or sixteen years of age, he was a fully productive member of the family unit and, in many cases, had begun his own family. Girls helped the mother in the house and worked on the farm until marriage when the girl took up the same subservient role in relation to her husband's family.

Education for the children of the peasants was, of necessity, short-lived and meager, even by American standards at the turn of the century. Each child was needed to work for the family unit, and, since the average work day was ten to eleven hours, little time was left for learning. Those children who did attend school during part of the year were rigidly segregated, boys and girls going to separate schools. Education terminated at age ten, and school-centered social activities simply did not exist.

Most marriages were endogamous by village and while it was customary for the parents to choose mates for their children, some degree of choice, subject to parental approval, was permitted. Marriage commonly took place in the early teens and it was not unusual for girls of fourteen and boys only a few years older to be married and accepted as young adults.

With very few exceptions, the people of Southern Italy were and remain Roman Catholics. Catholicism in Southern Italy, however, differed in practice from that found elsewhere in Italy; it differed even more significantly from the predominantly Irish-American Catholicism found in the United States. In Southern Italy, Catholicism was more ritualistic, more mystical, and permeated more of the daily life of the peasant than elsewhere. But, as was also true in other parts of Italy but not in the United States, the men of the villages held an almost antagonistic attitude toward the church and particularly toward the priesthood.

The village-centered family system of Southern Italy brought by the immigrants to the United States may be characterized, then, as typically patriarchal with a strong, family-community-centered culture. The children were an integral part of this family but subordinate as individuals, and parental authority stressed the duties rather than the rights of children. In return, however, the family provided for the child the means of satisfaction for most necessary affectional, social, educational, and economic needs. The teen-age adolescent was non-existent because by the time a child entered his teens he was already an active, producing member of the family. By the middle teens he had begun his own family, while still retaining membership in his father's family.

### The Immigrants and Their Children

The immigrant Italian peasant family was forced to make drastic and dramatic changes as soon as it arrived in the United States. The labor market in America drew them to the cities to become day laborers in industrial, construction, and transportation sectors of the economy. Very few became farmers or even farm laborers. The reasons were both economic and cultural. In Italy, farming had been conducted on small plots outside the villages in which the peasants lived. In the United States, however, farming was an individual enterprise with farms dispersed and isolated in the rural areas. Equally important was the fact that most Italian immigrants arrived with barely enough money to establish households in the cities, let alone enough to purchase or lease farms.

In these strange and hostile cities the Italians banded together into cultural enclaves and the "Little Italies" began to grow, often with old village neighbors as new neighbors here. Because of their close cultural contact with other Italian families, because of the belief of many that they were here for only a brief period before returning to Italy, and in spite of the many immediate pressures toward acculturation, the traditional Italian family pattern remained relatively intact during the first few years in the United States. But soon the realization that ethnicity was economically as well as socially retarding, the continued strong pressures toward acculturation, and the natural results of culture contact as the children had more and more to do with

Americans began to undermine and weaken the Old World peasant pattern.

In time, the family became only fictitiously patriarchal as the children, out of the home for long periods during the day, achieved new independence and the family-centered educational, recreational, economic, and religious functions were more and more fulfilled by the American community. The adolescent children of these families in conflict became the teenagers in conflict popularly identified with the Little Italies of the 1920's and 1930's. The street-corner gangs made famous by the press, as well as by William Foote Whyte, emerged as the teenagers, no longer encompassed by an integrated and need-satisfying family, took to the street corners and peer-group associations.[7] The family had neither the means nor the living space to provide recreation to replace the labor previously expected of the teenagers. New conflicts also appeared in the parent-child relationship as the teenager attempted to transmit his newly acquired American expectations of life into the weakened family structure. The teenage Italo-American children of the 1920's and 1930's were neither Italian nor American but occupied an uncomfortable and confused position somewhere between the two.

The teen-age life of the children of these marginal men was quite different, however. By the time of the adolescent years of the second-generation Italo-American teenager, whose parents were American-born children of Italian-born parentage, the family had moved even further from the traditional Italian pattern. This movement was physical as well as cultural, for, by the 1930's, Italo-Americans had begun to move in increasing numbers out of the colonies.

The forces which molded the second-generation teenager were as much, if not more, lower-class urban American as traditional Italian. In his childhood, this teenager attended an American public school or a parochial school where the nun-teachers and usually the pastor were Irish-American rather than immigrant-Italian or even Italo-American. The few Italian priests and nuns who had come to the United States were dying off, and they were not being replaced by Italo-Americans in anywhere near sufficient numbers to staff the churches in the colonies. In these churches, the teenager was encouraged to join a host of new church-centered social, religious, and recreational groups, such as the Catholic Youth Organization, the parish Boy Scout troop, or some other such organization. These groups, along with the youth centers, school social groups, and other

---

[7] William Foote Whyte, *Street Corner Society* (Chicago: University of Chicago Press, 1943).

civic activities designed to "keep him off the streets," brought him into increased and intensified contact with parent-substitutes who conveyed the values of urban American rather than Italo-American culture.

For those who had moved out of the colonies, the acculturative contact was even greater. Their peer-group associations were often with non-Italo-American youngsters. The old immigrant mutual-benefit societies and the *Bocce* clubs, organized to keep nostalgic contact with Old Country values, were as alien to the second-generation teenager as to his "American" friends. He did not feel at home in such associations as "The Patriotic Order of Sons of Italy in America."

In some cases, the adjustment of the second generation to this conflict was extreme—the name was changed, all association with the colony was cut off, and the individual rushed to become an American. In some cases, the reaction was equally extreme but in the other direction—second generation families re-embraced the Italo-American cultural pattern, preferred to remain in the colony close to the parental home, and insulated themselves against further pressures toward acculturation. The most common reaction, however, was to attempt some compromise adjustment, seeking integration into the American culture while still retaining intimate contact with the immigrant family and way of life.

These second-generation teenagers, many of whom married outside their ethnic group and many of whom served in the armed services in World War II, are the parents of today's third-generation Italo-American teenagers. The adjustment they made to the conflict between the small-village peasant Italian cultural orientation of their parents and the predominantly lower-class urban American culture in which they were reared represents the cultural baseline for the third-generation teenager.

### Today's Adolescent

Today's Italo-American teenager is the third-generation product of this heritage of peasant-village Italian culture exposed to forty-odd years of acculturation in the United States. A third set of forces, the general social change which has taken place in the teen-age culture of the United States over the last half century, combines with these forces to shape his cultural milieu. How individual Italo-American teenagers respond to these forces is, of course, dependent largely upon the type of adjustment made by their second-generation parents.

For those teen-age members of second-generation families who sought complete integration into the American culture, residual

Italian cultural characteristics are minimal or nonexistent. Living outside the ethnic colony, often with new or anglicized names, their only association with the Italo-American culture is the infrequent contact they have with their immigrant grandparents. On these occasions, the grandparents are often proud of the advances made by their "American" descendents but still retain some degree of resentment over the abandonment of the "old family" and its traditions. During a recent visit to a large Italian colony in Pennsylvania, I was introduced to the immigrant grandfather of a popular Italo-American rock-and-roll singer. The old man gave me a lengthy description of the beautiful and costly home the young star bought for his parents. His obvious pride in the accomplishment of his grandson was somewhat conditioned, however, by ill-hidden disappointment, for he added, "Of course, in that beautiful house with all those expensive paintings and pictures he didn't put up one picture or statue of a saint or even a crucifix."

For those "Capobiancos" who became "Whiteheads" and the "Campagnias" who became "Bells," the transition is almost complete. This total rejection of Italo-American ethnicity has been relatively rare, but, where it does exist, it necessarily becomes even more complete in the third-generation teenager. His parents have rejected Italo-American culture and he has been reared as an American. If his parents were accepted as Americans, then he has no ties with the immigrant culture. These teenagers are Italo-American only in ancestry and are virtually indistinguishable from their non-Italo-American peers.

In the few families which sought to maintain and, indeed, to re-embrace the Italian cultural pattern by a closer orientation with the Italian neighborhood, the course of social change and the compelling forces of acculturation have worked against any further re-Italianization. As movement out of the colonies continues, along with the increasing dilution of the cultural baseline of their ethnicity, they are now forty years removed from the traditional environment. Warm, family-centered life remains, but the importance of interfamilial community relationships has all but disappeared. The traditional religious *festas* where *paisani* from the same village or province celebrated the feast of the patron saint, the provincial mutual-benefit societies, and the interlocking system of godparenthood are becoming rarities. And, even where they do exist, the bonds they once signified are alien and meaningless to today's teenager. Even the neighborhoods are beginning to disappear as Italo-Americans move up the ladder of social acceptance and are replaced in the slum areas by recent Spanish-speaking immigrants and Negroes. As the immigrant grandparents die off in increasing numbers, there is no place to turn but to greater integration into the American culture. These teenagers may well become the new Italo-American generation in conflict for the decision of their parents to resist acculturation has merely postponed its inevitable occurrence.

The vast majority of today's teen-age Italo-Americans, however, comes from neither of these two types of second-generation families but rather from the marginal families which, both in and outside the colonies, sought Americanization while still retaining a bond with the old family and culture. The teenagers of this group are best described as typically American while still retaining elements of ethnic identification.

Since these Italo-American families fall predominantly in the lower socioeconomic classes, their teen-age children have greater representation in the earlier phases of teen-age culture. By late adolescence, they have usually entered the labor market, and those who do go on to college have no distinctive ethnic patterns to follow. Italo-Americans are still underrepresented in the higher socioeconomic classes, so Italo-American teenagers are not a significant group in the middle- and upper-class-oriented later-teen culture.

The role of the younger Italo-American teenager in the family is much the same as in other lower-class families. There is, perhaps, greater warmth and a stronger affectional bond, but only the affectional function remains of the once-strong family. The family is slightly more patriarchal than other lower-class families but tends toward the ideal of democracy.

Today's Italo-American teenager is also much more Irish-American in religious orientation than either his father or grandfather. The effect of religious and often academic education by the predominantly Irish-Catholic church in the United States has been to give this generation of Italo-American teenagers a much stronger religious orientation to life than previous generations. It is this orientation, more than any other, which will shape their attitudes toward family life and the rearing of the coming fourth generation.

Another factor which affects Italo-American participation in teen-age culture is their high degree of urbanization. Most Italo-American families continue to live in large and medium-sized cities, so that third-generation teenagers are underrepresented in the suburban and rural patterns of teen-age culture. In these cities, many of the characteristics associated with the Italo-American youth of the 1930's and 1940's are beginning to disappear. Street-corner gangs are still found in the larger cities but have nearly vanished from the smaller ones. Even in the larger cities, however, the structure and the functions of the gang have changed. The well-organized street-corner society which had a locus in a particular neighborhood and a specific territory to "protect" has given way to an organization which is likely to include non-Italo-Americans and even non-neighbors. Neither does the street-corner gang serve the same status-conferring function it did in earlier generations. The paths of advancement into adult status in the Italo-American community no longer depend upon the preservation of the reciprocal gang obligations described by Whyte in Cornerville.[8] In most cities, organized Italo-American communities no longer exist, so the teenager must prepare for a role in the general community rather than in the Italian community.

The declining importance of Italo-American teen-age gangs results from the disappearance of the factors which led to their original formation. Culturally, the sudden break from a strong family-centered adolescence made strong peer-centered associations inevitable. These conditions simply do not exist for the third-generation teenager. Psychologically, a large element in the formation of the neighborhood gangs was a sense of cultural inferiority to which the teenagers responded by banding together. As Italo-American social mobility has increased, this basis for gang organization has lessened in importance.

The final factor which preserves some element of ethnicity in the Italo-American teenager is the fact that he is still identified as being an Italian American by his peers and their parents. Attitudes toward Italo-Americans have changed over the last forty years and social acceptance is much greater today than in the past. Certainly, active discrimination against such groups as the Poles, Ukrainians, and Greeks has greatly subsided. But, while there is not the same hostility and social distance that existed for the second-generation teenager, Italo-Americans are still considered "different" and teased about Italian gangsters on TV shows ("Cops and Wops"), and about pizza and spaghetti. Most Italo-American teenagers accept this differentiation as a relatively minor part of American life and the teasing as the good-natured banter it usually is. Being considered different, however, cannot help but influence the teenager's self concept, and so he does not always participate as an equal in teen-age culture.

Most of these changes have been the result of the acculturative experience of the Italian family in the United States. During several recent visits to Italy I have been struck by the fact that many of the changes described above are also taking place among teenagers in the

---

[8] *Ibid.*, pp. 104–8.

Italian cities. In fact, the orientation of Italian urban teenagers is almost as much to American teen-age culture as it is to Italian culture.

The history of the Italo-American teenager indicates what seems to be true of all immigrant ethnic groups in the United States. The adolescent child of the recent immigrant is caught between the ethnic culture of his parents and the teen-age culture of his peers. After two or three generations, however, the ethnic factor all but disappears and social class factors become far more important than ethnic patterns.

## JEWISH TEEN-AGE CULTURE

Today's American Jewish subculture sprang from a more varied background than that of the Italo-Americans. While the Italian emigration was largely regional and restricted to the period from 1890 to 1924 (and heavily concentrated at the turn of the century), Jewish emigration covers a much longer period of time and a much wider area of origin. The first period of Jewish immigration to the United States was from the mid-1600's to 1830 when Sephardic Jews—followers of the Spanish rite—came to this country from Spain, Portugal, South America, and later Holland, England, and the West Indies.

After 1830 and up until 1881, large numbers of German Jews, despairing of opportunities at home, migrated to the United States. Settling largely in the cities, they became traders and peddlers but soon began to rise in economic and, to a lesser degree, social status. From 1881 to the restrictive immigration laws of 1924, the locus of Jewish emigration changed to Eastern Europe as Russian, Polish, Ukranian, and Rumanian Jews fled the restrictions and pogroms of Eastern Europe.[9] The bulk of the Eastern European Jewish immigrants settled in New York City and became workers and later entrepreneurs in the garment industries.

Two smaller periods of Jewish emigration resulted from Nazi oppression in Europe. From around 1936 to World War II, about 150,000 Jewish immigrants entered the United States, and after the war about the same number of survivors of the concentration camps arrived. Both these later groups contained large numbers of individuals who had at one time enjoyed high economic and social status in Europe. Though most arrived penniless and destitute, this group has adjusted itself well and has rapidly achieved responsible positions.

While most writers on current Jewish social life agree that this multiple cultural origin does not greatly affect modern American Jewish culture, it is important to note that it was not a common regional cul-

---

[9] Nathan Glazer, *American Judaism* (Chicago: University of Chicago Press, 1957), p. 62.

ture that held the Jews together in this country but rather a common religious cultural heritage. Consequently, American Jewish culture is essentially that of an *ethnic church* and religious identification has served as the chief guarantor of Jewish ethnic persistence and survival.[10] This shared religious ethnicity of Jews can and has survived social and residential mobility far better than the cultural ethnicity of the Italo-Americans.

Despite these differences in cultural focus and regional origin, there are striking similarities between the generational experiences of Jewish and Italian immigrants and their descendents. Like the Italians, the first-generation Jews had to make immediate adjustments for economic survival. Like the Italians, they banded together in ghettoes where they found the security of tradition and the community of *landsmans*.[11] Unlike the Italians, the European Jews had brought with them an existing pattern of ghetto life so that isolation from the dominant culture in the United States was more complete and probably less conflict generating. If the American cultural pattern was strange, ghetto life was not, for this pattern of isolated communal existence for social survival was not unique to America but had been very much a part of Jewish life in Europe. Unlike the Italians, the great wave of Jewish immigrants from Eastern Europe had been preceded by German and Latin co-religionists who could and did offer occupational opportunities which allowed the immigrants to continue to survive as Jews.

### The Second-generation Jew

The emergent generation of American Judaism, again like the Italo-American, became the marginal generation in conflict. The teenagers of this generation actively sought Americanization and rejected the security of the ghetto. If the first generation wanted merely to survive in an alien land, their teen-age children wanted to live as a part of the culture of that land.

The means by which this generation achieved its partial assimilation were once again the familiar patterns found among the Italo-Americans; occupational and residential mobility.[12] The second-

---

[10] Marshal Sklare, "The Function of Ethnic Churches: Judaism in the United States," in J. Milton Yinger, *Religion, Society and the Individual* (New York: The MacMillan Co., 1957), pp. 458–59.

[11] See Louis Wirth, *The Ghetto* (Chicago: University of Chicago Press, Phoenix Books, 1956).

[12] See Francis A. J. Ianni, "Occupational and Residential Mobility as Indices of the Acculturation of an Ethnic Group," *Social Forces*, Vol. 36, No. 1 (October 1957), pp. 65–72, and William Kephart, "What is Known about the Occupations of Jews," in Arnold Rose (ed.), *Race Prejudice and Discrimination* (New York: Knopf, 1951), pp. 131–46.

generation Jewish community which resulted from this partial assimilation has been called "the gilded ghetto," where the institutions were all middle-class American but the participants were all Jewish.[13]

In the second-generation ghetto, teen-age life moved rapidly and dramatically from what had been traditional in the first-generation ghetto to an emergent contraculture. This was also the age of the Jewish intellectual in protest as Jewish youth groped for meaning and identity and found escape from both binding orthodoxy and repugnant materialism in the broad intellectual formulations of Zionism, the labor movement, and socialism.

In the traditional Jewish family the father was the strong head of a patriarchal family steeped in moral and religious values and the home was regarded as the "Mikdash Me'at"—the miniature sanctuary. In the second-generation family the patriarchal dominance of the father began to disappear as the mother took on new duties. The strong drive for business and professional success which characterized the second-generation male left little time for active family management. But perhaps the most striking development in this generation was the inevitable change in religious attitudes. The orthodoxy of the ghetto was too cumbersome and too visible for the mobile second generation. New religious attitudes and institutions developed and the conservative synagogue—where Jewish identity was maintained without the all-encompassing religiosity of orthodoxy—became the religious and social center. Teaching the group loyalties necessary for group survival, yet giving teenagers a chance to participate in new middle-class youth activities as well as Hebrew classes, the "temple center" joined with community centers, YMHA, and the summer camps to provide for Jewish teenagers an experience in the middle-class life of America without the need to leave the ethnic fold. Jewish teenagers associated with other Jewish teenagers and social contact outside the group was not encouraged.

### Today's Jewish Adolescent

This is the cultural background of today's Jewish teenager. Like the Italo-American and other minority groups, the Jews had to adjust to new social, economic, and psychological imperatives generated by immigration to the United States. Unlike most other ethnic groups, however, the role of religion as the main expression of Jewish identity allowed for survival of group identification even after occupational and social mobility disrupted the ethnic community. Over-all Jewish

---

[13] Judith R. Kramer and Seymour Leventman, *Children of the Gilded Ghetto* (New Haven: Yale University Press, 1961).

identification has remained high and ethnic survival under religion auspices has had a lasting effect. Most accounts of modern Jewish teenage culture stress the fading of this sense of uniqueness and special destiny and the coherent sense of distinctive Jewish identity.[14] The same commentators, however, indicate that Jewish teenagers have created a culture which still has elements of ethnic uniqueness.

Jewish teenagers tend to view themselves as participating fully in American teen-age culture but most still hold some feeling of identification as Jews. There is some evidence, however, that the sensitivity in regard to being Jews, which Kurt Lewin and others saw as the basis of Jewish "self-hatred," has all but disappeared.[15] David Boroff, for example, in describing modern Jewish teen-age culture reports that among Jewish teenagers he interviewed, being Jewish is "no longer a burden or an obligation but merely a fact of life generating neither anguish or exaltation."[16] He sees even less feeling of uniqueness among younger Jewish teenagers.[17]

The younger teens have even less sense of being differentiated from the mass of American teen-agers than do the older Jewish teen-agers. In a series of interviews with groups of Jewish boys and girls between the ages of thirteen and sixteen, I found it difficult to elicit from them any coherent sense of their own distinctive Jewish identity. "We don't have to try to be like other teen-agers," a fifteen-year-old boy remarked. "We *are* like other teen-agers." A girl of the same age ventured the definition that they were merely "teen-agers of Jewish parents." In any case, they were emphatic about participating fully in American teen-age culture. There was no embarrassment, for example, at their passion for rock-and-roll music, although a few cultural status-seekers insisted that their musical tastes were catholic—"I like all kinds of music." And though they approved of current sartorial styles—"If a boy has a thirty inch waist, he wears trousers that measure 28 inches"—they showed some sophisticated amusement at sartorial excess. If there is any significant difference between Jewish teen-age culture and the dominant models, it is that the Jewish version is somewhat less cultistic and less sharply set off from adult life. One is not likely to find, for example, many Jewish teen-agers among the rabid enthusiasts who wait outside theaters for their rock-and-roll idols. There is a reason for the narrow margin between Jewish teen-age culture and adult life. Jewish middle class life is increasingly secular and hedonistic. This tendency, coupled with the traditional cohesiveness of Jewish family life, counteracts the impulse of Jewish teen-agers to seal themselves off from adult culture.

Religious behavior among Jewish teen-agers shows the result of

---

[14] See David Boroff, "Jewish Teen-Age Culture." *The Annals*, Vol. 338 (Nov. 1961), pp. 79–90; and Albert I. Gordon, *Jews in Suburbia* (Boston: the Beacon Press, 1959).

[15] Kurt Lewin, "Self-Hatred Among Jews," *Contemporary Jewish Record*, Vol. 4 (June, 1941), 219–32. Copyright 1941 by *Contemporary Jewish Record*. The article was reprinted in the posthumous collection of the author's esays under the title, "Resolving Social Conflicts" (New York: Harper & Brothers, 1948), 186–200. Copyright 1948 by Harper & Brothers.

[16] David Boroff, "Jewish Teen-Age Culture," *The Annals of the American Academy of Political and Social Science*, Vol. 338 (Nov. 1961), p. 80.

[17] *Ibid.*, p. 80.

years of adjustment and acculturation to middle-class American society. As pointed out earlier, religion has been the central theme in maintaining the ethnicity of Judaism. If the religious values and customs had remained immutable to the changing times, the religious conflict of the second generation would have been magnified for the third. Such is not the case, however, because mutual customary observances have been modified to fit the host culture and the emphasis has been placed on the ethical rather than religious and ritualistic elements of Judaism. Now there is nothing to rebel against since the ethical values are not greatly different from those of the dominant society. In *The Riverton Study,* for example, when Jewish adolescents were asked, "What do you think you will do when you are married and have your own family?" no evidence of impending conflict and rebellion appeared. Seventy-two per cent of the youngsters said they plan to observe the same customs their parents do; 11 per cent plan to be less strict, and 7 per cent believe they will be more observant than their parents.[18]

*The Riverton Study* also indicates the continued movement from orthodoxy is as true of the third-generation teenager as of the second. In this study, only 9 per cent of the teenagers, but 16 per cent of the parents and 81 per cent of the grandparents, described themselves as orthodox.[19] Reared in a thoroughly acculturated Judaism, today's Jewish teenager experiences little religious conflict and has little reason for religious rebellion.

Another factor in second-generation Jewish culture which persists into modern Jewish teen-age culture is the social differentiation which results in a multiclass society. If the second-generation Jew sought economic mobility as a means of advance, the third generation has settled into a pattern of accepting these social differences. Today, however, income alone does not distinguish one Jew from another; social stratification is based on occupational prestige, social level, and "class."

The effect of this stratification is felt particularly among the older Jewish teens for this is primarily a college-oriented culture—65 per cent of the college-age Jewish students attend colleges as contrasted to 46 per cent of the males and 29 per cent of the females in the population at large. The teen-age culture of the upper middle-class Jewish student at the Ivy League school or the large Midwestern university differs considerably from that of the lower middle-class Jewish student

[18] J. Marshall Sklare and Marc Vosk, *The Riverton Study* (New York: The American Jewish Committee, 1957), p. 15.
[19] *Ibid.,* p. 16.

at Temple, City University, Brooklyn College, or other urban universities. Generally, the degree of ethnicity and group identification seems to be inversely related to socioeconomic status among college-level Jewish teenagers.[20] These differences, based as they are on a social class rather than ethnicity, underscore the changing pattern of Jewish teen-age culture. As social mobility brings the Jewish teenager into increasing contact with the dominant American middle-class teen-age culture, ethnicity diminishes.

## THE NEGRO TEENAGER

Teen-age behavior among American Negroes results from conditions which differ dramatically from those of the Italo-American and the Jewish American teenager or any other teen-age group in America. As Joseph S. Himes points out, the quality of Negro teen-age culture is shaped by four decisive factors: "Race, inferiority, deprivation, and youthfulness." [21]

Youthfulness is, of course, a characteristic Negro teenagers share with all others; deprivation is also characteristic of some other minority groups, particularly during the immigrant period; and even social "inferiority" is not restricted to Negroes. The special characteristic of Negro teen-age culture is race and the visibility which is a part of racial membership. The unique group patterns characteristic of Negro teenagers are a blend of those same ingredients which motivate other teenagers, but they are filtered through barriers of deprivation and racial discrimination which tend to "trap Negro teen-agers by forces beyond their control [and] the school, the church, the mass media, city street and other institutions . . . serve to sharpen the sense of entrapment and deprivation." [22]

The seeds of this entrapment are to be found in the culture history of the Negro family. The well-developed familial and kinship patterns of the Africans were practically destroyed by forced migration to the New World and slavery. Unlike the Italian and the Jewish immigrant, the African was not given a period of adjustment in which his traditional family values and practices could be adjusted to the new environment. Indeed, the African was not an immigrant at all, but a slave, and the choice of place and mode of residence, and many of the familial arrangements we take for granted, were not his to make.

The family system which emerged in the plantation economy of the

[20] For an excellent account of various college-level Jewish cultural milieus, see David Boroff, *op. cit.*, pp. 83–88.

[21] Joseph S. Himes, "Negro Teen-age Culture," *The Annals,* Vol. 33 (Nov. 1961), p. 92.

[22] *Ibid.*, p. 93.

South was a matriarchal society in which the father not only played a minor role but often was not even present. The locus mobility of individuals which characterized the slave economy, the African heritage of polygymy, and the impossibility of any fixed, ordered family life combined to produce a situation where only the bond between the mother and her child could effectively resist disruptive effects of slavery on family life. The mother inevitably emerged as the dominant and dependable (rather than dependent) figure in the Negro family. A child, whether by a white or a Negro father, took the status of his mother and became a part of her "family"—often with no knowledge of who his father was and feeling kinship only with the maternal line.

As soon as the children were physically capable of labor, the boys worked either in the fields or on the grounds and the girls took over chores from the mother either in the cabin or in the manor house. Soon after puberty they were expected to procreate new slaves—often through selective breeding rather than actual permanent mating. Legitimacy and illegitimacy were not important considerations and in many cases a female's children had different biological fathers.

After emancipation the pattern established in slavery continued both in the South and in the developing Negro centers in the North. The characteristic Southern Negro family which grew out of slavery after emancipation is well described in Hortense Powdermaker's study in Mississippi.[23]

Among the middle and lower class Negroes in Cottonville, the woman is usually the head of the house in importance and authority and is frequently the chief economic support. Even where husband and wife share responsibility for maintaining and directing the family, the woman is likely to contribute the larger share of the income and to assume the larger share of family responsibility. The economic disparity is most evident in town, where employment is so much more available to the women than to the men. The matriarchal nature of the family organization obtains equally on the plantations. In many cases the woman is the sole breadwinner. Often there is no man in the household at all. In a number of instances, elderly women in their seventies and their middle-aged daughters, with or without children and often without husbands, form one household with the old woman as the head.

In the North, this family pattern continued, partly as the result of the persistence of a cultural pattern already established and partly as a result of economic factors which made Negro females more employable than males. After slavery, Negro women were able to find work as domestics while Negro males, restricted to unskilled labor, faced growing unemployment or became "hustlers," finding employment on a day-by-day basis. In more recent years, continued employ-

---

[23] Hortense Powdermaker, *After Freedom* (New York: The Viking Press, 1939), pp. 145–46.

ment discrimination and welfare regulations requiring an absent father for aid to dependent children have almost institutionalized the fatherless—whether physical or psychological—family by lower-class Negroes.[24]

There have been other patterns of Negro family organization—that which developed among the half-million freed slaves before the Civil War as well as the stable family organizations found among middle-class Negroes today—but the social heritage of the slave family is the cultural background within which the majority of lower-class Negro teenagers must function. More than any other segment of the population they are affected and afflicted by poor housing, job discrimination, inferior educational opportunities and—inevitably—the frustration that results from the knowledge that only a part of the promise and glittering affluence that beckons our country's teenagers is for them.

### The Position of the Negro Today

The results of this deprivation and dissemination and the reactions of the lower-class Negro teenager to this frustration are statistically clear:

· Negro teenagers have far higher rates of arrest; in Washington, D.C., for example, between June 1962 and July 1963, of the 2,366 offenders referred to juvenile courts 86 per cent were Negroes.

· In 1956, over 30 per cent of all reported arrests in cities of over 2,500 population were among Negroes while the Negro was only about 10 per cent of the population.

· While all crime and juvenile delinquency rates are enormously high among Negroes in most American communities, their rates for crimes of violence are even higher.[25]

The factors which lead to this situation are equally clear:

· The illiteracy rate among Negroes is four times that of whites.

· In the nation, 24 per cent of the nonwhite population is functionally illiterate (less than five years of schooling) compared with 7 per cent of the white population.

· Negroes made up nearly 60 per cent of selectees rejected for military service in World War II because of educational deficiency, though they formed only about 10 per cent of the population at that time.

· Nearly 70 per cent of the young white population, but only about 40 per cent of the nonwhite youngsters, have graduated from high school. To put it another way, 60 per cent of the nonwhite group were dropouts.

· On English usage tests, Southern Negro children in segregated schools score three years below the national average in elementary school and by high school are over four years behind.

· While 11.8 per cent of young adults (twenty-five to twenty-nine years of

---

[24]See St. Clair Drake and Horace R. Cayton, *Black Metropolis* (New York: Harcourt-Brace, 1945).

[25] Harry Manuel Shulman, *Juvenile Delinquency in American Society* (New York: Harper and Bros., 1961), p. 79.

age) in the white population have completed college, only 5.4 per cent of the young adults in the nonwhite population have done so.

· Eleven per cent of the total population is Negro but Negroes make up only 3.5 per cent of professional workers.

· When compared with the opportunities open to white children the Negro child has one third as much chance of completing college; one third as much chance of becoming a professional man; twice as much chance of becoming unemployed; about one seventh as much chance of earning $10,000 a year; and a life expectancy which is seven years shorter.

· The unemployment rate among Negroes is more than double that among whites (5.9 per cent for whites, 12.7 per cent for Negroes). The relative unemployment rates for teenagers are even more disturbing: 13.4 per cent of white teenagers, but almost 30 per cent of Negro teenagers, are reported out of work. In the largely Negro slum area of one city, 50 per cent of the boys aged sixteen to twenty-one were out of school and unemployed.

· Median income for those over fourteen years of age in 1959 was $1,519 for Negroes compared to $3,027 for whites. Three tenths of one per cent of the Negro incomes were over $10,000 compared to 4.7 per cent for whites.

It seems almost unnecessary to point out that these characteristics of deprivation and the statistics indicating the high Negro crime rate and obviously low achievement motivation are closely related. Early in life the Negro teenager acquires a sense of drab deprivation and, for some, violence and delinquency seem the only way to strike back.

### Negro Delinquency and Gang Behavior

While Negro teen-age youth still constitute a disproportionate number of cases of juvenile delinquency in the cities, both the pattern of the delinquency and the character of Negro gangs have begun to change in recent years. In the past, and in some cases today, delinquency among urban Negroes has been largely violent, inner-directed, and conflict oriented.[26]

The gangs formed under these conditions reflected the conflict which resulted from the economic and social deprivation of the Negro. Caught in this region of conflict, Negro gang behavior was characterized by inward-directed hostility and intra-Negro crime; it was further encouraged by white official and unofficial leniency toward intra-Negro crime. Violent gang activity provided an outlet for the aggression resulting in the frustration of marginality. The acute social disorganization of the Negro slum, the lack of facilities which made the street the dominant Negro social center, and the poverty combined to produce situations where Negro gangs differed considerably from their white equivalents.

---

[26] See Richard A. Cloward and Lloyd E. Ohlin, *Delinquency and Opportunity* (New York: The Free Press of Glencoe, 1961), pp. 199–203; Joseph S. Himes, *op. cit.*, p. 96; and E. Franklin Frazier, *The Negro in the United States* (New York: MacMillan Co., 1957), pp. 638–53.

The chief difference between white and Negro gangs seems to be in the psychological make-up of the individual members. Most observers of gang behavior hold that white gang members are usually more emotionally disturbed and this factor plays a greater role in motivating a white boy to belong to a gang than is true among Negroes.

Stanley Anderson, superintendent of the Roving Leaders, a detached program for delinquency prevention in Washington, D.C., reports that in working with Washington gangs he finds Negro boys more responsive to social-work methods than their white counterparts; Negroes can often be reached by offering jobs and recreation whereas white boys suffer not from lack of opportunities but from deeper emotional problems.[27]

Negro gangs also seem to contain a high percentage of boys who are slow learners, placed in remedial reading classes or the "basic group" in school. While the same is true of many white gang members, they appear on the whole to be more successful in school than the Negro youths.

In general, juvenile gangs provide a channel for acting out hostility and aggression but these characteristics of gang behavior appear less dominantly among Negroes than among white gang members. Where the white gang often commits senseless, random crimes, the Negro gang is more practical in its criminality. White teenagers tend to steal petty items, whether they need the article or not, because it is considered "cool." Negro teenagers, on the other hand, steal objects which have some immediate use. White teenagers seem to carry out their thefts for "kicks" much more than Negroes. Drug addiction, however, is more common among Negro gang members—a problem usually assessed to the Negro's attempt to escape the grim and dowdy world he must inhabit.[28]

Recent evidence, however, particularly from other than the larger cities, seems to indicate that tightly organized gangs have been disappearing among Negroes. The new pattern is one of "walking partners," small groups of boys consisting of three to seven members organized to carry out various crimes. These small bands do not contain the tight hierarchy of leadership—a "president," "war lord" and so on—found in the large thirty to sixty-five member gangs which were common and still are found in the larger cities. Apparently, organized gang behavior—actually a characteristic part of the Negro teen-age

---

[27] Personal contact.

[28] See Harrison E. Salisbury, *The Shook-up Generation* (New York: Harper and Bros., 1958), p. 208, *passim*.

pattern only in specific slum areas of the great cities—is becoming even less institutionalized. Never a significant feature of the lives of most Negro teenagers, the violent gangs seem to be on the wane.

The future of Negro delinquency and gang activity is peculiarly associated with growing social assent, in both the legitimate and the illegitimate worlds of the slum. As the Negro's life chances improve—in the numbers rackets as well as in legitimate business, in the crime syndicates as well as the labor market—violence as a feature of Negro teen-age life will diminish. Richard Cloward and Lloyd Ohlin predict just such a change.

> If our analysis is correct, drastic changes may be imminent in the character of Negro delinquency, not only in Harlem but also in many urban centers where the Negro's power is beginning to be felt. The growth of illegal wealth and political power will probably lead to the types of neighborhood integration that provide opportunities for legitimate as well as illegitimate social ascent. We may expect, therefore, that violence will diminish in Negro neighborhoods and that criminal modes of delinquency will increase. In addition, such defeatist adaptations as widespread drug use may be on the wane.[29]

The obvious distortion presented by the figures on Negro crime and the results of deprivation is to give a picture of a brooding, sullen, uneducated, and idle Negro teen-age subculture, striking out violently in frustrated aggression at the surrounding world. Of course, many more Negro teen-agers do not fit the lower-class, urban slum gang stereotype than do. There is now a well-established and stable Negro middle class and it is growing in importance. And even in the lower class, the usual pursuits of teenagers are followed by most Negro teen-agers. Himes describes teen-age behavior of both the middle-class (high prestige) and lower-class (low prestige) teenagers.[30]

> The craving for things is intense—cars, clothes, stereo, records, transistors, cameras, and the like. It is widely reported that the teen-agers work, save, and even—especially among the low-prestige category—steal for them. The teen-agers favor such activities as car riding, vigorous dancing, competitive sports, animated "yackity-yacking," transistor toting, record listening, and the like. For example, current dance vogues in Durham, North Carolina, include the "pony," the "continental," the "twist," the "rocking Charlie," the "shimmy," the "watusi," the "booty green," the "jack-the-ripper," the "stran," and the "stupidity."
>
> Field reports from all regions indicate that dress, grooming, and ornamentation are extreme and faddish. High-prestige boys and girls tend to follow the current national teen-age styles. Low-prestige teen-agers, however, are often slightly behind current vogues or distinguished by unique styles. Though there is much variety, some girls seem to favor colored sneakers, socks, flaring skirts, with crinoline petticoats, and sloppy Joe sweaters; others go for short tight skirts, burlap cloth being one current vogue, bulky sweaters with the ubiquitous sneakers and socks, and sometimes stockings. Older low-prestige boys feature caps or

---

[29] Richard A. Cloward and Lloyd E. Ohlin, *op. cit.*, p. 202.
[30] Himes, *op. cit.*, p. 94.

derbies, button-down collars, "continental" jackets, short tight-legged pants, and hard-heeled shoes. "Processed" (straightened and styled) or close-cropped hair for these boys and "shades" (sun glasses) for both sexes are popular. Girls feature heavy eye make-up, light matching shades of lipstick and nail polish, usually chosen to match some color of the outfit, which may include bright, unharmonious colors.

The reports show a universal interest in music, which seems to work like a narcotic. The Negro musical heritage is a folk tradition compounded of spirituals, gospel hymns, blues and jazz. The difference between high- and low-prestige teen-agers is less evident in musical taste than in most other areas.

The contracultural aspects of Negro gang and delinquency behavior are not the only such elements in Negro teen-age society. In the 1960's, a new contracultural movement, or at least the first nationwide evidences of it, began to appear among Negro teenagers—the racial protest. From the first "sit-in" demonstration on February 1, 1960, when four freshmen from the Agricultural and Technical College in Greensboro, North Carolina, requested service at a dimestore lunch counter in the town, through the freedom rides and the picketing of school boards and building sites, to the dramatic march on Washington of August 28, 1963, the protest has gathered staggering momentum and more and more it is the Negro teenager who is actually involved in this protest. Unlike his white teen-age peers whose protests have lacked much social-action orientation, the Negro teenager has become a rebel *with* a cause. That these demonstrations are something other than just a new and more legitimate means of handling aggression and hostility is shown by Himes' description of the planning involved in a sit-in demonstration.[31]

Behind the public phase of the sit-in demonstration, however, there is a great deal of planning and organization. Student leaders must arrange meetings to recruit demonstrators, make decisions, and prepare schedules and assignments. Sometimes, though not always, interested adults also participate in the sessions where skills and disciplines are discussed, analyzed, and rehearsed. Negotiating conferences have to be arranged and conducted with the establishments affected. Legal defense must be arranged for students who get arrested and jailed, and public relations efforts must be kept going at all times. Most of the sit-in demonstrations merged into long-time picket projects that entailed a prodigious amount of organization and management.

What the results of these demonstrations and the growing positive results will be for Negro teen-age culture of the future is difficult to predict but easy to envision. Certainly the future holds widespread improvement in the educational, economic, social, and political lot of the Negro American. This must mean a growing expansion of the op-

_____
[31] *Ibid.*, p. 99.

portunities for social participation and individual expression of the Negro teenager in the general teen-age culture.

## MINORITY GROUP STATUS AND ADOLESCENT BEHAVIOR

These brief views of cultural history and teen-age behavior in three different minority groups give some idea of the range of values and attitudes, activities, and behavior patterns of the groups in comparison to each other as well as to the dominant teen-age culture. Before attempting to draw some conclusions from these comparisons, however, it might be well to take a closer look at three related areas of group differences—parent-teen relationships, achievement motivation, and gang behavior—to see the how and the why of cultural influence on teen-age behavior.

### Parent-Youth Relationships

One of the universal characteristics of adolescence is the child's move toward independence from parental control. Societies differ considerably, however, in how they provide for this transition and in how much independence is given. Even within particular societies families vary, of course, in their handling of independence training during adolescence. Some families grant greater independence sooner than others; some families never seem to grant independence. Generally, however, it is possible to determine cultural or even subcultural patterns.

From the earlier descriptions, we can generalize that both the Italian and Jewish pattern of familial authority can be characterized as basically patriarchal rather than matriarchal as is the case among Negroes. There is, however, one important difference between the Italian and the Jewish pattern. In the traditional Italian family, the subordination was complete and covered all areas of the individual's life. Among the Jews, however, in one area—the intellectual—the parents not only did not demand subordination, they valued and even insisted upon individuality and independence from their children. The child was taught early in life to question authority in his schooling, to seek knowledge, and, in general, to value intellectual curiosity and attainment. In physical matters he was just as subservient as the Italian youngster. The Jewish parent's direct concern for the child's health and safety persisted even into adulthood and the Jewish mother seemed forever ready to provide both the love and the chicken broth necessary for proper recovery.

Among Negroes, where the matriarchal family inherited from slavery has been the traditional pattern, adolescent independence is quite different. Here independence comes very early, as it necessarily must with an absent father and working mother. The discontinuities and lack of strong direction of youth socialization among Negroes become important factors in the formation of the Negro adolescent's attitudes toward himself, the community, and life in general. The situation in many lower-class Negro families might almost be described as "acultural" rather than contracultural. Ethical and moral explanations for behavior control are usually absent. The child is told not to do something or to stop doing it—but not why. Behavior thus becomes reward evoking or punishment producing, but not valued or disvalued. What the Negro child and adolescent gain as they grow older is not independence from parental control but rather a growing lack of reliance in and dependence on their parents for guidance.

These differences in parent-adolescent relations among Italians, Jews, and Negroes lead to differences in striving behavior—in agression—among Italo-American, Jewish, and Negro teenagers. Since the parent interprets (or fails to interpret) the social world to the child-adolescent, what his self-conception is, what his view of his life chances is, what he sees as the valued rewards of a society, and to what degree he feels they are available to him, all spring from the parent-child relationship and are especially related to parental training for independence. As Allison Davis has pointed out, what is rewarding for one racial or ethnic group's teenagers need not be so for others and, "What they fear, what they abhor, what they desire, what they crave, what they will work for, or fight for; what they consider valuable or sacred differ in almost every basic area of human relationships."[32] These differences have an important bearing on two very different ways teenagers channel aggression: achievement motivation and membership in juvenile gangs.

### Racial and Ethnic Differences in Achievement Motivation

One of the important differences readily apparent among teenagers is the level of achievement motivation—the desire to get ahead in the world. Present thinking on the conditions that generate or inhibit achievement motivation as an active concern in the teenager's life seem to center on childhood influences. The demands parents make on their children, the values they stress, the taboos they impose, the behaviors, the rewards, the punishments—all these can enhance or inhibit a child's, and eventually a teenager's, general attitude of con-

[32] Allison Davis, "Socialization and Adolescent Personality," in Guy E. Swanson, Theodore M. Newcomb, and Eugene L. Hartley, *Readings in Social Psychology* (New York: Henry Holt & Co., 1952), p. 528.

cern or lack of concern toward achievement. Much of the recent research in this area has concentrated on the child-rearing demands stressed by cultures characterized by high or low levels of achievement motivation. Generally these studies have indicated that early stress on mastery—getting the child to do things well—helps develop achievement motivation while general intellectual restrictiveness in the home inhibits it. Further, these researches show that where there is a high prevalence of achievement concern in the values of an ethnic group, the child rearing values and practices of the group are consonant with the fostering of achievement motivation.

Returning to our three ethnic groups, the research evidence confirms what we would be led to believe by the cultural histories and the current teen-age orientations. Jewish, Italo-American, and Negro subcultures place different emphases on both independence training and achievement training in child-rearing values and practices. As a result, high achievement motivation is more characteristic of Jewish teenagers than of Italo-American teenagers, and is lowest among Negroes.[33]

As we have seen, the cultural traditions of handling child rearing and adolescence in each of the three groups shape these levels of achievement motivation. Jewish cultural traditions stress individual mastery and rational, intellectual independence for teenagers while the Italian peasant, who never really felt he could better his own lot, was willing to accept less from and for his child. Fred L. Strodtbeck and his colleagues have indicated this attitude does affect the teenager; while both Italo-American and Jewish boys generally guessed their parents would be pleased if they achieved the highest vocational positions, the Italo-American boys also thought their parents would be satisfied with less.[34]

Jackson Toby has described the differences in Jewish and Italian cultural orientation toward intellectual accomplishment, and its effect on achievement motivation as well.[35]

Jews and Italians came to the United States in large numbers at about the same time—the turn of the century—and both settled in urban areas. There was, however, a very different attitude toward intellectual accomplishment in the two

[33] Bernard C. Rosen: "Race, Ethnicity and Achievement," *American Sociological Review*, Vol. 24, No. 1 (February, 1959), p. 60. Additional information can be found in the various writings on this subject by Rosen, Fred L. Strodtbeck, and other members of the staff of the "Cultural Factors in Talent Development" project.

[34] Fred L. Strodtbeck, Margaret R. McDonald, and Bernard C. Rosen, "Evaluation of Occupations: A Reflection of Jewish and Italian Mobility Differences," *American Sociological Review*, Vol. 22, No. 5 (October, 1957), pp. 546–53.

[35] Jackson Toby, "Hoodlum or Businessman: An American Dilemma," in Marshall Sklare (ed.), *The Jews: Patterns of an American Group* (New York: The Free Press of Glencoe, 1958), pp. 548–50.

cultures. Jews from Eastern Europe regarded religious study as the most important activity for an adult male. The rabbi enjoyed great prestige because he was a scholar, a teacher, a logician. . . . Life in America gave a secular emphasis to the Jewish reverence for learning. Material success is a more important motive than salvation for American youngsters, Jewish as well as Christian, and secular education is better training for business and professional careers than Talmudic exegesis. Nevertheless, intellectual achievement continued to be valued by Jews—and to have measurable effects. Second-generation Jewish students did homework diligently, got high grades, went to college in disproportionate numbers, and scored high on intelligence tests. Two thousand years of preparation lay behind them.

Immigrants from Southern Italy, on the other hand, tended to regard formal education either as a frill or as a source of dangerous ideas from which the minds of the young should be protected. They remembered Sicily, where a child who attended school regularly was a rarity. In the United States, many Southern Italian immigrants maintained the same attitudes. They resented compulsory school-attendance laws and prodded their children to go to work and become economic assets as soon as possible. They did not realize that education has more importance in an urban-industrial society than in a semi-feudal one. . . . [Children] accepted their parent's conception of the school as worthless and thereby lost their best opportunity for social ascent.

The Negro teenager has, of course, never really had an opportunity to internalize the achievement values of American society, and his life situation simply does not encourage the belief that one can manipulate the world around him and improve his lot in life. Getting on is, for the Negro, more important and more attainable than getting ahead.

In general, it appears there is some persistence of subcultural values into the achievement values of teenagers. While it is probably true social class differences are more important than ethnic backgrounds in this respect, current research seems to reveal that when social class differences are taken into consideration, ethnicity and race continue to be important.

### Juvenile Gang Behavior as Characteristics of Racial and Ethnic Groups

Another means by which the teen-ager may expend energy and assert aggressiveness is through delinquent behavior. While many aspects of delinquency are interesting to examine from an ethnic-cultural point of view—differential delinquency rates for Jewish, Italo-American and Negro teenagers, for example—only one will be considered here: the teen-age gang. This aspect of delinquent, pre-delinquent, and even nondelinquent behavior is peculiarly associated with minority status.

Lewis Yablonsky has identified three types of teen-age gangs: the social gang organized for comradeship and only inadvertently related to delinquent acts; the delinquent gang, primarily organized to carry out illegal acts; and the violent gang primarily organized for emotional gratification through violence.[36] Each of these types of gangs has had some importance at different stages in the assimilation of ethnic groups. As was pointed out in describing the marginal second-generation Italo-American teenager, the first gangs were largely social. In most cases they were organized street-corner societies whose primary function was to give a locus to peer-group relations to youngsters who, but for parental emigration from Italy, would have been completely family rather than peer oriented. Although these gangs started out as social gangs they soon took on new functions of violence, delinquency, and crime as the social and emotional needs of the members changed.

Cloward and Ohlin have described the three stages in crime and delinquency which accompany the assimilation of a minority group: (1) in the first stage the acute social disorganization of the minority group leads to gang violence; (2) as assimilation proceeds, there is some social mobility and a considerable growth of illegal advance as the gangs become part of organized crime; until (3) finally there is a new physical and social deterioration in the ethnic neighborhood and violent gangs reappear.[37] This description accurately portrays what has happened to ethnic gangs in large cities but one must remember some ethnic gangs never proceeded beyond the initial social phase. Among Jews, for example, the phenomenon of the gang never really became established except on a minor basis in Jewish slum sections of large cities. Even here the gangs showed few signs of violence and, while thirty years ago the children of Eastern European Jews were frequently prominent figures in organized crime, delinquency has always been low among Jewish adolescents.

Gang organization among Negroes has already been discussed, but a few additional remarks concerning the future of Negro gangs seem in order. If the Negro follows the pattern of other ethnic groups, notably the Italians, we should expect violence and intragroup crime to diminish, paradoxically, as the Negro finds new opportunities for illegal wealth and political power. During this stage delinquent subcultures (Negro youth gangs) will take the form of apprenticeship to organized crime.[38]

Once again, the cultural traditions of the three minority groups appear to have had some influence on teen-age behavior. The Italo-American teenager, with no strong cultural impetus for education, failed in school, quit, and either tried unsuccessfully to find employment or gave up in despair. In either case his frustrations increased

---

[36] Lewis Yablonsky, *The Violent Gang* (New York: MacMillan Co., 1962), pp. 149–58.

[37] Cloward and Ohlin, *op. cit.*, pp. 194–203 *passim*.

[38] Cloward and Ohlin, *op. cit.*, 197–98.

and ultimately he turned to illegitimate activities. Jewish youngsters, on the other hand, were encouraged to seek education and gang behavior was never a serious problem. Even when Jews turned to crime, it was usually in the successful operation of a crime syndicate. The Negro, buffeted by prejudice and discrimination, used the gang as an understandable, culturally acceptable means of carrying out aggression while obtaining, albeit illegally, some of the valued objects he was denied.

## SUMMARY AND DISCUSSION

It appears that racial and ethnic minority group membership does have some effect on teen-age behavior. It is not ethnicity alone, however, which produces the effect, because each of the three groups we considered has had a somewhat different experience with its teenagers. Neither is it the development of an adolescent subculture within the minority group culture since, as we have seen, each generation of minority group teenagers makes a vastly different adjustment to minority group status. What, then, does account for the differences in and among minority group teenagers?

The difference, it seems, is simply that the minority group teenager must make an adjustment between the traditional ethnic cultural norms which he learned as a child and the social and cultural milieu in which he finds himself as an adolescent. While similar discontinuities exist for the nonminority teenager, the teenager from a racial or ethnic group has this extra differentiating factor with which to contend. The significant question for each generation is—is the difference of his ethnicity distinct enough from the dominant culture to make a difference? The important differences which occur in the minority group teenager are thus as much psychogenic as they are cultural, for each member of each generation must make his own adjustment. Norms and values for the minority group teenager are not learned, accepted, and taught to succeeding generations in the same way as custom and language. He acquires them alone or, at most, as part of a teen-age band or gang. The cultural elements of the norms come from what he learned as a child and what he views in his experience. If these two patterns are vastly different he can either retreat to the minority culture or reject it completely. If the dominant culture rejects him, he can strike back and then his norms become delinquent, nonutilitarian, and negative and often produce even greater conflict for him. If he is accepted by the dominant culture he must reject his ethnicity, at least until he is well-enough established and secure in the new society to indulge in self-deprecating humor.

Of the three situations we viewed—the cultural ethnicity of the Italo-American, the religious ethnicity of the American Jew, and the racial minority group identification of the American Negro, obvious differences exist in the amount of minority group culture which filters through to the teenager and in the persistence of his minority values. Where a regional culture seems to be the primary focus of group identification, as was the case among the Italo-American and is also true of other groups such as Irish-Americans and Polish-Americans, the culture cannot long endure in a new environment and social class differences become more important than ethnicity. Thus, among to-day's Italo-American teenagers, ethnicity has almost disappeared and the cultural modes of the lower middle-class shape their behavior.

Where religion forms the real basis of ethnic identification, ethnicity seems to have greater permanence. For American Jewish teenagers religious principles turned into ethical and secular values still seem to hold some importance. Thus, while social class status also makes for important differences in Jewish teen-age behavior, a measure of ethnic stability and permanence pervades the total Jewish group. Other ethnic-church minority groups such as the Amish, which have had much less extra-group contact, maintain even more of the ethnic differential than the Jews.

The teen-age behavior patterns of Negroes represent a distortion of the general teen-age culture as they filter through a barrier constructed of poverty, inferiority, and discrimination. In the case of the Negro, the disparity between high-prestige and low-prestige groups is even greater than elsewhere. While both are faced with the frustrations of prejudice in a democratic society, each protests in a different way; the low-prestige Negro strikes out in interpersonal aggression, the only way he knows. The high-prestige Negro has found a new vehicle and he attacks racial discrimination.

Ethnicity, race, and religion are significant factors in shaping teen-age behavior and they are closely related to class. While the child of recent immigrants is a marginal youth in conflict, after two or three generations the ethnic factor all but disappears. The racial factor, however, does not change as rapidly and despite any desire the racial-minority teenager has to become like other teenagers, much of the surrounding society seems to deny him that chance. In 1960 he decided to do something about it; what will our answer be?

# Chapter XIII

# A REVIEW OF
# YOUTH PROGRAMS

In this chapter we will attempt to draw together the main principles discussed earlier in this book to describe more precisely the sociological perspective on adolescence in the United States. We will also attempt to present a brief outline of the types of research which might lead to more help for the adolescent in his transition from childhood to manhood.

It is generally believed that recent decades have witnessed increasing concern over adolescence in the United States. If there is increased concern, it can be attributed in part to improved channels of communication for the discussion of adolescence. As has been shown, concern for the degeneration of the younger generations has always existed. There is, of course, a legitimate concern for the social development of adolescents, for every society must train the young to take on responsible adult roles. This concern is unique neither to our time nor to the United States. The Old Testament, Socrates, and Shakespeare represent three of a multitude of sources of worry, advice to the youth of the times, and lamentation.

Various causes have been discussed as sources of adolescent behavior now considered social problems: the city, the theater, deep psychological factors, industrialization, conflict in values between peers and adults, and the failure of first one institution and then another. Most of the literature on youth, historically, is based on impressionistic evidence because only recently have scientific methods been applied to human behavior. Impressionistic analysis is plagued by bias in the selection of cases, including the influence of dramatic, unusual, and extreme deviations from modal types of behavior.

Several studies, more nearly scientific in method, were done during the economic depression of the 1930's. These studies contributed greatly to our understanding of adolescence. Whatever they lacked in scientific rigor was compensated for by the great strides forward they provided in giving a background for the more refined studies currently taking place. Of particular importance, the classic research studies showed the error of applying any single generalization to all adolescents.

Most American authors indicate that a prime characteristic of adolescence is tension: with self, with parents, with school, and with the adult community generally. Although many factors may be hypothesized as explaining this tension, the universality of the tension itself needs further study in American society, for there is room for doubt. It is evident that some tension exists—a few tensions for all adolescents, and much tension for some adolescents. Part of the explanation may be found in the fact that adults still feel responsible for the actions of their offspring. Further, adults compare the behavior of their adolescent offspring with that of adults rather than with the behavior of themselves and their peers during their own adolescence. This comparison is made within the frame of reference of adult expectations. It is not surprising, then, that adolescents are viewed as irresponsible. This generally negative appraisal leads to guilt feelings on the part of the parent; he feels he has not reared his adolescent properly. The result often is to "nag" sons and daughters about relatively minor matters, which in turn produces even more undesirable behavior.

A second factor in tension may be the decreasing need for reliance on parents for the preparation for and achievement of occupational goals. While this factor operates most often where the parent wishes the son to take over the business or farm, it may also hold true when the son or daughter chooses an occupation which violates the value system of the parent. The difference of opinion between adult and adolescent on occupational choice may involve status considerations or, more particularly, negative images which carry over from generations past.

A number of authors refer to a distinct adolescent society. The American scene presents many factors which favor the development of a relatively autonomous adolescent society. There is a great amount of specialization throughout our society, with accompanying difficulties in communication and mutual understanding among persons in differing statuses. Offspring leave the status of their parents with relative ease and are often encouraged to begin preparing early to accept the norms and values of the anticipated status. The family surrenders much of the socializing function to the middle-class-oriented school. Youth are set apart. Only vaguely defined courses of action are recommended to them in defining and solving their problems. Adolescents therefore have developed their own culture and network of social relations. The press, in recognition of this, appeals to adolescent interests in special and distinctive ways. The adolescent is a distinctly different consumer.

Further, the adolescent is alienated from the central processes in most of our institutions. Most families are not democratic in the sense adolescents have an equal right to discussion and vote in family decisions. Further, adolescents influence the economy only in the aggregate sense of their consumer preferences. Churches invite the adolescent's attendance but hardly his contribution to decision making on matters of church policy. Traditionally, youth have been almost completely alienated from political processes of the state. Only a few schools have student government that goes beyond a facade of democratic process. Regardless of how one may feel about democratic process, without it adolescents can hardly receive the experience we believe one must have to learn the inherent connection between freedom and responsibility.

We may lay claim to a real and relatively autonomous adolescent society in at least one sense. There is a heavy concentration of interaction, shared values, and normative control among adolescent peers, and fewer such contacts and commonalities between adolescents and adults.

There is perhaps as much diversity among adolescents as in adult society. Part of this diversity is related to the social origin of the adolescent. Adolescents from different minority groups, residential backgrounds, religious memberships, and social classes have differing life chances, values, normative beliefs, and interaction patterns.

However, the diversity in the adolescent society is not merely a reflection of adult society. Some differences are generated within the adolescent society itself. One such set of factors is found in the way students of high school and college age react to the school. Some adolescents accept the demands of the school quietly and without much evasion. Others accept the oft-stated loftier ideals of intellectual curiosity and critical thought. Still others are oriented toward the extracurricular activities centered in the school and strongly supported by peers and the adult community. Another group is oriented toward the vocational functions of the school. If we look at the high schools, we may add a fifth group who reject and are rejected by all the main features of the school system. This last group includes, but is not exclusively composed of, those to whom the term "hood" is applied.

Another view of diversity among adolescents is comprised of more general reactions to the adult community. We hypothesize three such general orientations: the apprenticeship era, the adolescent rebellion, and the cool generation. Each of these may be found at any one time in our history, but we believe the three orientations represent a sequence of predominant themes historically.

The apprenticeship era was characteristic of the time when sons mainly followed their father's occupation and worked with the father in the fields or in the small shop. Girls helped their mothers in household chores. Recreation was a family activity in the home. School years were short and people quit school early. Few distractions from parental control were experienced. Relations between adolescent and adult were smooth and without overtly manifest conflict. Emulation of the father or mother was facilitated by constant contact and clear-cut goals for development.

The adolescent rebellion began gradually as school years became longer and more adolescents remained in school. The necessity of preparing for an occupation different from that of the father produced difficulty in taking anticipatory roles. The father was increasingly away from home. Appliances and smaller families made less important the help of the daughter in household chores. The peer groups reinforced whatever feelings of hostility existed even in the apprenticeship era. Further, the peer group gave support for overt conflict between adolescent and adult. Peer-group discussion doubtless made more explicit the difference between what adults said and what they did. Developmental tasks became more difficult to define. Adolescents began to recognize and resent a conspiracy of secrecy on the part of adults about certain types of information. The increase in channels of communication increased the opportunity for the adolescent's exposure to some aspects of cultural relativity and to question the inherent rightness of folkways within the individual's own community and family. Conflict resulted when the adult and adolescent were in contact. Evasion resulted as the automobile made possible an escape from direct observation.

As World War II ended and the cold war developed, people turned from concerns with nuclear bombs to concerns with the nuclear family. This inward orientation of the American family was facilitated by the affluent society. Families could pamper their children. More attention was paid to the feelings and desires of the adolescent. With little to fight, the adolescent in middle-class suburbia, and to some degree in the city and in the small community, quit fighting. The cool generation is much more seriously concerned with security than with individualism and achievement.

## Social Development

Adolescence is an age status, and the primary obligation of that status is development from childhood into manhood. Neither parents nor adolescents understand this development clearly. The tasks toward which development is to be directed are not clear, nor is the process by which these tasks are to be achieved. This is not the case in all societies, for in some societies adolescents have clear-cut tasks and well-defined roles. The lack of clarity in our society plays a major part in making American adolescence a period of stress.

Another important aspect of adolescence in our society is that both adolescents and parents feel ambivalent toward development. Parents want their children to become adults, but they also want to keep their child. Adolescents want the rights of adult status, but they also often want the security that goes with being a child. These feelings on the part of adults and adolescents are referred to as dual ambivalence. Therefore, the adolescent period is characterized by both ambiguity and ambivalence.

The adolescent must achieve many tasks if he is to be accepted eventually as an adult—to attain the rights and obligations that go with adulthood. One of the most difficult tasks occurs early in adolescence: learning to accept one's physical characteristics. The young person enters the adolescent period with physical changes at puberty which make this an especially acute problem to him. The emphasis in our culture on physical appearance and physical prowess adds to the problems of this task.

A second task to be achieved during adolescence involves adopting the appropriate masculine or feminine role. The question of whether the male or the female has more difficulty with this developmental task is moot. Girls find greater difficulty in verbalizing their role but boys are more often delinquent and more often in trouble with parents and teachers.

Generally, the transition from one age status to another is abrupt. There is little deliberate preparation. Further, the rights and obligations morally appropriate for the general age status of adolescence are vague and are not matters of general concensus. However, those age and sex roles determined by the peer group are more clearly defined. There are some distinct features of age status at each age grade in school.

In the relations between the sexes, a strong romantic theme underlies the entire complex of courtship. The adult community, and specifically parents, use devious means to interfere with courtship on the premise that dating leads to marriage and one should marry either "one of his own kind," or a better. There does appear to be a trend toward more interclass marriages.

The public school facilitates heterosexual association in leisure-time activities through much of its extracurricular activities. The great amount of concern with the opposite sex, especially prevalent among girls, does not reinforce serious attention to academic tasks. Indeed, "brains" are not popular romantic partners. It is apparent the double standard is accepted by both sexes in adolesence.

Another developmental task is achieving emotional independence from parents and other adults. The basic factor in this process is the dual ambivalence toward growing up experienced by both the adolescent and by the parent toward his offspring. The vagueness of rights and obligations in relations with parents contributes greatly to the difficulties in this task. The peer group reinforces the move to independence in the adolescent rebellion. Indeed, the adolescent rebellion can be viewed merely as one means of achieving this task—but a means costly to both adolescent and adult in terms of emotional stress. As the "cool generation" develops, the role of the peer group in helping the adolescent gain emotional independence may change. The evidence is inadequate.

The adolescent must lay the groundwork for economic independence in selecting and preparing for an occupation. The process by which this seems to occur, at least for boys, is a very early fantasy choice, then a tentative choice with gradual narrowing of the alternatives during adolescence, and finally a realistic choice. Occupational choice and preparation is not, therefore, a single decision but rather a series of decisions many of which are not made in terms of this developmental task but are crucial to the task nevertheless (such as the case of study habits). One of the most difficult features of preparing for economic independence is that the adolescent must anticipate changes in the labor force for several decades—a task that will become increasingly difficult due to the rapid changes expected in the labor force during the next few years. Of course, adults may change occupations without the necessity of anticipating such changes during adolescence. However, the extent of technological unemployment dramatically demonstrates that the avenues open to occupational changes in adulthood are not sufficient. A long-standing idea in occupational counseling is that adolescents aspire too high and the job of the counselor is to help them reach a more realistic and lower level of aspiration. That levels of occupational aspiration are lower than twenty years ago is evident. However, the changes in status in the labor force are ever upward in those occupations which will represent an increasing proportion of available jobs.

Another developmental task is the need of the society for adolescents to develop the intellectual skills and concepts necessary for civic competence. If such development occurs, it does so in a context in which the adolescent is alienated from real experience in political process. The adolescent society, with its informal relations and patterned evasion of adult demands, is the only experience in political process many adolescents have. For many we say, in effect, "Now you are twenty-one. Yesterday you were a child. Today you must be a man."

In a more general perspective, development for those children who remain in school until late adolescence follows a pattern which moves from adult domination to increasing influence by peers during high school and then back to concern, once again, with the attitudes, values, and expectations of the adult world. In spite of the greater orientation toward peers during middle adolescence, however, the adolescent appears to have a greater respect for and "idealization" of adults than adults have of either other adults or adolescents. This is in contrast to the expectation adults have of teenagers. Idealization does not necessarily imply the person idealized will have a dominant influence. The discrepancy between idealization and influence would, we believe, lessen if adult expectations of adolescents were more clearly defined. Since the high school is manifestly for the purpose of academic training, it is important to note the types of influences which affect the adolescent's conformity to academic demands. Adults expect achievement in school, as measured by grades. Adolescents, for their part, give high status to athletes but even higher status to athlete-scholars. However, the meaning of scholar is the ability to get "A" grades with a minimum of study. The grade, not the knowledge, counts with peers; in fact, in most schools the knowledgable adolescent is not highly appreciated by peers.

On the negative side of adolescent behavior, delinquency is clearly the matter of most concern in the popular press and probably with adults generally. About two thirds of the magazine articles dealing with the subject of adolescents are either directly or indirectly on delinquency. Although there is a general rise in the amount of reported delinquency, part of this increase is due to the greater willingness to report delinquent acts, especially in rural areas. Boys commit more delinquent acts than do girls. Among those brought into juvenile court, boys are often charged with acts involving property and girls with acts which are more direct measures of rebellion against strict norms and against parents.

Reported delinquency is much higher in slums and among children from broken homes. While there is evidence of a small amount of correlation between these two variables and delinquency, much of the supposed relationship is due to methods of measuring delinquency. Practically all adolescents commit delinquent acts, but lower-class adolescents are less likely to be released with only a warning and more likely to be brought into police stations and juvenile courts and to receive sentences. Therefore, most of the relationship between slum living and delinquency rests not in the slums but in the handling of juvenile cases by the police and the courts.

Family relationships seem to be related to delinquency. Discipline which is too lax, too stern, or erratic seems to be characteristic of families in which we find adolescents who are judged delinquent. Delinquents also come from homes in which there is less feeling of affection. The theories on lower-class gang delinquency disagree as to the acceptance of middle-class values. One current theory holds that lower-class gang members do not accept middle-class values but rather lower-class values which include manliness, physical prowess, disobedience, and the like. Another theory holds that lower-class gang members accept middle-class goals but do not have the means to achieve them. If these gang members live in a community in which there is an outlet for stolen goods, theft will be the means of achieving the middle-class goals. If there is no such outlet, gang members will turn to gang warfare in some communities and drugs and alcohol in others.

The juvenile court differs in practice from the criminal court in several ways; the result is that the due process of law is often violated. Hearings are private rather than public; there is usually no representation by counsel; nor is there a prosecutor. The philosophy in most juvenile cases is that the adjustment of the individual is the main point at issue, and not his guilt or innocence. The investigation conducted by a social worker or parole officer is more important than the hearing itself.

The adolescent period generally may be characterized as more problem-filled than we would like it to be and probably less antisocial and devious than many adults believe it to be. In the context of growing up in a confused situation, it is appropriate to turn some attention to how adolescents might be given more help in the transition from childhood to adulthood.

## PROGRAMS OF ACTION FOR ADOLESCENTS

One program of action that seems to correspond to the fact of peer control is student government, which is increasingly being employed in high schools as well as colleges. It would appear that when the student government body is given real authority and treated as an actual governing body, adolescents take the responsibility seriously and carry out the duties of their offices with dispatch. It would also appear that the discipline is handled on a more universal basis than is the discipline exercised by adults in the same situation. Fewer exceptions are made and extenuating circumstances are not considered as often. Punishment is frequently more severe than adults would give for the same offense. If we consider the increasing use of student government and its correspondence to the facts of adolescent society, we believe much research attention should be devoted to this program. We need to know the conditions under which student governing bodies will perform their duties adequately and conditions under which they will not. We may hypothesize that one major factor influencing the effectiveness of student government is whether the students feel their decisions are going to be reversed by adult authority. We also need to know more about the side effects of student government. Does student government help leaders in developmental processes? Does it help nonleaders? What effect does the presence of student government in a school have on the student who is rejected by the informal cliques in adolescent society? What effect is seen on the "hoods" when peers are sitting in judgment on their acts?

Another program used in many schools (colleges only, to the authors' knowledge) is the honor system under which examinations are not proctored by the instructor. When it is collegewide, the system seems to reduce cheating rates. We need to know to what extent such a system might work in high schools and whether it would work when it is adult-imposed. Several experiments show that among adolescents, even at the age of eleven, democratic action results in more conformity, more "we" feeling, and more group loyalty. The greater difficulty of planning a working honor system at the high school level might be reduced if students actually planned the program. We need to know the effect of the honor system on the achievement of the developmental tasks. We need to know its effect on different classes of adolescents. What would be the effect on the hoods? And what would be the effect on the upper middle-class adolescent whose parents are exerting extreme pressure for grades?

Still another program often used for youth development is the student ownership and management of recreation centers. Such management is efficient, imaginative, and strict on violation of rules. However, the persons most helped by this experience in leadership are usually those who are also helped by experience in club presidencies, class presidencies, and informal leadership positions within adolescent society.

Generally, the programs of action designed for youth are class-bound, whether by design or accident. Many programs to help "boys of the street" avoid experience with the police and juvenile courts are conducted exclusively for slum dwellers while the programs in the school are, in actual practice, usually for the middle- and upper middle-class adolescent. A multiple-program approach is likely needed if we are to help more than a few adolescents. It is also obvious from the literature on adolescence that such programs need to be organized on a tightly controlled, experimental basis and reports of success should be made available. In these two suggestions we are looking to the action program both as an experiment in furthering our understanding of adolescence and as a test to inform others who would use the program as to its expected effects.

## THE ROLES OF PARENTS AND COUNSELORS

Most special programs for adolescents are either conducted within the school or are designed by or for the high school population. Some attention should be turned to the role of the parent and the role of the counselor in adolescence.

Certainly much of what occurs in the adolescent's life may be best explained by what happens to him before he reaches the adolescent years. Many of his problems rest in the earlier socialization process—a process that involves primarily his interaction with his parents. If sociologists and psychologists are correct in these assumptions, parents might well look to the difficulties of adolescence in determining the course they will take in child rearing. Research on socialization generally shows that an accepting relationship with the child and the acceptance of his friends lead to better adjustment. But within the context of personal acceptance and appreciation, it is possible a planned program of help for the adolescent toward accepting independence would contribute valuably to his attitudes toward self and others. Earlier, we explained that the parent often finds this difficult because of his reluctance to surrender the affection which comes from the dependence of childhood. However, the appreciation and respect of the adolescent who has had real help in meeting developmental problems are also rewarding. Parents who anticipate this appreciation and who are aware of the emotional costs of the adolescent rebellion if real help is not forthcoming may find it easier to help rather than to try to control the adolescent.

Perhaps the greatest difficulty for the parent is learning to shift from the frequent exercise of control characteristic of rearing the child to "laying off" during adolescence. Frequent exercise of control by parents during adolescence only fosters tension and antagonism between the two generations. Again, this lesson in restraint may be easier to learn when parents understand that the major source of social control for the adolescent is his peer group, regardless of what the parent does. Of course, we are not recommending that parents ignore or refuse to exercise control on major infractions of important norms. We are, rather, suggesting the boy becomes a man earlier when parents try first to understand the more intimate details of the adolescent's problems and then render aid and comfort.

The role of the counselor is of interesting importance in the school system. The basic problem in counseling is the choice between two approaches: (1) to manipulate the environment to help the adolescent solve his immediate problem; or (2) to manipulate the environment in no way but rather to help the adolescent to understand himself and others, to help him restructure his personality to adjust to the real world about him, and to help him learn to manipulate his own environment.

Our cultural milieu has hundreds of agencies for social control. The counselor can add little to this already ponderous and complex organization. However, few agencies exist to help people understand themselves and almost none to help the adolescent in this regard. We therefore believe the primary role of the counselor should involve the second approach: to help the student understand himself and others and to work on personality structure. In this way the effects of the counseling may be enjoyed after the relationship with the counselor is ended. On the other hand, if the counselor manipulates the environment to help the adolescent, a dependence is begun which deters rather than helps the adolescent to come to terms with his environment.

The role we suggest for the counselor is a difficult one. Teachers refer a troublesome boy or girl to a counselor and are horrified to hear of the counselor seeming to agree with the adolescent in criticizing the teacher. Apparently, neither teachers nor school administrators understand the seeming agreement is not intended as condoning misconduct. Indeed, quite the contrary. Such seeming agreement is not agreement at all, but rather indication of acceptance of the adolescent as a person. It establishes sufficient rapport to aid the counselor in understanding the adolescent in order to help the adolescent later understand himself. It is entirely possible that only by this means can the counselor help the adolescent adjust. It is also entirely possible that the suggested role of the counselor can be played only when administrators and teachers understand counseling techniques and aims.

Youth programs outside the school are often designed to help adolescents in social development. The Boy Scout and Girl Scout programs, the 4-H Club programs and the like[1] have many features consistent with the principles we have been discussing. One excellent example of well-designed programs is the 4-H Club's junior leadership projects where adolescents are given training and responsibility in helping younger members in club work. However, it is significant that many of these youth programs lose large numbers of members at the beginning of the adolescent period.

## SUMMARY

In this chapter we have reviewed some of the more fundamental principles of adolescence. We have also reviewed briefly some of the youth programs found in schools and some of the considerations in making these programs effective. We turn now to a more intensive analysis of a newer type of program which we believe corresponds to the principles of adolescence. This program is described in the next chapter. It is, of course, not in any sense a complete solution to the problem of the isolation of the adolescent from the mainstream of adult life. However, we believe it illustrates the principles of an involvement consistent with social development.

---

[1] For an excellent discussion of an experiment along these lines see Glenn C. Dildine, *Citizenship Improvement Study* (Washington, D.C.: The National 4-H Club Foundation, 1962).

*Chapter XIV*

# THE STUDENT EDUCATION CORPS: A CASE STUDY OF A PARTIAL SOLUTION

A central theme of this text is that a substantial gap exists between what adolescents are taught to do and what they are in fact allowed to do. For a good part of the preadult years, youth are tutored carefully in the business of citizenship and responsibility to others. At the same time the young person is given little opportunity to put these moral values to some realistic practice. With the possible exception of civic youth organizations, "mayor-for-the-day" programs, and sporadic fund-raising campaigns (all, incidentally, directed primarily at the younger adolescent), the more mature adolescent is frequently kept on the sidelines until he overcomes the societally imposed hurdles of passage. This moratorium on the ability, motivation, and enthusiasm of the young no doubt contributes to the adolescent's feeling of alienation from the adult world and the maintenance of an adolescent subculture. As was noted earlier in this book, there is evidence to support the proposition that when adolescents are given an opportunity to work in meaningful activities they will respond in a positive manner. Certainly the continued success of the Peace Corps must be considered.

The Peace Corps is a unique organization in several ways. Unlike our traditional approach to youth, the Peace Corps does not operate under the assumption that being young is sufficient reason for exclusion from significant societal involvement. In addition, there is the belief that achieved statuses (in this case, the needed skills, abilities, and talents) are of greater importance than ascribed statuses such as chronological age and sex.

The success of the Peace Corps is indicated by both the response of American youth and the comments of individuals from host nations. By April, 1963, 5,003 volunteers were either at work overseas or in training for an overseas assignment.[1] While most volunteers cannot

---

[1] These data, as well as other materials on the Peace Corps discussed here, are taken from *Peace Corps Congressional Presentation*, Vols. I, II, III; Fy., 1964, Washington D.C.

be classified as adolescents, 514 are under twenty years of age. The average age of all volunteers is, in fact, 26.6 years. It is anticipated that with the necessary financial support the Corps could grow to 10,000 active volunteers by the early part of 1964.

The accomplishments of the Peace Corps are indeed impressive and have been documented in the mass media. For our purposes it will be sufficient to note that as of April, 1963, volunteers were working in forty-five different countries at a variety of tasks including teaching, rural and urban community action programs, public health, agriculture, public works, and others. It would be erroneous to give the impression that all Peace Corps efforts have been successful. Some projects have been distinguished more by good intentions than by good works. In some instances volunteers have been trained for a particular job that failed to materialize. No selectivity process is perfect and some volunteers have been sent home. Despite these shortcomings, the Peace Corps has accomplished many of its original goals. In a short period of time the volunteers have won the confidence of skeptics and new respect for the United States. More important perhaps, they have given of themselves in purposeful activities and they have gained insights that are rarely touched upon in the formal classroom setting.

Some notion of the real value of the Peace Corps can be seen from the following comments. The first is from the *Malayan Times,* March 29, 1963; the second from a volunteer in Nigeria.

> Now that they are here and working in remote areas among the rural people, Malayans are beginning to admire them for their self-sacrifice. They are setting an example to young Malayans. . . .

> The first months were strange and at times quite tense. They were not quite sure what our real motivations were. Since that time things have changed. I am teaching in a small school with thirty-four students in my class. They are bright and eager. In the evenings I work with a group of parents and this is really exciting. Slowly I begin to see the significance of our work. To be honest I think I will gain more than they. . . . It is a whole new world.
>
> —From a letter to one of the authors

The success of the Peace Corps overseas stimulated legislation for the organization of a domestic youth-service program in the form of VISTA (Volunteers in Service to America). In addition, college students in different parts of the country have undertaken community-oriented service projects. In this chapter we present a detailed account of one such program.[2]

During the early part of 1963 one of the authors (Gottlieb) was a

---

[2] Much of this discussion is based on "The Student Education Corps," a report written by Sandra A. Worden, Michigan State University, June 12, 1963.

consultant to the Board of Education in a fairly large industrial community. His task was to work with school personnel who were teaching children from socioeconomically limited backgrounds. These children enter the public school inadequately prepared for the established programs of the educational system. They come from families in which the parents' educational background is relatively low (few have completed high school); the fathers (where one is present) are frequently either chronically unemployed or at work in unskilled jobs; the mothers are often employed outside the home. The families tend to be large, highly mobile, and minority group members; large numbers of the children are deprived of the experiences that are so often part of middle-class socialization. Many children have no books or magazines in the home and frequently health and social problems carry over into the school situation.

In these schools, and others like them in urban areas throughout the nation, classroom overcrowding and wide discrepancies in the ability and/or performance of the pupils make the teaching task a difficult one. In addition to the normal subject matter, the schools find it necessary to provide students with citizenship training, learning motivation, and an awareness of expected school and future adult roles—in short, to fill the gap left by an inadequate home environment.

Borrowing some of the concepts of programs already in existence (Higher Horizons in New York and the Greater Cities Project of Detroit), a project for expanding the breadth of interest, knowledge, and experience of these children was proposed. It was apparent such a program would require support from sources outside the school system—but what source? It was this problem which led to the idea of the Student Education Corps.

The depressing situation of these socioeconomically deprived children as well as the problem of implementing a special program for them was discussed in a sociology class taught by the author. Group discussion led to the suggestion that college volunteer talent might be utilized in some way to help alleviate the problem. A large number of students indicated not only their concern and interest but also their willingness to help. Ironically, although part of the function of the university is to prepare young adults for responsible citizenship, all too often no outlet is provided for them to assume these responsibilities. The students' reaction was that citizenship is not an indefinable abstraction but is, rather, a concrete state of social consciousness which embodies both privilege and duty. Their enthusiasm to fulfill this duty was apparent—and the idea mushroomed.

On March 4 and 5, 1963, *The State News* (the school newspaper) published a two-part article by Paul Schnitt, editorial co-editor, in which the problem and tentative plans for the corps were outlined. The university administration expressed approval of the concept; a number of local area schools indicated interest; and the schools where the author was working welcomed the idea enthusiastically.

The ultimate aim of the corps is to help prevent premature dropouts among intellectually qualified students. This has become a serious problem in our age of advanced technology. It is the socioeconomically disadvantaged children who are often potential dropouts. In a few years these pupils will be unequally represented in the ranks of the habitually unemployed and unemployable—adding to nothing but the already-overflowing pool of unskilled labor and the welfare rolls. The purpose of the SEC is to help show these youngsters that education is an important key to a better life by providing needed inspiration and motivation to continue their schooling. One way to do this is to give individualized attention to students who are poorly motivated or academically inferior to their classmates. Another way to help is through offering broader experiences to children of limited background. This then was, and remains, the idea behind SEC.

## INCEPTION OF THE ORGANIZATION—FACTS AND FIGURES

Aspirations were high and interest keen but organization was needed. A meeting of all interested students was arranged; over 200 students came. Speakers at this meeting included the president of student government, representatives from several school districts, and community social workers.

It was decided to pursue the idea of a Student Education Corps on an experimental basis and to begin immediately. An office was established in the student service building. Student government also offered $200 in support of the program, which represented the total operating budget for the SEC's first three months. A graduate student in sociology was appointed co-ordinator. Application cards were made available to anyone interested in membership. Ninety-nine such cards were returned at the close of the meeting and for the next few days the applications poured into the SEC office. The process of checking references, compiling lists of areas of available skills, and of contacting the schools with information as to the nature of the organization and the talent available progressed as rapidly as possible.

The total of 153 volunteers ranged in age from eighteen to forty-eight and represented all levels of scholastic training from freshman to advanced graduate students. Their major fields were varied but nearly all had had experience as group leaders and teacher's aides in schools, youth organizations, or children's camps. A number of the volunteers were education majors and some had completed their student teaching. Many were active campus leaders. Some of the volunteers had had specialized experience in working with physically and/or mentally handicapped children. All those selected were deemed responsible and dependable young adults.

Student volunteer assistance was offered to the schools in these areas:

1. Classroom assistance in guiding and tutoring.
   a) Reading and English.
   b) Arithmetic and math.
   c) Social studies.
   d) Homemaking skills.
   e) General teacher aid.

2. Recreation and physical education.
   a) Games and playground activities.
   b) Organized team sports.
   c) Special activities: swimming, archery, tennis, etc.

3. Foreign language assistance.
   a) French.
   b) Spanish.
   c) German.

4. Science—both to work with interested children and to present programs.
   a) General science.
   b) Specific areas: astronomy, biology, nature study, zoology, etc.

5. Fine arts—both to work with interested children and to present programs.
   a) Art: crafts through art history.
   b) Drama: acting through puppetry.
   c) Music: vocal and instrumental.
   d) Dance: folk to ballet.

The Corps also offered a variety of special programs.

1. A "Career Caravan"—an assembly program presented by students to give information and advice about modern career opportunities, including:
   a) Skill and educational requirements.
   b) "How-to" of financing a college education.
   c) Academic life of a college student.

2. Folk and classical music—an all-student assembly program concerned with rhythm fundamentals, the instruments and their uses, and composers, in addition to an entertaining performance of a variety of compositions.

3. Foreign students—to discuss and demonstrate customs, dress, and products of their native lands.

Within a few weeks of the initial organizational meeting a total of 124 volunteers were given assignments in nineteen different schools. They have been involved with a total of over 700 school children.

## WHAT THEY DID

The enthusiasm of the volunteer corpsmen has, if anything, increased after their experiences. This is true too of teachers, some of whom initially saw SEC as an interruption or interference in normal school routines. Some misunderstandings were encountered and certain organizational problems had to be resolved. Nevertheless, the project encountered no major obstacles of any kind and has proven to be a thoroughly gratifying experience to all those involved. Volunteers worked, as was indicated earlier, at a variety of tasks. The following comments, written by volunteers, reflect the nature of their assignments.

My experience at "X" School has largely centered around the activities of a particular group of fifth-grade students. I have been working with the slowest, less able group. . . . After having observed them in their normal classroom situation, I was given the opportunity to look through the cumulative record folder for each of these children. . . . On the California Test of Mental Maturity, which was given last fall, the IQ's of all the children were in the eighty range . . . with the amount of lag between their reading level and their grade level varying from a few months to two years. In no case was the parents' educational standing reported to be higher than the upper grades of high school. . . . With this amount of background, I began to meet individually with some of the students from the class for periods ranging from about fifteen minutes up to an hour. . . . I attempted to find some area that was particularly interesting to the child and then spent some time on that until he relaxed a bit. Sometimes I was successful during the first session, at other times this did not happen until the second or third interview. We were then able to move on to discussing other things. Almost everyone professed some liking for school and his teachers, although usually one or two subjects were preferred above the others. . . . Our discussions of family life and activities outside of school seemed to indicate that most of these children are left pretty much on their own a good part of the time. . . . Future plans of the children often included college careers to prepare themselves for the professions, although some of the fellows wanted to be professional athletes or soldiers. . . . A technique which we used several times was a modified kind of group therapy during which I met with two, three, or four students at a time. Sometimes we discussed questions which were important to the counselees, and other times we dealt with problems that had come up in classroom behavior, relationships with others, etc. At times I was able to make suggestions that the children involved spend a trial period of new behavior patterns when such a suggestion seemed the logical outcome of our discussion.

It seems fair now to ask if there have been any results after having made the efforts involved in a program such as this, and in response, I have to be honest and say that I do not know how these few hours together will affect the lives of these students for the next fifty years. But I do know that there have been some immediate and tangible rewards for me and for them. At one of the last sessions, I asked some of the boys if they enjoyed having someone come into their classroom and then to take them aside for a while to talk things over. Naturally we would expect them to reply in the affirmative, and some were honest enough to admit that the reason they liked it was that they could get out of class. But two of them gave me all the reward I needed when they agreed that they enjoyed such opportunities because they appreciated having "a friend to talk to." If we accomplished nothing more in these weeks than to indicate to these children that we care about them as individuals, that we accept them for what they are, and that we are interested in their affairs, then we have been successful in our efforts.

Thomas Englund—M.A. candidate in counseling

Tom's experiences and efforts are typical of the volunteers assigned to the more deprived schools. Those children who needed special attention were chosen by the school staff who welcomed the SEC "counselors" with open arms and aided them in every possible way. It is early to attempt an evaluation of the long-range effect of such a student-counselor program but all indications are that this is a good beginning of a truly worthwhile project of deep significance dealing with a problem concerning our society today.

Bruce Keidan, a senior in social science, helped teach social studies to a sixth-grade classroom at "Y" School. He says of his experiences:

When we first met, [the teacher with whom he worked] explained to me that her class was studying the history of the world, and the present conditions in all the countries in the world. . . . She had ideas about what I could do, but was also open for my suggestions. . . . As a result of my suggestions and her enthusiastic support, I proceeded to build a program around the human interest part of the lives of people in a foreign country. Of prime importance to me in this was to destroy some of the ethnocentricism of the students and to show that people all over the world are only human. I chose to use a movie and taped interviews with foreign students as well as class discussions in order to make the children think things over for themselves. The movie was "Four Families" [Margaret Mead's film, obtained from the audiovisual center by SEC] . . . dealing with children and values in Japan, India, France, and Canada. In the taped interviews I used students from Iraq, India, Pakistan, and Turkey. The interviews dealt with what the students had thought about the United States before they came here, what they thought now, and the social, economic and religious aspects of their countries; with special attention to the lives of children in their countries.

Working with the foreign students and trying to find the answers to simple yet penetrating questions which the children asked, I too found this a real learning experience. If the children learned half as much as I, then I am sure the program did much to further understanding and appreciation of what we have. When I say "appreciation of what we have," I refer to the underlying stress of the program on the benefits we Americans have and the need not to take them for granted or let them be ignored.

Susan Palmer, a college junior majoring in music, worked in several different areas with younger school children. She reports:

When I filled out my card I listed academic work first and, as an afterthought, added art and music as areas where I might be able to help. Therefore, upon receiving my assignment to teach music, I became skeptical as to the intensity of my musical ability. I knew there was only one way to find out and that was to make my observations in the classroom itself. . . . Needless to say a beautiful new elementary-school building doesn't necessarily mean a wealthy community—as was proven inside the door. . . . However, I was determined that depression would not overcome my enthusiasm. It was then that I fully realized what my middle-class set of values could do to this class—possibly ruin it! I wasn't expecting to find the girls dressed in jeans and sweatshirts. . . . I observed most of the day in a first-grade classroom and came to realize fully why the SEC was in this particular town. (I might add here that I had two first grades and one fourth-grade music class so my observations are not confined to one classroom.)

As I wandered about the classroom I made many friends who wanted to squeeze my hand. I tried to be exceedingly warm and friendly as I felt these children needed this most of all. The teacher in charge just sat coldly at her desk for six weeks of my visits. I learned that Bobbie's father had more land than Tommie's and I was introduced to pet snakes kept in their desks, carefully concealed. Pris, another SEC volunteer, and I were both working in this class and the children were thrilled to have two special teachers.

We took over the class while the teacher sat back and observed. Because these boys and girls didn't have any physical education program, we decided to teach them rhythms. First we learned the song, with piano accompaniment, and then we did rhythm. There was always a battle to see who would hold the teacher's hand and we tried to work it so the more shy children were given a chance to shine. It upset us to think the regular teacher sat back and didn't give us any help. Although the teachers were anxious to have the SEC they weren't quite sure what to do with our enthusiastic attitudes. Perhaps their feelings could be attributed to a misunderstanding between themselves and their "helpers." As soon as they learned our purpose as "helpers" and not "replacers" the tension was greatly reduced.

I enjoyed going outside on the playground and joining in with the girls who were jumping rope. I taught them several new rhymes and was well rewarded the following week when these rhymes were a part of their fun. . . . By sharing experiences and talents the SEC volunteers are promoting good will between the school and community; this program is helping the children enrich their experiences and will, hopefully, promote a lasting interest in and enthusiasm for schooling.

Marel Lee Bolger, a home economics senior who had already completed her student teaching, made another of the outstanding contributions to the SEC pilot project in "X" community. She traveled to "X" every Wednesday for six weeks and her abilities were fully utilized in a variety of ways. One hour each week was spent in tutoring slow readers on a first- to third-grade level; another hour she tutored slow readers from the fourth and fifth grades. Marel devoted one hour each week to helping with a number of individual student problems. Her fourth hour was devoted to teaching a tenth-grade home economics class for which she established her own schedule and made up her own lesson plans. The last hour of each Wednesday she taught art to seventh-grade girls. In addition, she prepared a questionnaire which she asked a number of teachers and other volunteers to complete in an effort to get some objective evaluation of the SEC program. She concludes her lengthy report with these words: "It is hoped that I helped somewhat to further the goal of the SEC program. Again, it was a tremendous opportunity for me—an opportunity I'll always remember."

Another of the SEC volunteers assigned to "X" was Joanne Schrier, a social work major from New York city who had, admittedly, only a stereotyped conception of small rural communities. She volunteered, and was selected, to teach folk dancing and dramatics. She says:

I entered the school ready for apathy, but filled with enthusiasm and "illusions of grandeur" as to what I would accomplish. Throughout numerous conversations the teachers frankly admitted to the cultural defects within the school system, and on the whole didn't feel themselves qualified to furnish the required improvement. . . . They repeatedly expressed their gratitude to me and seemed entirely confident in my abilities. Because of this I was given little instruction as to what they required, and most of the time was left to my own devices to teach and conduct the classes.

I taught folk dance to a co-ed sixth grade and an all-girls seventh- and eighth-grade gym class. In both the response was one of enthusiasm and eagerness. . . . My impressions and experiences with the eighth-grade dramatics class concurred with those in the dance groups. Although there was some bashfulness at the outset these kids also responded quickly, and soon were participating in skits, improvisations, etc. They expressed an insatiable inquisitiveness about the theater and related my bits of information with experiences and facts of their own. . . . An observation I would like to note came to my attention when the topic of a college education popped up for discussion. From my prodding I soon learned that most of the students wanted to continue with a higher educational experience, but doubt was expressed as to this ever becoming a tangible reality. They based their opinions on low scholastic ratings and subsequently held the belief that a college wouldn't take many of them.

As to the worthiness of this type of project, I'm quite sure my feelings are self-evident. (I even dread continuation along these lines for fear that my written words will become too sentimental and dramatic.) I have found this newly instituted program an ennobling and enriching idea. This holds true not only for the people involved within the program, but for the university as a whole. For, if the SEC is continued, the university will not only be able to provide the knowledge for a future vocational goal to its students, but a field-work experience as well. . . . For instance an expectant education major could be provided with the opportunity to observe and realize the need for her type of training, and the marvelous effects it could have to awaken and stimulate children in these culturally and educationally deprived areas. . . . To me my primary aim had become fulfilled, for I had given of myself to others.

Some small indication of the impact these and other SEC volunteers had on the school system may be seen in the fact that two of the volunteers were offered permanent teaching positions in the school. One of these students is not an education major and had never seriously considered the possibility of teaching as a career.

One of the art assistants was Lynn Ann Maynard and she says:

Liking art and loving children, I was very excited when one of my sorority sisters and I received an assignment from the Student Education Corps. We worked as a team, teaching art to first, second, and third graders. . . . We were not notified as to what grades we were to teach and we had no idea of either the materials we had to work with or the length of time we would have with each class. Thus, we were not able to prepare a lesson. We had a couple of "emergency" ideas though. . . . The children did not seem to be familiar with anything but crayons and cut paper—their art experiences were not too varied. Therefore, we were warmly welcomed by the children and the teachers. . . . Although some of our students were from middle-class families, the majority were of lower-class background and many had special problems stemming from their home situations. Certain students had a need for approval and security and if we had known from the first who they were we could have helped by choosing them as our helpers more often. . . .

The teachers we worked with frequently expressed their appreciation for our work, and one of them gave us some pansy plants. They felt that along with our fresh ideas and prepared lessons, just the presence of new faces was a stimulus to the children. Our students were very cooperative and enthusiastic.

Aside from the feeling of helping someone through participation in a worthwhile program, I feel that I gained valuable experience from my work in the corps. . . . When the little boy who "couldn't do anything right" (and wouldn't try) finally came up with his completed card holder to ask for criticism, when a girl described by her teacher as "backward" painted a beautiful picture, when a usually uncooperative child volunteered to clean up paper scraps (and did), and when an excited second grader jumped up in the middle of the class period to say how much he liked art—then I began to realize for the first time the influence a teacher can have with her students. I felt that I had really made a contribution to these classes.

The university athletic department was extremely cooperative in loaning volunteers the necessary equipment to conduct a recreational program. This special program is only a part of the effort put forth by SEC volunteers in recreation. Dan Riley, who went to his assigned school every Friday and taught a third grade, a fifth grade, and a special education class, had this to say of his experiences:

I went to "W" community with the Student Education Corps the first Friday and have gone every Friday since. My experience has been both enjoyable and enlightening. My biggest reservation about the program lies in the fact that now the program is over, at least for the summer, and just when I was beginning to cultivate a relationship with the children which was more than just an "excitement" for them. Spending only about forty minutes with each class it took about three weeks for us—the class and I—to get up a working relationship, but it was indeed worth the effort.

I found the fifth-grade students accustomed to the various outdoor sports and, to some degree at least, used to group activity. The third graders, however, were not only unaccustomed to group activity but they seemed to lack any orientation toward sports in general. It was not uncommon in this class for the boys, who were generally smaller, to look upon some of the more adept girls with respect and admiration. . . . These two classes—the third and fifth grade—showed a great divergence in the way in which they regarded my presence. While my presence was still important to the fifth graders, the largest concern of each individual was with his peers. My first experiences with the third graders was entirely different; each individual member of the class hung on my every word. . . . To my dismay the degree of obedience instilled in these youngsters was phenomenal and until I got used to the absolute necessity of being literal whenever I spoke I ran into difficulty. One example of this still sticks with me: I had, to my knowledge, explained a relay race in full and almost painful detail, divided the class up into teams, designated which would run and which would wait for the exchange, etc. At the word "go" I watched with exasperation as forty small bodies hurled themselves across the field, twenty from one direction and twenty from the other. . . . One thing I still wonder about: why is it so difficult to get third graders into a line shoulder to shoulder facing the front? It is amazing the configurations they come up with when you try and explain the formation.

These two classes were made up of average lower middle-class youngsters of average ability, but my third class was average in neither of these respects. They were a class of what they [the teachers and principal] . . . referred to as "special education." The youngsters were generally older (ranging probably to twelve or thirteen) and of very limited ability. All of these students had less than third-grade reading ability and in many there was an observable deviation from the other children—their age, hostility, aggressiveness, moodiness, depression, etc.; while some, otherwise emotionally normal, were simply feeble-minded. These children, from my observations, were not proficient in any sport but I was unable to determine whether this arose out of their own inability or out of the aversion of their teacher to sports; I think rather the latter. . . . The first time I tried to get them to play very few were any good and one student absolutely refused to participate. Another who was hesitant, but who consented to play, took two swipes at the ball, threw down the bat in disgust and humiliation, and retreated to sit and observe from about fifty yards back. When I got a chance I went over and tried to "big-brother" him back into the game. . . . When I mentioned it to his teacher she scowled and passed the incident off as an excuse on the part of the child to escape the necessity of participating in the game. Whether or not this is true, and I think it is not, there is still something that this child needs. . . . My contact with these children, though short, was I think beneficial to them, as would be any continued contact. It is with children such as these that the corps has its work cut out—these are the children who merit our time and efforts. I hope that the work of the Corps in the future can be carried on with emphasis on depth.

One of the more noteworthy contributions in the university area was made by Mark Krastof, who worked several evenings each week with a group of twelve boys at the "Z" Community Center. Mark devoted much time and effort to befriending these boys, visiting their homes, and supplying some direction to their leisure-time activities. He arranged to bring his group to the campus on baby-animal day. On that same day the boys were given access to the wrestling gym in the intramural building and two members of the university wrestling team volunteered their time to demonstrate techniques.

The experiences of these volunteers are typical of the experiences of those who worked in schools where large populations of the student body were from deprived homes.

I did my work at the Main Street School which is located on the west side of town. The school is composed of all Negroes except for fifteen white children; there were two white children in my class. I was assigned to a fifth-grade class in which I tutored the underachievers primarily in arithmetic but also in reading. I took these children out of the classroom in groups of five, and on occasion worked with children individually. Besides doing this, I was available to answer questions while the teacher gave individual help to other students. . . . Both the principal and the teachers that I talked to felt that the Student Education Corps had worked quite successfully. . . . I cannot express how much it has meant to me to be a part of this worthwhile project; it has given me so much.

Judy Donoghue

I started in the middle of the term and went to the school every Tuesday and Thursday afternoon from 12:30 to 4:00. I helped two second-grade rooms. . . . There were about sixty-five students in these two second-grade rooms. One room had most of the slow learners in it, and the other room had the average and above-average learners. Throughout the time I spent in the school I tutored these children in reading and arithmetic. I usually took these students out of their classrooms and worked with them as a group, but on a few occasions I worked with them alone. . . . The teachers and principal felt that the main objective in the program was to give these children who had difficulty in learning added attention, which the regular classroom teacher cannot do when she has thirty-five students. They felt it was very effective, and said they were sorry to have the SEC members leave. They also told me that they think it would be a wonderful idea if this could extend over a whole year, with the same students in the SEC working the whole year through. . . . I found it very rewarding to work with these children, for the small accomplishments you made with them seemed like a great step forward.

Nancy Carlson

The school has 180 students. As a Student Education Corps member my task was to tutor slow readers. There is a regular remedial reading teacher who comes in once or twice a week to help slow readers. However, there are still some students in need of special attention who are not included in this special reading class. These are the students that I worked with. I tutored these students in small groups. One group consisted of two third-grade boys, who both read at about a late first-grade level. I also worked with a group which consisted of two girls and one boy, all in the fifth grade. None of these students read past the fourth-grade level.

Being a social science major I have had no training in any field of education. So, before my first visit, I spoke to some senior elementary education majors and to one elementary education teacher for some help in techniques which would be of good use in helping slow readers. . . . Aside from the students, the principal and the two teachers, with whom I spoke frequently, were quite cooperative. . . . I would like to say that I am personally very enthusiastic about the program and its future.

Marsha Hilton

Working with a first-grade class at this school has been such an enlightening experience for me. The environment was one in which I had never before spent much time, and I learned from those children much more than they learned from me, I'm sure. . . . This school, near downtown, is in a lower-class section of town and, therefore, the majority of children are from lower-class families. . . . My job was to aid the teacher generally, taking the reading groups sometimes; or if the teacher listened to the reading groups, I would help the rest of the class with their arithmetic, walking around and working with individual students. . . . I went to the school only on Tuesday and Thursday afternoons. and the afternoon was spent in reading, arithmetic, art, singing, and story reading, all conducted in the same classroom by the same teacher. I assisted in whatever area I was most needed. . . . This was a very worthwhile and profitable experience for me; and as far as my doing good for the school, I feel I helped most in giving these children more individual attention, which they all need so badly.

Sally Meyer

It is obvious the Student Education Corps has meant many things to many people. Volunteers have worked with pupils in groups and on an individual basis. They have acted in many capacities—from virtual baby sitting to the actual conducting of classes without supervision. There have been personality conflicts and misunderstandings and some confusion. There have also been some valuable contributions to the education of both the elementary pupils and the student volunteers.

In their reports, written at the close of the pilot project, the corpsmen expressed their personal reactions.

> I wish to state here, without being maudlin or sentimental, that my work with the Student Education Corps has been of great personal satisfaction to me. I feel like a thief. I have taken so much from this experience, I can only hope I have given the equivalent.
>
> Priscilla Moorman

> The Student Education Corps is a rewarding experience beyond a doubt. It probably does more to open eyes to the problems faced by the present educational system than any other single thing could. Also to be included would be the problems of communities in general. Whether or not a student is an education major or a physics major I am convinced that *all* can contribute a great deal to this program. I have gained a knowledge of a sampling of subjects in the past three years of college but, for the first time, in this program I feel I have gained more understanding. I felt that I was finally making some contribution instead of soaking up lectures in a classroom like a sponge.
>
> Robert D. Warner

> Now it is time to tell how I personally gained from SEC. To begin, I have mentioned that I truly disliked children. I have always felt uneasy and perfectly frustrated with them. This is due, I'm sure, in part to the fact that I have never had small children in my home or near us in the neighborhood. I no longer dislike children. I have come to realize their intelligence, abilities, and interests. I feel much more at ease around them and do not conceive of them so much as "monsters." (They still are frustrating at times I will not deny.) I cannot emphasize enough that in all sincerity I am sure this experience has enhanced my adjustment as an adult. All in all I benefited; I only hope they did. Thank you for this opportunity.
>
> Shelley Lynn Hecht

Of course, any attempt to evaluate the true effectiveness of the program in the schools must come in part from the teachers who participated directly in the project. Many of their reactions were included in the reports the volunteers submitted, but a number of teachers took the time and trouble to write directly to the SEC office. Typical of their observations are such statements as:

> I guess I was one of the teachers who at first was skeptical about the effectiveness of such a program. Needless to say I have changed my mind. What a difference one outsider made to these children. I know it sounds farfetched but I honestly believe that the children are showing more interest in school than they did before. The college students working in our school have introduced new ideas and a new enthusiasm. I look forward to them being here again next year.
>
> Fifth-grade teacher

It is a pity that the volunteers came here so late in the year. The young man who worked with my slow readers did a fine job. Not only because he helped them in their reading but because of the extra boost he gave these children.

Third-grade teacher

This year we had five volunteers in our school; next year I hope we have ten.

School principal

## IMPLICATIONS

It should be apparent to the reader that with few exceptions student volunteers, school children, and school personnel gained from this project. Of specific interest to our discussion is the young people's response to a problem they perceived as worthy of their time and talent. In this case, the volunteers were college students who, in addition to their regular responsibilities, devoted themselves to the program. Some would suggest there is little that 124 students can do on a parttime basis, and we would agree. Perhaps the reply to this type of criticism would be the one expressed by a volunteer who said, "It is only a drop in the bucket but it is in the right bucket." Still another response might be that if college students and upperclassmen in high schools throughout the country were engaged in similar service programs much could be accomplished.

More important, and not unlike the Peace Corps, a program such as SEC becomes a partial solution to the problem of moving young people into positions of responsibility within their community and nation.

Finally, programs such as the one outlined here seem to fulfill, in part at least, three needs frequently expressed by the young. The first is a need for *visibility*—the opportunity to be seen by others. The second is a need for *recognition*—the opportunity to be seen as an individual, independent and respected for the contribution he makes. The third is a need for *fidelity*—the opportunity to become attached to someone or some idea in a full and dedicated manner.

# INDEX

*This book has been set on the Linotype in 11 point Caledonia, leaded 2 points, and 9 point Caledonia, leaded 1 point. Chapter numbers and titles are in 18 point Tempo Medium. The size of the type page is 27 by 46½ picas.*